Library of
Davidson College

THE BROOK FARM BOOK

GARLAND REFERENCE LIBRARY
OF THE HUMANITIES
(VOL. 730)

THE BROOK FARM BOOK
A Collection of First-Hand Accounts of the Community

Joel Myerson

Garland Publishing, Inc. • New York & London
1987

© 1987 Joel Myerson
All rights reserved

Library of Congress Cataloging-in-Publication Data

The Brook Farm book.

(Garland reference library of the humanities ; vol. 730)
"Reprints important published notices, descriptions, and recollections of Brook Farm by the press, participants, and visitors"—Introd.
Bibliography: p.
Includes index.
1. Brook Farm—History—Sources. 2. Collective settlements—Massachusetts—Boston—History—Sources. 3. Transcendentalism (New England)—History—Sources. 4. Authors, American—Massachusetts—Boston—Biography. 5. Authors, American—19th century—Biography. 6. American literature—Massachusetts—Boston—History and criticism. 7. American literature—19th century—History and criticism. 8. Brook Farm Phalanx (West Roxbury, Boston, Mass.)—History—Sources. I. Myerson, Joel. II. Series: Garland reference library of the humanities ; v. 730.
HX656.B8B76 1987   335'.974461   86-25811
ISBN 0-8240-8507-8 (alk. paper)

Printed on acid-free, 250-year-life paper
Manufactured in the United States of America

CONTENTS

Introduction	ix
"Agricultural School"	1-3
"The Community at West Roxbury, Mass."	4-10
Elizabeth Palmer Peabody, "Plan of the West Roxbury Community"	11-23
"The West Roxbury Community"	24-25
Orestes A. Brownson, "Brook Farm"	26-38
"The West Roxbury Community"	39-40
Charles Lane, "American Correspondence"	41-42
"The Roxbury Community"	43
Charles Lane, "Brook Farm"	44-50
John Finch, "Letter on Brook Farm"	51
"The Brook Farm Association"	52
John Finch, "Notes on Travel in the United States"	53-55
A. Bloomer Hart, "Brook Farm"	56-62
"Letter from Charles A. Dana"	63-67
John A. Collins, "Fourierism"	68-71
"Celebration of Fourier's Birthday at Brook Farm"	72-74
George Ripley, "Fire at Brook Farm"	75-79
George Ripley, "Brook Farm School"	80-81
John Sullivan Dwight, "How Stands the Cause?"	82-84

George Ripley, "The Angels of the Past"	85
Margaret Fuller, "Brook Farm"	86-91
George William Curtis, "Hawthorne, Brook Farm, and Transcendentalism"	92-100
Georgiana Bruce Kirby, "My First Visit to Brook Farm"	101-118
Georgiana Bruce Kirby, "Reminiscences of Brook Farm"	119-175
George William Curtis, "Brook Farm and Transcendentalism"	176-181
"The Brook Farm Coterie"	182-184
Belle C. Barrows, "Brook Farm Recollections"	185-190
Thomas Wentworth Higginson, "The Brook Farm Period in New England"	191-195
George P. Bradford, "Reminiscences of Brook Farm"	196-213
Arthur Sumner, "A Boy's Recollections of Brook Farm"	214-221
J. Homer Doucet, "Reminiscences of the Brook Farm Association"	222-239
Annie M. Salisbury, "Brook Farm"	240-252
M. Betham-Edwards, "A Survivor of Brook Farm"	253-255
John T. Codman, "The Brook Farm Association"	256-267
Ora Gannett Sedgwick, "A Girl of Sixteen at Brook Farm"	268-283
Frederic Dan Huntington, "Brook Farm"	284-285
M. Gertrude Cutter, "Brook Farm Reminiscences"	286-298

Contents

Kate Sloan Gaskill, "A Girl's
    Recollections of Brook Farm School"   299-312

S. Willard Saxton, "A Few Reminiscences
    of Brook Farm"   313-328

Joel Myerson, "Two Unpublished
    Reminiscences of Brook Farm"   329-338

Index   341-349

INTRODUCTION

The Brook Farm Book: A Collection of First-Hand Accounts of the Community reprints important published notices, descriptions, and recollections of Brook Farm by the press, participants, and visitors. Many of these works were originally published in obscure or hard-to-locate periodicals. The present collection is intended to complement book-length accounts of Brook Farm,[1] unpublished manuscript accounts easily available by photocopying,[2] and published journals and letters by members of the community which are readily available in scholarly books and periodicals.[3] Nearly two-thirds of the present collection represents material now reprinted in full for the first time.

Brook Farm, a community established by George and Sophia Ripley at West Roxbury, Massachusetts, near Boston, lasted from April 1841 to September 1847. It is one of America's most famous communal experiments and the best representation of the social aspect of Transcendentalism. When Ripley began the community, he wrote Ralph Waldo Emerson, "Our objects . . . are to insure a more natural union between intellectual and manual labor than now exists; to combine the thinker and the worker, as far as possible, in the same individual; to guarantee the highest mental freedom, by providing all with labor, adapted to their tastes and talents, and securing to them the fruits of their industry; to do away [with] the necessity of menial services, by opening the benefits of education and the profits of labor to all; and thus to prepare a society of liberal, intelligent, and cultivated persons, whose relations with each other would permit a more simple and wholesome life, than can be lead amidst the pressure of our competitive institutions."[4] Emerson declined to join the community and his reply shows a basic difference between the two men: "It seems to me a circuitous & operose way of relieving myself of any irksome circumstances, to put on your community the task of my emancipation which I ought to take on myself."[5]

That is, while Ripley felt that just laws and good living would produce good people, Emerson believed that the individual must first be reformed and that just people would then--and only then--make just laws.

Ripley had hoped to raise some $50,000 capital, but soon lowered his sights to $30,000. Yet when he purchased the 170-acre Ellis Farm in West Roxbury for $10,500, he immediately had to take out two mortgages because of a lack of working funds. In September 1841, the "Brook Farm Institute of Agriculture and Education" was chartered, with twenty-four shares at $500 apiece pledged, one-third of that sum in cash. Each shareholder was to receive free tuition for his children in the Brook Farm school or five per cent annual interest. Membership in the community would be granted by a two-thirds vote after a two-month probationary period. Those who worked received free board; those who did not paid four dollars a week.

The early period of Brook Farm went fairly well. Ripley wanted a community where everyone shared in the work and in the profits, yet had time for contemplation and artistic endeavors. Not everyone found it possible to do all these things, and Nathaniel Hawthorne, an original shareholder, left when he discovered that his workload was too heavy to permit him time to write. (He later fictionalized Brook Farm in his novel, The Blithedale Romance.) Activities were distributed in these areas: teaching in the school, farming, working in the manufacturing shops (such as the shoemaker's), domestic tasks (such as waiting tables), maintenance of buildings and grounds, and group recreation. Of these, the only unqualified successes were the school and recreation. Life was hard but pleasant, and visitors included Bronson Alcott, Orestes Brownson, Emerson, Margaret Fuller, and Theodore Parker.

A dramatic change of direction occurred in March 1845, when the community was reorganized as the "Brook Farm Phalanx." Patterned after the ideal community of the French utopian Charles Fourier, the phalanx structured its life around various "groups." Each person served in a number of groups--Dinner Waiters, Farmers, Washers, Printers, and so on--and, in theory, could work in

Introduction   xi

any of them. The strict regimentation brought about by this change upset many people, and the community's fortunes declined. The death blow was delivered in March 1846, when the new central building being constructed, the Phalanstery, caught fire and burned to the ground, for an uninsured loss of $7,000. Brook Farm never recovered and collapsed in September 1847.

One reason for the community's demise was the declining public interest in the late 1840s in utopian and communitarian ventures. Another--and more important--reason was Brook Farm's shaky financial base. Immediately after buying the land for Brook Farm, Ripley took out two mortgages, one for $6,000 and another for $5,000; that is, he mortgaged the property for $500 more than he had paid for it. A third mortgage of $1,000 was taken out in April 1843 and a fourth mortgage of $2,500 in August 1845. Small wonder, then, that the loss of the Phalanstery--and the money invested in it--signaled the end of the community. Ripley sold his library to help pay off the debts and eventually paid all creditors personally.

Two excellent guides exist for the study of Brook Farm. My 1978 Brook Farm: An Annotated Bibliography and Resources Guide lists and annotates material by and about members, visitors, and contemporaries; discusses general histories of Brook Farm and its publication, the Harbinger; lists miscellaneous material such as poetry about Brook Farm; and fully describes manuscript collections of Brook Farm-related materials.[6] Carol Johnston's 1984 "Transcendentalist Communities" is an excellent survey and evaluation of the major works by participants and later commentators.[7] The following works, which have appeared since the publication of my bibliography, are of especial interest: Myerson's "James Burrill Curtis and Brook Farm" edits seventeen letters by George William Curtis' brother written from Brook Farm in 1842 and 1843;[8] James M. Mathews' "An Early Brook Farm Letter" edits a letter written by George P. Bradford in 1841;[9] Anne C. Rose's Transcendentalism as a Social Movement is an interesting socio-economic study of the community using manuscript records;[10] Stephen Garrison and Myerson's

"Elizabeth Curson's Letters from Brook Farm" edits sixteen letters written from Brook Farm between 1845 and 1847;[11] Sterling F. Delano's "The Harbinger" and New England Transcendentalism is the definitive study of the Brook Farm periodical;[12] Myerson's "New Light on George Ripley and the Harbinger's New York Years" edits twelve letters from Ripley to Dwight written in 1847 and 1848 which trace the Harbinger's demise;[13] and Daniel Shealy's "Ralph Waldo Emerson's Lecture on Brook Farm" reprints an account of an 1868 lecture on the community by one of its most famous non-participants.[14]

The Brook Farm Book: A Collection of First-Hand Accounts of the Community provides a valuable first-hand account of the life of the community and the people who lived it. When taken together with other book-length accounts and published journals and letters by participants, it is now possible to have easily available all the major works on Brook Farm by the people who lived and worked there.

Joel Myerson
Edisto Beach, South Carolina
17 August 1986

Introduction   xiii

                            NOTES

   ¹ See John Thomas Codman, Brook Farm: Historic
and Personal Memoirs (Boston: Arena, 1894); Amelia
E. Russell, Home Life of the Brook Farm Association
(Boston: Little, Brown, 1900; revised and expanded
from her "Home Life of the Brook Farm Association,"
Atlantic Monthly Magazine, 42 [October, November
1878]: 458-466, 556-563); and John Van Der Zee
Sears, My Friends at Brook Farm (New York: Desmond
FitzGerald, 1912).
   ² The major manuscript collections are the
John Sullivan Dwight Collection at the Boston
Public Library, the John Stillman Brown Family
Papers at the Kansas State Historical Society, the
Brook Farm Collection at the Massachusetts
Historical Society (which includes Marianne
Dwight's letters and the journals and day books of
the community), the Abernethy Library of Middlebury
College, and the Orestes Augustus Brownson
Collection at the University of Notre Dame Library.
All except the Middlebury materials have been
microfilmed and are available for sale.
   ³ For the most important works, see, by
members of the community, Early Letters of George
Wm. Curtis to John S. Dwight: Brook Farm and
Concord (New York: Harpers, 1898); Marianne Dwight
(Orvis), Letters from Brook Farm 1844-1847, ed. Amy
L. Reed (Poughkeepsie, N.Y.: Vassar College, 1928);
Nathaniel Hawthorne, The American Notebooks, ed.
Claude M. Simpson (Columbus: Ohio State University
Press, 1972), and The Letters, 1813-1843, ed.
Thomas Woodson, L. Neal Smith, and Norman Holmes
Pearson (Columbus: Ohio State University Press,
1984); Isaac Hecker's diaries and letters printed
in Walter Elliott, The Life of Father Hecker (New
York: Columbus Press, 1891), and Vincent F. Holden,
The Early Years of Isaac Thomas Hecker (1819-1844)
(Washington: Catholic University of America, 1939);
and, by visitors, Henry F. Brownson, Orestes A.
Bronson's Early Life: From 1803 to 1844 (Detroit:
H. F. Brownson, 1898); Emerson's comments in The
Journals and Miscellaneous Notebooks of Ralph Waldo
Emerson, ed. William H. Gilman, Ralph H. Orth, et
al., 16 vols. (Cambridge: Harvard University Press,
1960-82), and The Letters of Ralph Waldo Emerson,
ed. Ralph L. Rusk, 6 vols. (New York: Columbia
University Press, 1939); and Clarence Gohdes,

"Three Letters by James Kay Dealing with Brook Farm," Philological Quarterly, 17 (October 1938): 377-388.
  [4] 9 November 1840, in Octavius Brooks Frothingham, George Ripley (Boston: Houghton, Mifflin, 1882), pp. 307-308.
  [5] 15 December 1840, in Letters, 2:369.
  [6] Joel Myerson, Brook Farm: An Annotated Bibliography and Resources Guide (New York: Garland, 1978),
  [7] Carol Johnston, "Transcendentalist Communities," in The Transcendentalists: A Review of Research and Criticism, ed. Myerson (New York: Modern Language Association, 1984), pp. 56-68.
  [8] Joel Myerson, "James Burrill Curtis and Brook Farm," New England Quarterly, 51 (September 1978): 396-423.
  [9] James M. Mathews, "An Early Brook Farm Letter," New England Quarterly, 53 (June 1980): 226-230.
  [10] Anne C. Rose, Transcendentalism as a Social Movement (New Haven: Yale University Press, 1981).
  [11] Stephen Garrison and Joel Myerson, "Elizabeth Curson's Letters from Brook Farm," Resources for American Literary Study, 12 (Spring 1982): 1-28.
  [12] Sterling F. Delano, "The Harbinger" and New England Transcendentalism (Rutherford, N.J.: Fairleigh Dickinson University Press, 1983).
  [13] Joel Myerson, "New Light on George Ripley and the Harbinger's New York Years," Harvard Library Bulletin, 32 (Summer 1985): 213-236.
  [14] Daniel Shealy, "Ralph Waldo Emerson's Lecture on Brook Farm," Concord Saunterer, 18, no. 2 (December 1985): 28-29.

The Brook Farm Book

AGRICULTURAL SCHOOL*

We understand that an association has been formed by several gentlemen in this city and vicinity, for the purpose of establishing a "Practical Institute of Agriculture and Education." The design of this institution is to furnish the means of a liberal education to those who are not intended for the learned professions. The principles of science, which lie at the foundation of the practical arts of life, will form the chief objects of attention, while the study of the languages will occupy a subordinate sphere. It is intended to combine the study of scientific agriculture with its practical operations, to illustrate the great improvements of modern husbandry by actual experiment; to increase the attachment of the farmer to the cultivation of the soil, by showing the dignity of the pursuit, and the knowledge and ability which it demands, and thus to prepare young men, who propose to make agriculture the business of their lives, for the intelligent discharge of the duties of their calling.

The want of an institution of this kind has been deeply felt and loudly expressed. No branch of education has been more neglected, though its unspeakable importance is admitted, than the professional education of those who seek their subsistence by tilling the earth. Our most enlightened agricultural publications have been urgent in their appeals to the community in behalf of such an institution; the friends of popular education have set forth its claims in a convincing manner; legislative patronage has been earnestly solicited both in Massachusetts and New York for the establishment of one on a large scale; proposals have been made to connect a department for this purpose with some of our most distinguished colleges; and no one acquainted with the character of our New England population can doubt for a moment, that an institution of this description, conducted in a judicious and effective manner, would receive the favor of the public, and prove of wide practical utility. The eminent success of Van Thaer, in Prussia, and of

Fellenberg, in Switzerland, it would seem, ought not to surpass that of an institution so congenial with the spirit of our government and the character and habits of our citizens.

"When we consider," says the late lamented Judge Bael, of Albany, among the last words probably which ever fell from his pen--"when we consider that agriculture is the great business of the nation--of mankind; that its successful prosecution depends upon a knowledge in the cultivation of the soil, of the principles of natural science, and that our agriculture stands in special need of this auxiliary aid--we cannot withhold our surprise and regret, that we have not long since established professional schools, in which our youth, or such of them as are designed to manage this branch of national labor, might be taught, simultaneously, the principles and practice of their future business of life, and on which, more than any other branch of business, the fortunes of our country, moral, political and national essentially depend. We require an initiatory study of years in the principles of law and medicine, before we permit the pupils to practice in these professions. We require a like preliminary study in our military and naval schools, in the science of war and navigation, ere the student is deemed qualified to command. And yet in agriculture, by which, under the blessing of Providence, we virtually "live and move and have our being," and which truly embraces a wider range of useful science than either law, medicine, war, or navigation, we have no schools, we give no instruction, we bestow no governmental patronage."

The proposed institution is undertaken on the sole responsibility of a few individuals, whose interest in agriculture and science has led them to engage in the enterprise; and the internal arrangements they have made, we learn, are of a character which those who are concerned trust will ensure the management of the institution with great economy, efficiency, and completeness.

It is contemplated, we also understand, to connect with the institution a department for classical learning, in which pupils will be prepared for admission to any of the New England colleges, or be instructed in a course similar to that which is pursued by under-graduates, while at the same time, they will have an opportunity to study the sciences on which agriculture is founded, and to engage in its practical details to such extent as may be desired.

It is intended, if a suitable degree of encouragement should be given to the enterprize, to open the institution for the reception of a limited number of pupils, in the course of the ensuing season, and to enlarge its operations in proportion to the favor it shall receive from those for whose benefit it is designed.

We have here given what we understand to be the objects of the gentlemen concerned; and we hope that prudence and efficiency will so mark the course as to win and secure to the projectors public favor. We are pleased that they have no design to ask for legislative aid, because we doubt whether such an animal as this body would be long suffered to feed quietly at the public crib.

*"Agricultural School," New England Farmer and Horticultural Register, 19 (27 January 1841): 238-239. This is the first known published notice of Brook Farm.

THE COMMUNITY AT WEST ROXBURY, MASS.*

Some curiosity having been excited respecting the Establishment for Agriculture and Education at West Roxbury, we have asked and received leave to print the following extract from a letter written by a friend--not a member of the new Community--to a lady in England.
"And what hinders,--say these associates,-- that we should have an organization of society on Christian ideas, if those who have these ideas only come out from the world, and communicate and live;--live wholly,--live in the body by a constant increase of health, live in the spirit by a complete unfolding of heart, intellect, and moral nature?"
On consideration it was seen, that the labour of society might be lessened by machinery and cooperation of numbers, while the desirable fruits of labour would not be in the least sacrificed; that there was no need of any drudge in society, provided there was no drone; that a diffusion of bodily labour would be equally a means of health to those who do not work at all, and to those who work too much; that there need be no want, if there were indulged no superfluity; no perpetual sacrifice by many of the higher pleasures of life, were there a reasonable and righteous sacrifice by some of mere bodily luxuries.
This insight could hardly exist without stimulating the conscience, and the question arising,--how <u>dare</u> I be a drone when others are drudges? How dare I sacrifice not only my own, but others' health, in sequestrating myself from my share of bodily labour, or neglecting a due mental cultivation? How dare I have superfluities, when others are in want? How dare I oppose the unfolding of the spiritual progress of my whole race, by all the force of my personal selfishness and indolence? In short, is it not the sin against the Holy Ghost, with this newfound insight, to hesitate to enter immediately upon the immortal life?
The associates were not previously acquainted with each other. The protest of Mr. R[ipley]

against a situation in life, which, taking society as it is, is undoubtedly one of the most disinterested, had excited inquiry among other earnest livers, in the most dissimilar external situations,--scholars, candidates for the ministry, teachers, mechanics, farmers, young men and young women with no especial vocation; and this inquiry led to mutual understanding. They said to one another:--"We belong together, let us unite and realize our principles. Some of us have bodily strength and skill of labour, some of us have scientific education, some of us have knowledge of the domestic arts; each of us wishes to be enriched with the power of the other, be it manual, intellectual, or moral. Let us put together our means and buy a farm, and cultivate it. Let us go together and teach one another our various knowledges and skills; above all, let us teach our children according to their genius, and according to the genius of humanity, neglecting all those customs and prejudices which have no life in them."
But here the question came up of the disadvantages. Surely <u>community</u> has its advantages, but let us not sacrifice individuality. Every man must be wholly himself before he can be a desirable associate. Private property and personal isolation have their indispensable good influences; this was acknowledged. But why not have an organization in which both these principles shall be combined? In a family, these two poles of society act. Individuality and the intensest social action are united there. Why may they not be in God's great family? They planned then that every one should retain some property,--enough to be so far independent that each one could leave the Association, if it were necessary or desirable, and not be cast penniless on the world. This is effected by an arrangement of which I will endeavour to give you a general outline.
Each man and woman who has any money puts it in, and it is understood that each shall have five per cent interest. They also put themselves in as labourers; whose labour is worth the same number of cents an hour, whatever is the office or service. For it is not supposed that money is the only or chief compensation for labour. There are compensations of a different kind, which this community provides by its constitution;--freedom to

work in the vocation adapted to your disposition and genius; freedom from care respecting the temporal future of your children, or your own old age; in short, freedom to live, which our "merchant princes" seldom redeem from the calls of business, with their incomes of ten thousand a year; how much less the majority of society! With two thirds of the stock of money put in, the Community as such would buy a farm, stock it, provide it with implements of agriculture, build a sufficient number of houses on a very simple scale and one large house for general purposes, and furnish a warehouse with all such merchandise as is necessary for comfortable subsistence, purchased at such advantage as the quantity they would want makes possible, and sold at cost. The Community as such also provides gratuitously for all the individual members houses, medical attendance, nursing, education in all departments, amusements; and to all persons over seventy and under ten years of age, and too all persons who are sick, free board, unless their five per cent interest can support them. But every capable person must pay board, calculated at cost; and it is believed that the board will not amount to the labour, and therefore that it will not be necessary, after they have fairly got under weigh, for a well gifted person to bring any other contribution than his labour, even though he have the usual number of helpless dependents; which, by the way, children over ten years of age are not considered, for they will be credited at half price by the hour for their light labours until they are twenty, when they will in ordinary cases have accumulated three or four hundred dollars, to be paid to them at that time. This, with a perfect education, would be a very good beginning of life for a young person who should incline to leave the Community and seek his or her fortune in the world at large.

    It seems to me that here we see brought about, in the most peaceable manner in the world, that very rectification of things which Mr. Brownson in his Article on the Labouring Classes is understood to declare will require a bloody revolution, a war such as the world has not heard of; viz., that no child shall be born richer or poorer than another, except by inward gift of God, but all shall inherit from society a good education and an independent place. Then might there not be good hope that these gifts of God would be used, as Jesus used his, purely for disinterested purposes; the energy now thrown into the brute law of self-preservation, becoming love of God and man?

It is calculated that, once in operation, the Community will have annually an overplus of money, instead of the population's pressing upon the means of subsistence, as is the common fact in the society of competition. This overplus is to be divided among the associates according to their labour, and they can throw it back again into the common fund to increase the common advantages, according to personal disposition, since all the necessaries of life are secured to them at all events. You see that private property, so necessary to secure personal isolation at will, is reconciled with community of labour. Persons who enter upon this scheme will indeed forego forever the hope of great individual accumulation, but, as a vast overpayment for this, infancy and old age are to be maintained sacred, sickness provided for, and "carking care" taken forever out of life.

Family integrity is also to be sacred. Any married couple with their children may live together, eat together, and have a paramount right to each other; or they may go to the commons. Social intercourse is to be so free as to be under individual choice, as it is not now. Rooms for intercourse are to be open every evening, which can be used for religious exercises, religious teaching, scientific and literary lectures, benevolent associations, or mere conversation, or amusements--such as dancing, music, (and I hope dramatic exhibitions, but I do not know, for I never heard that subject mentioned). All are to go freely to these rooms, but any are to stay at home when they please, and no questions asked. This facility and universality of intercourse will preclude all excuse for invading people's leisure. The principle they wish to establish is, that every man has a primary right to decide for himself as to what are his social duties, as well as all other duties; nor be appropriated without his own consent.

The "governmental" machinery is to be very simple. The Directions of Agriculture, of Domestic Labour, of Education, &c. are at certain times to state in general meeting what is to be done; and the people are to volunteer to the several departments for certain hours, which they shall specify,--being credited so much the hour at the general rate of labour. If any thing is left undone, it is to be restated, and if none volunteer, the Community as such is to hire it done, until persons are found who have taste or genius for this department, or who, for the sake of society or the education of their children, are desirous to become associates on the condition of doing these duties. The associates vote about the admission of new members, in order that none should enter who are not in sympathy with the idea; and they pledge themselves to take care of each other. The associates may also vote out any member for moral turpitude proved, or for idleness; but things will so work, that ungenial or unworthy members will doubtless take themselves off before it is put to vote.

These associates have some money among them, though not more than half enough to commence their operations. But in point of personal power,-- although they have bodily power, and habits of labour too, among them, abundantly sufficient for the work of the place, as they are proving this summer by working (a few of them) as hired men to one of their number who has taken the farm for a year on his own responsibility,--they are richest in intellectual power. Consequently on this account, as well as because it is the natural business of a true society to be doing the work of education, they will receive children to be educated with their children, and be paid for it; but only so many as can be domesticated in their families, and as will enter into all the labours like the children of the Community, according as these are desirable for the development of their bodies and minds.

Here is the germ of the true University. Moral education will not be here <u>exparte</u> life. It will be the life of the Community pervading the life of the members. They lay out to have science and literature and art taught in all branches. Scientific agriculture will naturally take the lead, but boys are to be fitted, from the first, for our colleges; and in the end, all that is taught in our colleges will be involved in the course of instruction. Female education will also be there more complete than it has ever been, because they will be able to combine the retirement of private education with all that is desirable of public education. They begin also with infancy. The infant education will be divided among such women as come forward to do this work; and the parents will have the liberty of choosing among these those whose genius they think most adapted to their children, or of keeping their children under their own sole care. The number of teachers will also make it so easy for each, that there will be no danger of the genius of instruction becoming wearied down by confinement and fagging.

How can education growing so naturally out of life be otherwise than perpetually advancing? The Faculty is neither dependent on government patronage, nor on popular favour. The Instructors stand on the soil, having earned their subsistence, and with the leisure and intellectual power they offer to carry on the great work of man--human education. I feel that the spectacle of this Community will stand in society as the Constitution of the United States does among the nations, and for more; for the Constitution is but a human instrument, while this Community is a divine life.

I have said that they have begun agricultural labour in a private sort of way already. They have also commenced their school operations upon the very few whom Mr. and Mrs. R[ipley]. could take into their small house; and they have received applications in behalf of many more pupils whom they cannot accommodate. But if they had their thirty thousand dollars now, they would buy the farm they have hired, and put up the buildings for the accommodation of all their families, and go into operation as a Community this autumn, or next spring at latest. And I have not the slightest doubt that, were a knowledge of the idea and details of the plan, even so far as this letter gives, widely diffused, there would be found many a person in this broad land who would rejoice to buy the stock, and take the interest in the education of his children. One or two subscribers would be enough.

My letter is so long, I must defer to another time the account of the school in more detail, and of the individuals who are to compose the association. You see I have lost entirely my horror of community, --now that I have found it can be so restricted, as to leave personal liberty and family integrity sacred. If it succeeds, two of the most important problems of human life will be settled, viz. the reconciliation of labour with cultivation and elegance of mind and manners, and the independence of the Faculty of education. I think too it can be proved the true church;--but of that another time.

*"The Community at West Roxbury, Mass.," Monthly Miscellany of Religion and Letters, 5 (August 1841): 113-118. Orestes A. Brownson's "The Laboring Classes" appeared in the July 1840 Boston Quarterly Review.

PLAN OF THE WEST ROXBURY COMMUNITY*

Elizabeth Palmer Peabody

In the last number of the Dial were some remarks, under the perhaps ambitious title, of "A Glimpse of Christ's Idea of Society"; in a note to which, it was intimated, that in this number, would be given an account of an attempt to realize in some degree this great Ideal, by a little company in the midst of us, as yet without name or visible existence. The attempt is made on a very small scale. A few individuals, who, unknown to each other, under different disciplines of life, reacting from different social evils, but aiming at the same object,--of being wholly true to their natures as men and women; have been made acquainted with one another, and have determined to become the Faculty of the Embryo University.

In order to live a religious and moral life worthy of the name, they feel it is necessary to come out in some degree from the world, and to form themselves into a community of property, so far as to exclude competition and the ordinary rules of trade;--while they reserve sufficient private property, or the means of obtaining it, for all purposes of independence, and isolation at will. They have bought a farm, in order to make agriculture the basis of their life, it being the most direct and simple in relation to nature.

A true life, although it aims beyond the highest star, is redolent of the healthy earth. The perfume of clover lingers about it. The lowing of cattle is the natural bass to the melody of human voices.

On the other hand, what absurdity can be imagined greater than the institution of cities? They originated not in love, but in war. It was war that drove men together in multitudes, and compelled them to stand so close, and build walls around them. This crowded condition produces wants of an unnatural character, which resulted in occupations that regenerated the evil, by creating artificial wants. Even when that thought of grief,

"I know, where'er I go

That there hath passed away a glory from the Earth."

came to our first parents, as they saw the angel, with the flaming sword of self-consciousness, standing between them and the recovery of spontaneous Life and Joy, we cannot believe they could have anticipated at time would come, when the sensuous apprehension of Creation--the great symbol of God--would be taken away from their unfortunate children,--crowded together in such a manner as to shut out the free breath and the Universal Dome of Heaven, some opening their eyes in the dark cellars of the narrow, crowded streets of walled cities. How could they have believed in such a conspiracy against the soul, as to deprive it of the sun and sky, and glorious apparelled Earth!--The growth of cities, which were the embryo of nations hostile to each other, is a subject worthy the thoughts and pens of the philosophic historian. Perhaps nothing would stimulate courage to seek, and hope to attain social good, so much, as a profound history of the origin, in the mixed nature of man, and the exasperation by society, of the various organized Evils under which humanity groans. Is there anything, which exists in social or political life, contrary to the soul's Ideal? That thing is not eternal, but finite, saith the Pure Reason. It has a beginning, and so a history. What man has done, man may <u>undo</u>. "By man came death; by man also cometh the resurrection from the dead."

The plan of the Community, as an Economy, is in brief this; for all who have property to take stock, and receive a fixed interest thereon; then to keep house or board in commons, as they shall severally desire, at the cost of provisions purchased at wholesale, or raised on the farm; and for all to labor in community, and be paid at a certain rate an hour, choosing their own number of hours, and their own kind of work. With the results of this labor, and their interest, they are to pay their board, and also purchase whatever else they require at cost, at the warehouses of the Community, which are to be filled by the Community as such. To perfect this economy, in the course of time they must have all trades, and all modes of business carried on among themselves, from the lowest mechanical trade, which contributes to the health and comfort of life, to the finest art which adorns it with food or drapery for the mind. All labor, whether bodily or intellectual, is to be paid at the same rate of wages; on the principle, that as the labor becomes merely bodily, it is a greater sacrifice to the individual laborer, to give his time to it; because time is desirable for the cultivation of the intellect, in exact proportion to ignorance. Besides, intellectual labor involves in itself higher pleasures, and is more its own reward, than bodily labor.

Another reason, for setting the same pecuniary value on every kind of labor, is, to give outward expression to the great truth, that all labor is sacred, when done for a common interest. Saints and philosophers already know this, but the childish world does not; and very decided measures must be taken to equalize labors, in the eyes of the young of the community, who are not beyond the moral influence of the world without them. The community will have nothing done within its precincts, but what is done by its own members, who stand all in social equality;--that the children may not "learn to expect one kind of service from Love and Goodwill, and another from the obligation of others to render it,"--a grievance of the common society stated, by one of the associated mothers, as destructive of the soul's simplicity. Consequently, as the Universal Education will involve all kinds of operation, necessary to the comforts and elegances of life, every associate, even if he be the digger of a ditch as his highest accomplishment, will be an instructer in that to the young members. Nor will this elevation of bodily labor be liable to lower the tone of manners and refinement in the community. The "children of light" are not altogether unwise in their generation. They have an invisible but all-powerful guard of principles. Minds incapable of refinement, will not be attracted into this association. It is an Ideal community, and only to the ideally inclined will it be attractive; but these are to be found in every rank of life, under every shadow of circumstance. Even among the diggers in the ditch are to be found some, who through religious cultivation, can look down, in meek superiority, upon the outwardly refined, and the book-learned.

Besides, after becoming members of this community, none will be engaged merely in bodily labor. The hours of labor for the Association will be limited by a general law, and can be curtailed at the will of the individual still more; and means will be given to all for intellectual improvement and for social intercourse, calculated to refine and expand. The hours redeemed from labor by community, will not be reapplied to the acquisition of wealth, but to the production of intellectual goods. This community aims to be rich, not in the metallic representative of wealth, but in the wealth itself, which money should represent; namely, LEISURE TO LIVE IN ALL THE FACULTIES OF THE SOUL. As a community, it will traffic with the world at large, in the products of Agricultural labor; and it will sell education to as many young persons as can be domesticated in the families, and enter into the common life with their own children. In the end, it hopes to be enabled to provide--not only all the necessaries, but all the elegances desirable for bodily and for spiritual health; books, apparatus, collections for science, works of art, means of beautiful amusement. These things are to be common to all; and thus that object, which alone gilds and refines the passion for individual accumulation, will no longer exist for desire, and whenever the Sordid passion appears, it will be seen in its naked selfishness. In its ultimate success, the community will realize all the ends which selfishness seeks, but involved in spiritual blessings, which only greatness of soul can aspire after.

And the requisitions on the individuals, it is believed, will make this the order forever. The spiritual good will always be the condition of the temporal. Every one must labor for the community in a reasonable degree, or not taste its benefits. The principles of the organization therefore, and not its probable results in future time, will determine its members. These principles are cooperation in social matters, instead of competition or balance of interests; and individual self-unfolding, in the faith that the whole soul of humanity is in each man and woman. The former is the application of the love of man; the latter, of the love of God, to life. Whoever is satisfied with society, as it is; whose sense of justice is not wounded by its common action, institutions, spirit of commerce, has no business with this community; neither has any one who is willing to have other men (needing more time for intellectual cultivation than himself) give their best hours and strength to bodily labor, to secure himself immunity therefrom. And whoever does not measure what society owes to its members of cherishing and instruction, by the needs of the individuals that compose it, has no lot in this new society. Whoever is willing to receive from his fellow men that, for which he gives no equivalent, will stay away from its precincts forever.

But whoever shall surrender himself to its principles, shall find that its yoke is easy and its burden light. Everything can be said of it, in a degree, which Christ said of his kingdom, and therefore it is believed that in some measure it does embody his Idea. For its Gate of entrance is strait and narrow. It is literally a pearl <u>hidden in a field</u>. Those only who are willing to lose their life for its sake shall find it. Its voice is that which sent the young man sorrowing away. "Go sell all thy goods and give to the poor, and then come and follow me." "Seek first the kingdom of Heaven, and its righteousness, and all other things shall be added to you."

This principle, with regard to labor, lies at the root of moral and religious life; for it is not more true that "money is the root of all evil," than that <u>labor</u> <u>is</u> <u>the</u> <u>germ</u> <u>of</u> <u>all</u> <u>good</u>.

All the work is to be offered for the free choice of the members of the community, at stated seasons, and such as is not chosen, will be hired. But it is not anticipated that any work will be set aside to be hired, for which there is actual ability in the community. It is so desirable that the hired labor should be avoided, that it is believed the work will all be done freely, even though at voluntary sacrifice. If there is some exception at first, it is because the material means are inadequate to the reception of all who desire to go. They cannot go, unless they have shelter; and in this climate, they cannot have shelter unless they can build houses; and they cannot build houses unless they have money. It is not here as in Robinson Crusoe's Island, or in the prairies and rocky mountains of the far west, where the land and the wood are not appropriated. A single farm, in the midst of Massachusetts, does not afford range enough for men to create out of the Earth a living, with no other means; as the wild Indians, or the United States Army in Florida may do.

This plan, of letting all persons choose their own departments of action, will immediately place the Genius of Instruction on its throne. Communication is the life of spiritual life. Knowledge pours itself out upon ignorance by a native impulse. All the arts crave response. "WISDOM CRIES." If every man and woman taught only what they loved, and so many hours as they could naturally communicate, instruction would cease to be a drudgery, and we may add, learning would be no longer a task. The known accomplishments of many of the members of this association have already secured it an interest in the public mind, as a school of literary advantages quite superior. Most of the associates have had long practical experience in the details of teaching, and have groaned under the necessity of taking their method and law from custom and caprice, when they would rather have found it in the nature of the thing taught, and the condition of the pupil to be instructed. Each instructer appoints his hours of study or recitation, and the scholars, or the parents of the children, or the educational committee, choose the studies, for the time, and the pupils submit, as long as they pursue their studies with any teacher, to his regulations.

As agriculture is the basis of their external life, scientific agriculture, connected with practice, will be a prominent part of the instruction from the first. This obviously involves the natural sciences, mathematics, and accounts. But to classical learning justice is also to be done. Boys may be fitted for our colleges there, and even be carried through the college course. The particular studies of the individual pupils, whether old or young, male or female, are to be strictly regulated, according to their individual needs. As the children of the community can remain in the community after they become of age, as associates, if they will; there will not be an entire subserviency to the end of preparing the means of earning a material

subsistence, as is frequently the case now.
Nevertheless, as they will have had an opportunity,
in the course of their minority, to earn three or
four hundred dollars, they can leave the community
at twenty years of age, if they will, with that
sufficient capital, which, together with their
extensive education, will gain a_ subsistence
anywhere, in the best society of the world. It is
this feature of the plan, which may preclude from
parents any question as to their right to go into
this community, and forego forever all hope of
great individual accumulation for their children; a
customary plea for spending life in making money.
Their children will be supported at free board,
until they are ten years of age; educated
gratuitously; taken care of in case of their
parents' sickness and death; and they themselves
will be supported, after seventy years of age, by
the community, unless their accumulated capital
supports them.
 There are some persons who have entered the
community without money. It is believed that these
will be able to support themselves and dependents,
by less work, more completely, and with more ease
than elsewhere; while their labor will be of
advantage to the community. It is in no sense an
eleemosynary establishment, but it is hoped that in
the end it will be able to receive all who have the
spiritual qualifications.
 It seems impossible that the little
organization can be looked on with any unkindness
by the world without it. Those, who have not the
faith that the principles of Christ's kingdom are
applicable to real life in the world, will smile at
it, as a visionary attempt. But even they must
acknowledge it can do no harm, in any event. If it
realizes the hope of its founders, it will
immediately become a manifold blessing. Its moral
aura must be salutary. As long as it lasts, it
will be an example of the beauty of brotherly love.
If it succeeds in uniting successful labor with
improvement in mind and manners, it will teach a
noble lesson to the agricultural population, and do
something to check that rush from the country to
the city, which is now stimulated by ambition, and
by something better, even a desire for learning.
Many a young man leaves the farmer's life, because
only by so doing can he have intellectual

companionship and opportunity; and yet, did he but know it, professional life is ordinarily more unfavorable to the perfection of the mind, than the farmer's life; if the latter is lived with wisdom and moderation, and the labor mingled as it might be with study. This community will be a school for young agriculturalists, who may learn within its precincts, not only the skilful practice, but the scientific reasons of their work, and be enabled afterwards to improve their art continuously. It will also prove the best of normal schools, and as such, may claim the interest of those, who mourn over the inefficiency of our common school system, with its present ill-instructed teachers.

It should be understood also, that after all the working and teaching, which individuals of the community may do, they will still have leisure, and in that leisure can employ themselves in connexion with the world around them. Some will not teach at all; and those especially can write books, pursue the Fine Arts, for private emolument if they will, and exercise various functions of men.--From this community might go forth preachers of the gospel of Christ, who would not have upon them the odium, or the burthen, that now diminishes the power of the clergy. And even if pastors were to go from this community, to reside among congregations as now, for a salary given, the fact that they would have something to retreat upon, at any moment, would save them from that virtual dependence on their congregations, which now corrupts the relation. There are doubtless beautiful instances of the old true relation of pastor and people, even of teacher and taught, in the decaying churches around us, but it is in vain to attempt to conceal the ghastly fact, that many a taper is burning dimly in the candlestick, no longer silver or golden, because compassion forbids to put it quite out. But let the spirit again blow "where it listeth," and not circumscribe itself by salary and other commodity,--and the Preached word might reassume the awful Dignity which is its appropriate garment; and though it sit down with publicans and sinners, again speak "with authority and not as the scribes."

We write, as is evident perhaps, not as members, which we are not, but interested spectators of the growth of this little community.

It is due to their modesty to apologize for bringing out so openly, what they have done simply and without pretension. We rest on the spirit of the day, which is that of communication. No sooner does the life of man become visible, but it is a part of the great phenomenon of nature, which never seeks display, but suffers all to speculate thereon. When this speculation is made in respect, and in love of truth, it is most to be defended. We shall now proceed to make some observations that may sound like criticism, but this we do without apology, for earnest seekers of a true life are not liable to be petulant.

The very liberality, and truth to nature of the plan, is a legitimate reason for fearing it will not succeed as a special community in any given time. The vineyard does not always yield according to the reasonable expectation of its Lord. When he looks for grapes, behold it brings forth wild grapes. For outward success there must always be compromise, and where it is so much the object to avoid the dangers of compromise, as there very properly is here, there is perhaps danger of not taking advantage of such as nature offers.

One of these is the principle of antagonism. It is fair to take advantage of this in one respect. The members may be stimulated to faithfulness and hope, by the spectacle of society around them, whose unnecessary evils can be clearly seen to be folly, as well as sin, from their retreat. The spirit of liberality must be discriminated from the spirit of accommodation. Love is a stern principle, a severe winnower, when it is one with the pure Reason; as it must be, to be holy, and to be effective. It is a very different thing from indulgence. Some persons have said that in order to a true experiment, and to enact a really generous faith in man, there should be any neighborhood taken without discrimination, with the proportion that may happen to be in it, of the good and bad, the strong and weak. But we differ as to the application in this instance. They are so little fenced about with rules and barriers, that they have no chance but by being strong in the spirit. "Touch not, taste not, handle not," must be their watchword, with respect to the organized falsehoods they have protested against; and with respect to means of successful manifestation, the aphorism of St. Augustine, "God is patient because he is Eternal."

To be a little more explicit. The men and women of the world, as they rise, are not at the present moment wise enough, in the Hebrew sense of the word wisdom, even if they are good-intentioned enough, to enter into a plan of so great mutual confidence. To all the evils arising from constitutional infirmity and perversion they must, especially at first, be exposed. There will always be natures too cold to satisfy the warm-hearted, too narrow for the enjoyment of the wide-visioned, some will be deficient in reason, and some in sensibility, and there will be many who, from defect in personal power, will let run to waste beautiful hearts, and not turn to account great insight of natural wisdom. Love, justice, patience, forbearance, every virtue under heaven, are always necessary in order to do the social duties. There is no knot that magnanimity cannot untie; but the Almighty Wisdom and Goodness will not allow any tower to be builded by the children of men, where they can understand one another without this solvent magnanimity. There must ever be sincerity of good design, and organic truth, for the evolution of Beauty.

Now there can be only one way of selecting and winnowing their company. The power to do this must be inherent in their constitution; they must keep sternly true to their principles.

In the first place, they must not compromise their principle of labor, in receiving members. Every one, who has any personal power, whether bodily or mental, must bring the contribution of personal service, no matter how much money he brings besides. This personal service is not to amount to drudgery in any instance, but in every able-bodied or sound-minded person, it should be at least equivalent to the care of their own persons. Exchange, or barter of labor, so as to distribute to each according to his genius, is to be the means of ease, indefinitely, but no absolute dispensation should be given, except for actual infirmity. "My Father worketh hitherto, and I work," is always the word of the divine humanity.

But granting that they keep the gate of entrance narrow, as the gate to life, which is being as liberal as the moral Law, a subtle temptation assails them from the side of their Organization. Wo be unto them if they lean upon it; if they ever forget that it is only what they have made it, and what they sustain it to be. It not only must be ever instinct with spirit, but it must never be thought, even then, to circumscribe the spirit. It can do nothing more, even if it work miracles, than make bread out of stones, and after all, man liveth not by bread alone, but by every word that proceedeth out of the mouth of God. Another temptation assails them, clothed as an angel of light. The lover of man finds in his benevolence a persuasive advocate, when the Devil proposes to him to begin by taking possession of the kingdoms of this world, according to his ability. In their ardor for means of success, they may touch the mammon of unrighteousness. They will be exposed to endowment. Many persons, enlightened enough to be unwilling to let the wealth, they have gained by accident of birth or of personal talent, go to exasperate the evil of present society, will be disposed to give it, or to leave it as a legacy to this community, and it would be asceticism to refuse it absolutely. But they should receive it greatly. "Thou shalt worship the Lord thy God, and Him only shalt thou serve." No person who proposes to endow the community as a University, or the true system of life, understands what he does, unless he surrenders what he gives, unconditionally, in the same spirit of faith, with which the members throw themselves in, with their lives, their property, and sacred honor. At all events it would violate their principle of progress to accept anything with conditions: unless indeed it may be considered a condition, that they remain an association, governed by the majority of members, according to its present general constitution.

It were better even to forego the advantage of good buildings, apparatus, library, than to have these shackles.--Though space cannot now be given to do more than state these points, it might be demonstrated that to keep to them is essential to independence, and can alone justify the conscience of endower and endowed.

Another danger that should be largely treated is the spirit of coterie. The breadth of their platform, which admits all sects; and the generality of their plan, which demands all degrees of intellectual culture to begin with, is some security against this. But the ultimate security must be in numbers. Some may say, "already this taint has come upon them, for they are doubtless transcendentalists." But to mass a few protestants together and call them transcendentalists, is a popular cant. Transcendentalism belongs to no sect of religion, and no social party. It is the common ground to which all sects may rise, and be purified of their narrowness; for it consists in seeking the spiritual ground of all manifestations. As already in the pages of this periodical, Calvinist, and Unitarian, and Episcopalian, and Baptist, and Quaker, and Swedenborgian, have met and spoken in love and freedom, on this common basis; so it would be seen, if the word were understood, that transcendentalism, notwithstanding its name is taken in vain by many moonshiny youths and misses who assume it, would be the best of all guards against the spirit of coterie. Much as we respect our friends of the community, we dare not hope for them quite so much, as to aver that they transcend, as yet, all the limitations that separate men from love and mutual trust.

> Serene will be our days and bright,
> And happy will our nature be,
> When Love is an unerring light
> And Joy its own security.
> And blest are they who in the main
> This faith, even now, do entertain;
> Live in the spirit of this creed;
> Yet find the strength of Law according to their need!

We had intended to subjoin some further remarks, by way of inquiry, into the possibility of other portions of society, not able to emancipate themselves from the thralldom of city life, beginning also to act, in a degree, on the principles of co-operation. Ameliorations of present evils, initiations into truer life, may be made we believe everywhere. Worldly wisdom, for its own purposes, avails itself of what is outward in the community plan; at least of the labor-saving element. Why may not the children of light be equally wise?

There may be some persons, at a distance, who will ask, to what degree has this community gone into operation? We cannot answer this with precision, for we do not write as organs of this association, and have reason to feel, that if we applied to them for information, they would refuse it, out of their dislike to appear in public. We desire this to be distinctly understood. But we can see, and think we have a right to say, that it has purchased the Farm, which some of its members cultivated for a year with success, by way of trying their love and skill for agricultural labor;--that in the only house they are as yet rich enough to own, is collected a large family, including several boarding scholars, and that all work and study together. They seem to be glad to know of all, who desire to join them in the spirit, that at any moment, when they are able to enlarge their habitations, they may call together those that belong to them.

*E[lizabeth]. P[almer]. P[eabody]., "Plan of the West Roxbury Community," Dial, 2 (January 1842): 361-372. Peabody's "A Glimpse of Christ's Idea of Society" (Dial, 2 [October 1841]: 214-228) provides an introduction to the ideas in the present article.

THE WEST ROXBURY COMMUNITY*

BROOK FARM, August 3, 1842.
Our confidence in our movement is increased by every step we take. We know that we are infinitely nearer a true social state than Society generally, and this assurance cheers us in all sorts of circumstances. We are not doubtful either that an outward life expressive purely of Holiness, Beauty, Heroism, can finally be attained, and thus our courage is fresh and hopeful. We number now about seventy souls, of whom some fifteen are associates, the remainder pupils, boarders, and persons whose labor we are obliged to hire. We own two finished houses, hire another, and are building two more. As soon as these are done, we shall have not less than a hundred persons. Our department of Education is fully organized and efficient, and has thus far had remarkable success. Herein, too, we think we have something better than the ordinary, one-sided forcing method. We want mechanics. A shoemaker, a blacksmith and a carpenter would serve us greatly, and keep within ourselves large sums which we now have to pay out.

We congratulate ourselves especially that our organization is not fixed and finished, but constantly tending toward something better. I am persuaded that our Association could not exist long if it were not so. And here I fear that an Association on Fourier's system might suffer.--That system seems to leave little to be done by circumstances, but starts with definite rules for every possible case. Still I desire to speak with great diffidence on this point, especially as my own experience shows me more and more the immense practical wisdom embodied in Fourier's plan. Particularly, I see the advantages of a large edifice sufficient for all the operations of an Association over detached buildings. Our plan is to have one large building for a dining-hall and kitchen, and to have the dwelling-houses and other buildings separate. Perhaps a combination of both plans would be better than either. I should not willingly give up the simple beauties of cottage architecture for the palace of a Phalanx.

The greatest difficulty we find is, what you would expect, the want of money. This limits us in every way. To remedy this we rely upon the toil of our hands more than any thing else. This is no play, but toil indeed. By and by we hope to have easier times.

Adin Ballou's Community is going on well, as we hear. They lack the aesthetic features which a just state of society must wear. They are, moreover, a sect, and thus cannot act universally, and will always embody certain vicious tendencies. But here they have an infinite compensation in the Idealism belonging to purely religious movements.

Of our Northampton friends we have good accounts also.

When are we to see an organization on the plan of Fourier? Be assured we look with great interest upon your proceedings, for though we cannot hope so much as if you started purely from Ideas, we do full justice to your generous zeal.

The impulses that move the heart of the age are not to be mistaken. Fairer than the dream of a prophet the Future glimmers upon us. On all the currents of the time, clear or muddy as they may be, we are urged toward a larger Manhood than Man has yet conceived. The Kingdom of God, that has always filled now and then a soul, is descending into all men. These attempts after a perfect society are plainly the most important things now doing. All other philanthropic effort is fragmentary and superficial, as if one would destroy a tree by cutting off here and there a branch.

*"The West Roxbury Community," New-York Daily Tribune, 13 August 1842, p. 1. Introduced as "a private letter from a gentleman who is a member of the Community known as Rev. Mr. Ripley's at West Roxbury, Mass."

BROOK FARM*

Orestes A. Brownson

The subjoined letter from a highly esteemed friend and distinguished literary lady, giving some notice of Brook Farm, or the Community at West Roxbury, Mass., was addressed to me while Editor of the Boston Quarterly Review, and would have appeared in the last number of that journal, but for the want of room. This will explain its personal address and allusions. It is laid before the readers of the Democratic Review, because its details can hardly fail to interest them, and because it gives me an opportunity to offer some additional remarks on the importance of establishments like that of Brook Farm, in working out the moral, intellectual, and physical amelioration of mankind, especially of the poorest and most numerous class.

. . . .

It is proper, however, to remark, that Brook Farm is not an establishment for the indolent, nor for those who are in need of charity. It is an INDUSTRIAL ESTABLISHMENT. Industry is its basis and its object. It is established on the principle that man must obtain his bread by the sweat of his face. This must be borne in mind in attempting like establishments. The founder of this establishment very justly remarks: "Every community should have its leading purpose, some one main object to which it directs its energies. We are a company of teachers. The branch of industry which we pursue as our primary object, and chief means of support, is teaching. Others may be companies of manufacturers or of agriculturists; or may engage in some particular branch of manufacture or of agriculture. Whatever the branch of industry agreed upon, it will be necessary to make that the principal object of pursuit, as the only way in which unity and efficiency can be secured to the labors of the community."

Of the advantages of associated and attractive industry there is no occasion to speak. They are well known, and have been ably presented by Mr.

Brisbane, in the pages of this Journal and elsewhere. The common merit, and the chief merit of the schemes of Owen and Fourier, is in their proposing associated and attractive industry. These Mr. Ripley secures at Brook Farm, without their complicated machinery, and multiplicity of details,--of details often frivolous; at any rate foreign to the habits, tastes, and convictions of the American people. Families of moderate means associating in this way, by their union and co-operation may obtain an industrial and pecuniary independence to which they cannot aspire under existing social relations. What we most want, is such an arrangement as shall secure to every man a competence as the reward of his industry, and which shall render industry in any or all of its branches compatible with the highest moral and intellectual culture, and the greatest delicacy and refinement of manners. This we cannot have as things are; but this by means of association on the principles of the Brook Farm establishment we may have. And when once this is obtained, when I am once sure that by the labor of my hands I can earn and honest and an honorable livelihood, and without being obliged to forego any of the real advantages, pleasures, and refinements of society and social intercourse, I shall no longer feel that I was cursed by my Maker, when he commanded me to "eat my bread in the sweat of my face."

. . . .

"August, 1842.

"MY DEAR SIR: I have made my visit to the Community, as it is called, at West Roxbury, and find that it more than answers the expectation held out in that account of it, which appeared in the Dial last January. I mean that the degree of success already attained, is greater than it was there intimated it could be, for many years to come. In a pecuniary point of view it is not failing, and that is success, considering the great embarrassments under which they began. There are seventeen associates. Had each of these been able to contribute one thousand dollars a-piece, they would be at this moment under no embarrassment at all, but instead of that, not one third of the sum was contributed. For the cost of their farm, as I understood it, they are paying interest; but by

means of the farm and the school, they are able to
pay this interest and to <u>feed</u> themselves; although
there are seventy people already there, and the
number will be one hundred in the course of the
winter. The joining of a few associates or even
one with some money, would render them quite
independent. But they feel they have gained so
much morally and intellectually, by having been so
poor, as to have had none join but those to whom
the accomplishment of the <u>Idea</u> appears worth
working and suffering for, that it is no longer to
be feared, that they will be tempted to receive
among them any, of whom money is the chief
recommendation. They prefer to sacrifice many
conveniences, to endangering the social and ideal
character of their company. Several mechanics who
have been hired to do jobs upon the place, I mean
carpenters, blacksmiths, shoemakers, tailors, have
at first expressed themselves amazed, that people
should go together, of such apparent inequality,
and make a common cause, and share the fruits of
their labors equally among themselves; but after
seeing the operation for weeks, they have desired
to join, and to forego some of the income they were
already receiving from their trades, in order to
have the enjoyment, the moral advantage, and the
intellectual improvement, of a social life on
principles so consistently democratic and
Christian; and more especially, in order to have
all their children have every advantage of
education to which their abilities can do justice.
I speak of facts. The association has actually
under consideration such propositions. Also, one
of the farmers, the most thriving one, whose farm
joins theirs, has for the sake of his children made
them the offer, if they can meet him half way, of
throwing in his farm and becoming one. He would be
richer in dollars and cents to remain as he is, but
this additional money could not buy for him that
education of all his children, which he must
receive in this community, if he is one of them; to
say nothing of his own enjoyment and improvement.
To me, it is an inspiring thought, that they have
already showed to the agricultural population
around them, that with the cultivation of the earth
may be combined an intellectual and tasteful life,
and that the true democratic equality may be
obtained by <u>levelling up</u>, instead of <u>levelling
down</u>.

But let me speak of the education in detail, and show that the children of the actual associates have even greater advantages than those sent there, though for the latter, it is, I think, the best school I ever saw. I will begin with the a-b-c-d-arians. There is one lady among the associates, who loves to keep a regular school on the old-fashioned plan, with a kind but efficient discipline of rules and lessons. She has as many of the younger scholars as the parents wish. But some parents prefer a different system--in which their children are only confined a very short time, while they can be individually attended to by the teacher. And there are among the young women, several who take two or three at once--making one little class, and enlist their undivided, unwavering attention for an hour, or an hour and a half, and then let them play all the rest of the day. These children, in this way, get more instruction and do more intellectual work, than in ordinary schools, and yet have none of the weariness and bad physical and moral effect of confinement. They are never obliged to sit still and do nothing; nor do they in this plan become troublesome to others. There is so much room, they can spread round, and find infinite amusement on the place. I never saw children at once so happy and so little in the way of other people. There seemed to be great love for the little things, in all the men and boys, as well as the women; and I observed that when the young men went to walk in the woods, or about any out-of-door occupation, they would let two or three children go too, and keep their eye upon them, and so relieve the mothers and make the children happy, and this without troubling themselves either. Children from the ages of nine or ten up to thirteen and fourteen, go to the school of a gentleman who has been a very successful teacher for many years, and understands the drilling processes. But of this class also, if there are any, whose parents, on account of their health, or peculiar genius, or sex, wish to receive separate attention, there are found those who will attend to them in a very desirable way. Then there is a very fine teacher of Greek, and another of Latin, and another of Mathematics, among the gentlemen associates. Several teach German, French, Italian and Spanish, and I do not know how many other things. One lady has classes in History, Moral Philosophy, various branches of elegant literature, and with all her cares, (one of which is the care of a house of fourteen rooms), she told me she had not for more than a year set aside two recitations! This will show what real method lies under the graceful exterior, where not mathematical lines, but only the curves of beauty appear. This lady told me, too, that never in her life had she had so much leisure and enjoyment of herself, for hours together, and never had the occupations of life been so little fatiguing to her.

I would have you observe that grown up persons, as well as children, are members of these various classes. The workmen in the field partake just as much as they please, of these means of education. One man, who does as much hard work, if not more than any one on the place, and who never learnt any language, and is forty years old, a husband and father, having been engaged in a mechanical trade all his life, studied German last winter, on Ollendorf's method, with the greatest perseverance. They had eighty recitations a week, last winter. All have access also to all the books owned by any of the members, the most of them being collected in a charming room, designated as the "Library," of which all are free, young and old.

In another common parlor there is a piano-forte, and there, in the evening, the lovers or music congregate, and hear fine music from some of their number, sometimes songs, and sometimes psalms, and sometimes the deep music of Beethoven. Mr. J. S. D[wight]. superintends the musical department of the teaching. The very little children have to sing by rote; those who are old enough, are taught by the Manual of the Academy of Music. Instrumental music is also taught to all who have the ability and the desire to learn. It struck me how beautiful it would be, if some of those noble Italian exiles should go and join their number, who could throw in their music and their beautiful language, and receive in return the realization of the dreams of their youth; but all this will come in good time.

To go back to the children. The greatest advantage is, that the life is so natural, it makes a discipline without the ugly forms. Every body works and studies, and so the children work and study from imitation and in spirit. I never saw such 'habits of disinterestedness--so little personal selfishness. Children were requested by all parties to do all sorts of things; and if one had refused, another would only have been called upon, as the only rebuke. The punishment of appearing selfish, and not being in the general spirit, precludes all others. Of course, I do not mean to imply that any circumstances of social arrangement will destroy all moral evil. I know there are those which originate in the constitution of every finite creature, and which are only to be set aside in their principles and consequences, by a deep internal struggle, where there is no witness but God, by whose sovereign mercy alone is the great victory accomplished, and each individual introduced into "the company of the first born." But there are innumerable social vices, and deformities of character, which are exasperated, if not produced, by the unsanctified conventions of our common life, and which here do not appear; and there is no telling how much more those who are good have the advantage of their goodness, and those who are morally inferior are assisted, by living where there is such a general spirit and such habits among the adults. Country employments and country scenery, too, has an immeasurable effect upon children's tempers. I would repeat, that I am not one of those who believe that the issues of the human constitution, under any earthly circumstances, can be perfect goodness;--that finite creatures can ever be other than <u>pensioners</u> of the Love revealed in Jesus Christ; but I do believe that infancy and youth would shine with moral beauty, as a general rule, if society and education did their part. Some people seem to be dreadfully afraid that God will not have anything to forgive, and so the doctrine of forgiveness be proved unnecessary, if we admit that children can grow up, unselfish in their habits and lovely in their general characters. Such persons have, it seems to me, very little appreciation of the depth, and extent, and excellence of that Law, the violation of which is sin; for it seems to me that we may be very high in the scale of excellence, in the eyes of our fellow creatures; your faults may be not even perceptible to them; and yet we may be so far below that Ideal, which shines into us from God, that we shall yet require all the comfort of St. Paul's doctrine of justification by faith. I see less self-righteousness likely to be generated, under the views and habits of this community, than ordinarily; and to stand a better chance of being corrected. Should man, in the progress of wisdom and love, be elevated above all social crime and wrong, there will yet, as I think, be sin possible to him, great enough to have him feel the whole opposition between the law of finite natures, and that Law of the Infinite God, which Christ mysteriously reveals to him, as a glory to be had.

This is rather an episode in my letter, dear sir, but I must needs dwell a little upon the subject, because the majority of people I hear talk, seem to be in one of two extremes, equally erroneous. One set of people make no evil but social evil, and seem to think that if wars and theft and deception, are driven from the earth, the whole holiness and glory of humanity is attained, even up to the measure of Christ Jesus; while others think, that because the Bible and the Spirit of God within us teach that man, even when pure as the heaven or heavens, is not clean BEFORE God, he must necessarily unfold, in the process of his development, all the crimes to which he can be degraded; and that a systematical effort to prevent this, by removing occasions and exasperating causes of crime, is opposing the systems of Providence, and practically denying the philosophy of Christianity. I have heard it gravely urged against this little community, that it aimed at a state of enjoyment and general excellence, which would result, if it succeeded, in a state contrary to what the Bible declares to be the general character of human nature. I dispute the fact. I believe human nature may attain to a state of excellence that shall seem to realize Isaiah's visions of the millennium, and still the inhabitants of the earth will be even more disposed to use, with respect to themselves, the deepest language of contrition and humility which the Bible contains; for then they shall <u>see</u> <u>God</u>, by reason of their purity, so much more, that they shall still more earnestly feel the prayer,

"Forgive our <u>virtues</u> too--

Those lesser faults--half converts to the right."

It is because I think thus, that I do not condemn utterly that other class of errorists, who suppose evil so very superficial; and that if we could eschew bad organization of society, and act out our instincts, we should be as perfect, as human beings, as the animal creation is pefect in its way, and the vegetable creation in its way. In their faith in the better issues of human instincts under favorable circumstances, they go upon a fact. Human nature is capable of great excellence, beauty, and purity, when it draws only upon the original gifts of the good God of nature, common to all men; and there is a sort of blasphemy to me, in speaking irreverently of the virtues of Solon and Aristides, Anaxagoras, and Plato, and Socrates; of Regulus, and Brutus, and the Antonines; and even of many a beautiful child and adult of the present day, although he has not yet entered into all the depths of the unsearchable riches of Christ. To be arrested at the point of attainment of any of these persons, would indeed be to be damned, (if I may use old-fashioned phraseology). Such minds we may call a sort of heaven, But I think these persons would say, that to be condemned to an everlasting self-development in that same heaven, and receive nothing from without, or from the deeper within which is a without to the individual; in short, to have no more grace of God, would make it to them a hell. Indeed, the Swedenborgian hells are neither more nor less than for the individual to be given up to his individuality; and so Swedenborg says that the damned are often not without their enjoyments; which whole system shows how deeply he looked into things. But what is such enjoyment to the action upon an infinite good? The joy of immortality, and the only doctrine of immortality which is not a misnomer, consists in believing that man never is absorbed in the Infinite, but is CONSCIOUSLY RELATIVE for ever and ever. This is, if I read it aright, your own doctrine of life, as you have stated it in your letter to Dr. Channing, which I believe people do not understand, because you have couched it so much in theological formulas, that they do not see it to be something they have not thought.

At Brook Farm there may be more inclination to the error of believing that self-development, on the original stock of human nature, is the true way, than to the equal error of supposing it necessary to undervalue and be unfaithful to this original stock, which prevails in the world. But there are those there, who are the predominating life and strength of the place, who transcend both errors; and there is nothing in the plan of their life which favors either.

But I will leave moralising and theologising, and return to an account of what I saw in my visit.

With respect to the labor, which is the material wealth of the establishment, and the body of its life, they intend to have all trades and occupations which contribute to necessities and healthy elegancies, within their own borders, so as not to buy them from without, which is too expensive; but at present their labor is agriculture, and the simplest housekeeping. They have above a dozen cows that they take care of, and sell all their milk at the door; they cultivate vegetables extensively, and sell them in the markets of Roxbury and Boston, and this branch of their industry may be almost indefinitely extended. They cultivate grass also, and sell hay very profitably. I do not know about their grain, not being wise enough in those matters to understand what I saw. The farm is not wholly under cultivation, because they have not yet force enough to do all they wish. Fifty more men might be profitably employed on it. Teachers, scholars, and all, work. Their Greek teacher spends several hours a day in taking care of the fruit, which hereafter, they think, will constitute a great part of their wealth. Every one prescribes his own hours of labor, controlled only by his conscience, and the spirit of place, which tends to great industry, and almost to too much exertion. A drone would soon find himself isolated and neglected, and could not live there. The new comers, especially if they come from the city, have to begin gradually, but soon learn to increase the labor of one hour a day in the field, to six or seven hours, and some work all day long; but there can be no drudgery where there is no constraint. As all eat together, they change their dress for their meals; and so after tea they are all ready for grouping, in the parlors of the ladies, or in the library, or in the music-room, or they can go to their private rooms, or into the woods, or anywhere. They visit a good deal; and when they have business out of the community, nothing seems more easy than for them to arrange with others of their own number, to take their work or teaching for the time being; so that while they may work more than people out of the community, none seem such prisoners of their duties. The association of labor makes distribution according to taste and ability easy, and this takes the sting out of fatigue. Then I believe bodily labor does not fatigue so much, when the mind is active and elevated by noble sentiments; and certainly, intelligence and the spirit of improvement, give the advantage of saving themselves drudgery, by all the devices of our mechanical age. Perhaps they might go into vagaries in labor-saving expedients, but that their narrow pecuniary means checks all freakishness of mind in this respect. They put their hands to the plough in good earnest, and do their work by main strength, and not by stratagem. As the pupils work more or less, it makes the school a most desirable one for farmers' children; and I hope many a young man will be saved to the healthy pursuits of agricultural life, by this establishment, whose laudable desire for intellectual improvement and for bettering his condition in life, would drive him into our crowded professions and city warehouses.

For the women, there is, besides many branches of teaching, washing and ironing, housekeeping, sewing for the other sex, and for the children, and conducting all the social life. They have to hire one washerwoman now, but hope, bye and bye, to do all the washing within themselves. By the wide distribution of these labors, no one has any great weight of any one thing. They iron every forenoon but one; but they take turns, and each irons as long as she thinks right. The care of the houses is also distributed among those who are most active, in a way mutually satisfactory. And so of the cooking. In nothing did they seem to feel so immediate a desirableness of improvement, as in the kitchen department, and the eating rooms. These are all in the old house, and not at all convenient. Their next building is to be a kitchen establishment, and convenient dining hall, which will enable them to appear much more to advantage; besides leaving the old house, which they called "the Hive," to be entirely used for sleeping rooms and parlors. A more spacious and convenient dining-hall will enable them to be less confused and more elegant at table, than which nothing is more important for the general tone of manners. There is no vulgarity now, because all the people have the sentiment and desire of improvement; but many have not been in society, and these need to have things so arranged that the table manners of the more educated and best bred should have a chance to be observed, and do their work of refinement. The manners of the children also can then be more easily attended to; and when this is brought about it seems to me that in the article of elegance they will not fall behind the rest of the world. Without any wearisome etiquette there would be the beauty that naturally hovers round "plain living and high thinking"; and of which nothing now hinders the full development, but their crowded and inconvenient eating apartments. I ought to say that though a common table is preferable to most, yet any individual family, by taking the trouble on themselves, can have some or all of their meals at their own rooms; and now any individuals who wish, on account of ill health or for any other reason, to take a meal alone, can easily do so; and constantly there are those who are thus favored. You would hardly imagine that so many individuals should have their own way so constantly without clashing. For a time they did not have any regular housekeeper, but this office passed from one to the other; for they were afraid that the pride and tyranny of office might interfere with the freedom of individuals, and they preferred the inconveniences of frequent change, to the evil of that fixed vexation. But at last a housekeeper appeared, so fit, that they created for her the office! This woman went out to sew for them a week as a sempstress, during which time she used her eyes and ears and mind to such purpose that at the end of the week she wanted to join. The associates proposed that she should remain two months, without committing herself; and then, if she continued in the same mind, she should be considered to have joined from the first. During these two months she employed herself variously, and showed so much delicacy and tact, as well as ability and housekeeping talent, that they all agreed that she should be queen in that department, and they would obey. I do not know what measures they would take to dethrone her if she should grow naughty, but at present she reigns by the greatest of King Alfred's titles, the divine right of might and virtue.

I do not seem to myself to have told you a moiety of the good which I saw; I have only indicated some of it. But is it not enough to justify me in saying they have succeeded? It seems to me, if their highest objects were appreciated, they would challenge some of the devotedness which makes the Sisters of Charity throw large fortunes into their institution, and give themselves, body and soul, to its duties. It is truly a most religious life, and does it not realize in miniature that identity of church and state which you think is the deepest idea of our American government? It seems to me that this community, point by point, corresponds with the great community of the Republic, whose divine lineaments are so much obscured by the rubbish of reported abuses (that, however, only lie on the surface, and may be shaken off, "like dewdrops from the lion's mane";) and whose divine proportions are now lost to our sight by the majestic grandeur with which they tower beyond the apprehension of our time-bound senses. For the theory of our government also proposes education (the freest development of the individual, according to the law of God) as its main end; an equal distribution of the results of labor among the laborers, as its means; and a mutual respect of each man by his neighbor as the basis. Only in America, I think, could such a community have so succeeded as I have described, composed of persons coming by chance, as it were, from all circumstances of life, and united only by a common idea and plan of life. They have succeeded, because they are the children of a government the ideal of which is the same as their own, although, as a mass, we are unconscious of it; so little do we understand our high vocation, and act up to it. But these miniatures of the great original shall educate us to the apprehension and realization of it, as a nation.

Some people make objection to this community, because it has no chapel in it. But I think this is an excellent feature of it. There are churches all round it, to which any can go as they please; and there has been a service within it, which such might attend as were not pleased with any neighboring church; and this might be resumed if there were not seen to be a general preference in the church-goers to go out. The children are gathered on Sundays spontaneously, to sing hymns, the natural devotion of children, and to be read to by those who wish to do so; and there is a perfect freedom to do anything for social religious worship, that is felt desirable, by any, provided only nothing is prescribed to another authoritatively.

I meant to have asked you in some detail whether it would not be possible for this community system to be introduced into our cities by persons of different employments who were willing to associate, and thrown in their small capitals, combining and living together in some large hotel, or block of houses, agreeably situated, and perhaps having a country house attached? I have no head to make arrangements, but I should like much to have such a thing planned out. What do you think?

I am truly your friend,
&c., &c.

*O. A. Brownson, "Brook Farm," United States Magazine, and Democratic Review, 11 (November 1842): 481-496. This was reprinted in the New-York Daily Tribune, 20 January 1843, p. 4. Material not referring to Brook Farm has been omitted. The article in the Dial referred to is Peabody's "Plan of the West Roxbury Community," printed above. Brownson's The Mediatorial Life of Jesus. A Letter to Rev. William Ellery Channing, D. D. was published in 1842.

THE WEST ROXBURY COMMUNITY*

The West Roxbury Community (nine miles from Boston,) having enlarged their buildings and other accommodations, offer to receive and educate a few more children and young persons on terms not dissimilar from the higher Academical institutions throughout the Country. The peculiarities of Education at this Seminary are so marked that we are induced to mention some of the more prominent as hints to Instructors and themes of reflection for Parents generally.

In the first place, the least possible restraint is used over the children placed there for Education, and the least practicable manifestation of Authority or Superiority made on the part of their Teachers and elders. The design is to inculcate ideas of Freedom, Equality and Responsibility in tender years. Every child is made to feel that what is elsewhere enforced by Punishment is here confidently expected from his Self-Respect, Intelligence, Gratitude and Love.

Again: Children, especially the very young, are not rigidly required to devote so many hours per day to the study of their lessons, but every effort is made to awaken their interest in the acquisition of Knowledge, to lead them to <u>solicit</u> instruction, and, having a liberal range of hours and fields for exercise and recreation, to feel no constraint, formality or irksomeness in the School-room, but to enjoy the lesson as much as the holiday intermission.

Thirdly: It is intended that the <u>whole</u> Intellectual and Moral being of the pupils shall be here by developed in perfect harmony with the Physical, so that no child shall be occupied with the technicalities of the Latin Grammar before it has learned the meaning of an English sentence; or have its head filled with barren <u>terms</u> before it has acquired any Knowledge of the <u>things</u> which they signify.

Such are some of the peculiarities, as we understand them, of this Experimental Seminary.-- Should any desire to learn farther of it, they will address Geo. Ripley, Esq. Principal, West Roxbury, Mass.

*"The West Roxbury Community," New-York Weekly Tribune, 25 February 1843, p. 2.

AMERICAN CORRESPONDENCE*

Charles Lane

Our friend Charles Lane writes to us, from Fruitlands, Harvard, Massachusetts, dated July 30, 1843, as follows, which we trust will be interesting to many of our readers:--
"Mr. Alcott and I returned last evening from a short visit to Boston, to purchase a few articles; and while there we went out one evening to Roxbury, where there are eighty or ninety persons playing away their youth and day-time in a miserably joyous frivolous manner. There are not above four or five who could be selected as really and truly progressing beings. Most of the adults are there to pass "a good time"; the children are taught languages, &c. The animals occupy a prominent position, there being no less than sixteen cows, besides four oxen, a herd of swine, a horse or two, &c. The milk is sold in Boston, and they buy butter, to the extent of 500 dollars a year. We had a pleasant summer evening conversation with many of them, but it is only in a few individuals that anything deeper than ordinary is to be found. The Northampton Community is one of industry--the one at Hopedale aims at practical theology--this of Roxbury is one of taste; yet it is the best which exists here, and perhaps we shall have to say it is the best which can exist. At all events, we can go no further than to keep open fields, and, as far as we have it, open house to all comers. We know very well that if they come not in the right name and nature, they will not long remain. Our dietetic system is a test quite sufficient for many. As far as acres of fine land are concerned, you may offer their free use to any free souls who will come here and work them, and any aid we can offer shall be freely given. The aid of sympathetic companionship is not small, and that at least we can render. To bridge the Atlantic is a trifle, if the heart is really set on the attainment of better conditions. Here are they freely presented, at a day's walk from the shore, without a long and expensive journey to the West. Please to advertize these

facts to all youthful men and women, for such are much wanted here. There is now a certain opportunity for planting a love colony, the influence of which may be felt for many generations, and more than felt: it may be the beginning for a state of things which shall far transcend itself. They to whom our work seems not good enough, may come and set out a better.

"I could send you a description of works and crops--our mowing, hoeing, reaping, ploughing in tall crops of clover and grass for next year's manure, and various other operations; but although they have some degree of relation to the grand principle to which they are obedient, they are worth little in the exoteric sense alone. Perhaps the internal revelations of success ought always to be kept secret, for every improvement discovered is only turned to a money-making account, and to the further degradation of man, as we see in the march of science to this very moment. If we knew how to double the crops of the earth, it is scarcely to be hoped that any good would come by revealing the mode. On the contrary, the bounties of God are already made the means by which man debases himself more and more. We will, therefore, say little concerning the sources of external wealth, until man is himself secured to the End which rightly uses these means."

Should any of our friends consider emigration a favourable step towards human elevation, and be disposed to avail themselves of the above invitation of our friend Charles Lane, we shall be happy to advise with such parties, and enter into such arrangements as will render the undertaking easy to be put in practice.-- Editor.

*Charles Lane, "American Correspondence," New Age, Concordian Gazette, and Temperance Advocate (England), 1 (1 September 1843): 90. Lane and Bronson Alcott had started the Fruitlands community in June 1843.

THE ROXBURY COMMUNITY*

This is almost exclusively an Educational establishment, relying mainly upon the income of an excellent school, which, from the peculiar nature of its organization and management is, in our opinion, the best in the country, and depends but slightly upon its industrial income. It is situated about 8 miles from Boston, and possesses at present about 250 acres of fine land; the cultivation of which constitutes its only branch of industry. It is, however, wished to establish some branches of mechanics, and good mechanics who have some capital would find an advantageous location there. Letters may be addressed, <u>post paid</u>, to the Rev. Geo. Ripley, Roxbury, Mass.

*"The Roxbury Community," <u>Phalanx</u>, 1 (5 October 1843): 15-16. The <u>Phalanx</u>, started with this number, was the semi-official journal of the American Associationists, and was succeeded by the Brook Farm <u>Harbinger</u> after its collapse in May 1845.

BROOK FARM*

Charles Lane

Wherever we recognize the principle of progress, our sympathies and affections are engaged. However small may be the innovation, however limited the effort towards the attainment for pure good, that effort is worthy of our best encouragement and succor. The Institution at Brook Farm, West Roxbury, though sufficiently extensive in respect to number of persons, perhaps is not to be considered an experiment of large intent. Its aims are moderate; too humble indeed to satisfy the extreme demands of the age; yet, for that reason probably, the effort is more valuable, as likely to exhibit a larger share of actual success.

Though familiarly designated a "Community," it is only so in the process of eating in commons; a practice at least, as antiquated, as the collegiate halls of old England, where it still continues without producing, as far as we can learn, any of the Spartan virtues. A residence at Brook Farm does not involve either a community of money, of opinions, or of sympathy. The motives which bring individuals there, may be as various as their members. In fact, the present residents are divisible into three distinct classes; and if the majority in numbers were considered, it is possible that a vote in favor of self-sacrifice for the common good would not be very strongly carried. The leading portion of the adult inmates, they whose presence imparts the greatest peculiarity and the fraternal tone to the household, believe that an improved state of existence would be developed in association, and are therefore anxious to promote it. Another class consists of those who join with the view of bettering their condition, by being exempted from some portion of worldly strife. The third portion, comprises those who have their own development or education, for their principal object. Practically, too, the institution manifests a threefold improvement over the world at large, corresponding to these three motives. In consequence of the first, the companionship, the personal intercourse, the social bearing are of a marked, and very superior character. There may possibly, to some minds, long accustomed to other modes, appear a want of homeness, and of the private fireside; but all observers must acknowledge a brotherly and softening condition, highly conducive to the permanent, and pleasant growth of all the better human qualities. If the life is not of a deeply religious cast, it is at least not inferior to that which is exemplified elsewhere; and there is the advantage of an entire absence of assumption and pretence. The moral atmosphere so far is pure; and there is found a strong desire to walk ever on the mountain tops of life; though taste, rather than piety, is the aspect presented to the eye.

In the second class of motives, we have enumerated, there is a strong tendency to an important improvement in meeting the terrestrial necessities of humanity. The banishment of servitude, the renouncement of hireling labor, and the elevation of all unavoidable work to its true station, are problems whose solution seems to be charged upon association; for the dissociate systems have in vain sought remedies for this unfavorable portion of human condition. It is impossible to introduce into separate families even one half of the economies, which the present state of science furnishes to man. In that particular, it is probable that even the feudal system is superior to the civic: for its combinations permit many domestic arrangements of an economic character, which are impracticable in small households. In order to economize labor, and dignify the laborer, it is absolutely necessary that men should cease to work in the present isolate competitive mode, and adopt that of cooperative union or association. It is as false and as ruinous to call any "master" in secular business, as it is in theological opinions. Those persons, therefore, who congregate for the purpose, as it is called, of bettering their outward relations, on principles so high and universal as we have endeavoured to describe, are not engaged in a petty design, bounded by their own selfish or temporary improvement. Every one who is here found giving up the usual chances of individual aggrandizement, may not be thus influenced; but whether it be so or not, the outward demonstration will probably be equally certain. In education, Brook Farm appears to present greater mental freedom than most other institutions. The tuition being more heart-rendered, is in its effects more heart-stirring. The younger pupils as well as the more advanced students are held, mostly if not wholly, by the power of love. In this particular, Brook farm is a much improved model for the oft-praised schools of New England. It is time that the imitative and book-learned systems of the latter should be superseded or liberalized by some plan, better calculated to excite originality of thought, and the native energies of the mind. The deeper, kindly sympathies of the heart, too, should not be forgotten; but the germination of these must be despaired of under a rigid hireling system. Hence, Brook farm, with its spontaneous teachers, presents the unusual and cheering condition of a really "free school."

By watchful and diligent economy, there can be no doubt that a community would attain greater pecuniary success, than is within the hope of honest individuals working separately. But Brook Farm is not a Community, and in the variety of motives with which persons associate there, a double diligence, and a watchfulness perhaps too costly, will be needful to preserve financial prosperity. While, however, this security is an essential element in success, riches would, on the other hand, be as fatal as poverty, to the true progress of such an institution. Even in the case of those foundations which have assumed a religious character, all history proves the fatality of wealth. The just and happy mean between riches and poverty, is, indeed, more likely to be attained when, as in this instance, all thought of acquiring great wealth in a brief time, is necessarily abandoned, as a condition of membership. On the other hand, the presence of many persons, who congregate merely for the attainment of some individual end, must weigh heavily and unfairly upon those whose hearts are really expanded to universal results. As a whole, even the imitative powers of Brook Farm have, as is found almost every where, the design of a life much too objective, too much derived from objects in the exterior world.

The subjective life, that in which the soul finds the living source and the true communion within itself, is not sufficiently prevalent to impart to the establishment the permanent and sedate character it should enjoy. Undeniably, many devoted individuals are there; several who have as generously as wisely relinquished what are considered great social and pecuniary advantages; and by throwing their skill and energies into a course of the most ordinary labors, at once prove their disinterestedness, and lay the foundation of industrial nobility.

An assemblage of persons, not brought together by the principles of community, will necessarily be subject to many of the inconveniences of ordinary life, as well as to burdens peculiar to such a condition. Now Brook Farm is at present such an institution. It is not a community; it is not truly an association; it is merely an aggregation of persons, and lacks that oneness of spirit, which is probably needful to make it of deep and lasting value to mankind. It seems, even after three years' continuance, uncertain, whether it is to be resolved more into an educational, or an industrial institution, or into one combined of both. Placed so near a large city, and in a populous neighborhood, the original liability for land, &c., was so large, as still to leave a considerable burden of debt. This state of things seems fairly to entitle the establishment to re-draw from the old world in fees for education, or in the sale of produce, sufficient to pay the annual interest of such liabilities. Hence the necessity for a more intimate intercourse with the trading world, and a deeper involvement in money affairs than would have attended a more retired effort of the like kind. To enter into the corrupting modes of the world, with the view of diminishing or destroying them, is a delusive hope. It will, notwithstanding, be a labor of no little worth, to induce improvements in the two grand departments of industry and education. We say <u>improvement</u>, as distinct from <u>progress</u>; for with any association short of community, we do not see how it is possible for an institution to stand so high above the present world, as to conduct its affairs on principles entirely different from those which now influence men in general.

There are other considerations also suggested by a glance at Brook Farm, which are worthy the attention of the many minds now attracted by the deeply interesting subject of human association. We are gratified by observing several external improvements during the past year; such as larger and a more convenient dining room, a labor-saving cooking apparatus, a purer diet, a more orderly and quiet attendance at the refections, superior arrangements for industry, and generally an increased seriousness in respect to the value of the example, which those who are there assembled may constitute to their fellow beings.

Of about seventy persons now assembled there, about thirty are children sent thither for education; some adult persons also place themselves there chiefly for mental assistance; and in the society there are only four married couples. With such materials it is almost certain that the sensitive and vital points of communication cannot well be tested. A joint-stock company, working with some of its own members and with others as agents, cannot bring to issue the great question, whether the existence of the marital family is compatible with that of the universal family, which the term "Community" signifies. This is now the grand problem. By mothers it has ever been felt to be so. The maternal instinct, as hitherto educated, has declared itself so strongly in favor of the separate fire-side, that association, which appears so beautiful to the young and unattached soul, has yet accomplished little progress in the affections of that important section of the human race--the mothers. With fathers, the feeling in favor of the separate family is certainly less strong; but there is an undefinable tie, a sort of magnetic *rapport*, an invisible, inseverable, umbilical cord between the mother and child, which in most cases circumscribes her desires and ambition to her own immediate family. All the accepted adages and wise saws of society, all the precepts of morality, all the sanctions of theology, have for ages been employed to confirm this feeling. This is the chief corner stone of present society; and to this maternal instinct have, till very lately, our most heartfelt appeals been made for the progress of the human race, by means of a deeper and more vital education. Pestalozzi and his most enlightened disciples are distinguished by this sentiment. And are we all at once to abandon, to deny, to destroy this supposed stronghold of virtue? Is it questioned whether the family arrangement of mankind is to be preserved? Is it discovered that the sanctuary, till now deemed the holiest on earth, is to be invaded by intermeddling skepticism, and its altars sacrilegiously destroyed by the rude hands of innovating progress? Here "social science" must be brought to issue. The question of association and of marriage are one. If, as we have been popularly led to believe, the individual or separate family is in the true order of Providence, then the associative life is a false effort. If the associative life is true, then is the separate family a false arrangement. By the maternal feeling, it appears to be decided that the coexistence of both is incompatible, is impossible. So also say some religious sects. Social science ventures to assert their harmony. This is the grand problem now remaining to be solved, for at least, the enlightening, if not for the vital elevation of humanity. That the affections can be divided or bent with equal ardor on two objects, so opposed as universal and individual love, may at least be rationally doubted. History has not yet exhibited such phenomena in an associate body, and scarcely perhaps in any individual. The monasteries and convents, which have existed in all ages, have been maintained solely by the annihilation of that peculiar affection on which the separate family is based. The Shaker families, in which the two sexes are not entirely dissociated, can yet only maintain their union by forbidding and preventing the growth of personal affection other than that of spiritual character. And this in fact is not personal in the sense of individual, but ever a manifestation of universal affection. Spite of the speculations of hopeful bachelors and aesthetic spinsters, there is somewhat in the marriage bond which is found to counteract the universal nature of the affections, to a degree tending at least to make the considerate pause, before they assert that, by any social arrangements whatever, the two can be blended into one harmony. The general condition of married persons at this time is some evidence of the existence of such a doubt in their minds. Were they as convinced as the unmarried of the beauty and truth of associate life, the demonstration would be now presented. But might it not be enforced that the two family ideas really neutralize each other? Is it not quite certain that the human heart cannot be set in two places; that man cannot worship at two altars? It is only the determination to do what parents consider the best for themselves and their families, which renders the o'er populous world such a wilderness of selfhood as it is. Destroy this feeling, they say, and you prohibit every motive to exertion. Much truth is there in this affirmation. For to them, no other motive remains, nor indeed to any one else, save that of the universal good, which does not permit the building up of supposed self-good; and therefore, forecloses all possibility of an individual family.

These observations, of course, equally apply to all the associative attempts, now attracting so much public attention; and perhaps most especially to such as have more of Fourier's designs than are observable at Brook Farm. The slight allusion in all the writers of the "Phalansterian" class, to the subject of marriage, is rather remarkable. They are acute and eloquent in deploring Woman's oppressed and degraded position in past and present times, but are almost silent as to the future. In the mean while, it is gratifying to observe the successes which in some departments attend every effort, and that Brook Farm is likely to become comparatively eminent in the highly important and praiseworthy attempts, to render labor of the hands more dignified and noble, and mental education more free and loveful.

*C[harles]. L[ane]., "Brook Farm," _Dial_, 4 (January 1844): 351-357. See also Lane's "American Correspondence," printed above.

LETTER ON BROOK FARM*

John Finch

To the Editor of the New Moral World.
Liverpool, Dec. 23, 1843.
. . . .
From Boston we made excursions by railroads, &c., to the great manufacturing towns of Lowell, Springfield, Providence, Hartford, and other places. Visited the communities lately formed at Brook Farm, near Roxberry [sic], conducted by the Rev. Mr. Ripley, Unitarian Minister; and the Northampton Industrial Association, under the Rev. Mr. Adam, Unitarian Minister, lately from Calcutta, where he was converted from a Baptist Missionary, to an Unitarian, by the instrumentality of the late celebrated Indian Brahmin, Rammohun Roy,--of these communities I shall have to speak more particularly on some future occasion, suffice it now to say, that the leaders of these institutions have some property, and that they are of the highest respectability as to attainments and moral character. Brook Farm Institute is a superior educational establishment, where farming, gardening, and some useful trades are taught, similar to our own at Harmony--and that at Northampton is more of an industrial community; they have a saw mill for sawing timber, they have a silk mill, and they rear silk worms to supply it, and they have a school; each of these communities has purchased about three hundred acres of land where they are located, and there is every reason at present to believe that they will succeed, they expect they will be self-supporting before the end of another year.
. . . .

*John Finch, "Correspondence," New Moral World (England), 12 (13 January 1844): 232. Material not referring to Brook Farm has been omitted.

THE BROOK FARM ASSOCIATION*

The Brook Farm Association, near Boston, is now in process of transformation and extension from the former condition of an educational establishment mainly, to a regularly organized Association--embracing the various departments of industry, art, and science. At the head of this movement, are George Ripley, Minot Pratt, and Charles A. Dana. We cannot speak in too high terms of these men and their enterprize. They are gentlemen of high standing in the community, and unite in an eminent degree, talent, scientific attainments and refinement, with great practical energy and experience. This Association has a fine spiritual basis in those already connected with it, and we hope that it will be able to rally in its aid, the industrial skill and capital necessary to organize an Association, in which productive labor, art, science, and the social and religious affections,will be so wisely and beautifully blended and combined, that they will lend reciprocal strength, support, elevation and refinement to each other, and secure abundance, give health to the body, development and expansion to the mind, and exaltation to the soul. We are convinced that there are abundant means and material in New England now ready to form a fine Association; they have only to be sought out and brought together.

We shall publish, in our next, the Constitution adapted for the new Organization, and an introductory statement;--our paper was set up before we received them.

*Phalanx, 1 (5 February 1844): 68.

NOTES ON TRAVEL IN THE UNITED STATES*

John Finch

Letter XIV.

To the Editor of the New Moral World.

Liverpool, April 10, 1844.

Dear Sir,--I am now to give an account of our visits to "The Brook Farm Institute" and "The Northampton Association of Education and Industry," Communities in Massachusetts.

On the 10th of May last year we hired a car in the morning, at Tremont House, Boston, for the use of which we paid three dollars for the day, and went in company with the Rev. Mr. Giles, late Unitarian minister at Park Chapel, Liverpool, (who is now lecturing to large and most respectable audiences in Boston and the neighbourhood, on the Poets, on Ireland, and other subjects, and occasionally preaching, and it will give his friends here pleasure to know that he is doing well, and is highly respected for his talents and conduct by all who know him), on a visit to the Rev. Mr. Ripley's Community at Brook Farm, near Roxbury, about nine miles from Boston, and returned to Boston in the evening.

Brook Farm Estate contains about 200 acres of tolerably well cultivated land. There are about fifty residents and thirty pupils. They have only three hired servants, and will do without these as soon as possible. The object they have in view is the formation of a very superior boarding-school, where the children shall learn every branch of useful science, a superior system of agriculture, and various useful trades, and by their labour after a time assist in defraying the expenses of their education. They have eleven teachers in the school, all of first-rate talents, highly educated, and of respectable family connexions; these all turn out to labour in the fields and gardens, and in domestic occupations of every kind, when they are not in the school. The Rev. Mr. Ripley, one of the most learned and eloquent Unitarian ministers of Boston, was dressed in a smock-frock, and driving a cart; <u>all useful occupations are considered equally honourable</u> at Brook Farm. No salaries are paid to any of the teachers or members, but an account is taken of the time of each teacher and member, and they propose taking stock at the end of each year, debiting each member with a certain sum for board for themselves and families, giving each credit for labour performed, and then passing each member's share of the net profits to the credit of his account in the books of the Society, which amount he will be entitled to if he leaves the Society. I told Mr. Ripley that he would find this part of his scheme so difficult and complicated that it would be quite impracticable. The Society is governed by a committee of twelve members, and they choose the Executive, consisting of the president and two counsellors, who have the general superintendence; and the committee meet once each week to examine the accounts and devise plans of proceeding. They intend to raise agricultural produce, to supply themselves and the children in the school with food; to keep smiths, builders, tailors, shoemakers, and other domestic trades, for farming operations, clothing, and building, and to pay interest of money for sums which they have borrowed, and to purchase other articles which they require, from the income derived from the boarders. Children above ten years of age pay 200 dolllars per annum for instruction, board, washing, fuel and lights; children under ten pay 160 dollars; and they have children in the schools from the very first families in the neighbourhood. The Society has not yet been formed more than two years, but the farm is much improved, and they have erected four handsome new houses, which they call "The Beehive," "The Cottage," "The Eagle's Nest," and "The Pilgrim's House." They have also erected cow-houses, stables, and other out-buildings. They have twenty cows, two oxen, four horses, six pigs, carts, agricultural implements, &c. They all eat at the same table, and all the children receive the same education, and that the very best they can give. The teachers in the schools are--

1. The Rev. George Ripley, instructor in intellectual and natural philosophy and mathematics.

2. John S. Brown, and 3, George P. Bradford, teachers.
4. John S. Dwight, instructor in Latin and music.
5. Charles A. Dana, instructor in Greek and German.
6. Manuel Diaz, instructor in Spanish.
7. Sophia W. Ripley, instructor in history and Italian.
8. Amelia E. Russell, instructor in French and dancing.
9. Hannah B. Ripley, instructor in drawing.
10. Marianne Ripley, and 11, Ann M. Dana, teachers.

Such is the Brook Farm Community, and from the knowledge, zeal, diligence, good feeling, cleanliness, and order everywhere seen, there is not the least reason to doubt of its complete success. Almost every individual of the teachers are from among the most intellectual members of the Unitarian body; but the Bible is not used, and no sectarian opinions are taught in the schools. Success to Brook Farm Institute! We will now relate our visit to the Northampton Community.

. . . .

*John Finch, "Notes of Travel in the United States," New Moral World (England), 12 (13 April 1844): 329. Material referring to the Northampton Community has been omitted.

BROOK FARM*

A. Bloomer Hart

Nine or ten miles from the city of Boston, amidst a pleasant country, is the abode of a growing Association whose aim is the unity of human interests. Figure to yourself a rural domain, its present extent two or three hundred acres of undulating land, traversed by a shallow brook, decked with a half dozen buildings, and contiguous to a wood, and you have the appearance of this farm. First on the site is the edifice called "the Hive," where strangers are received, where some of the classes are instructed, and the associates assemble for meals. At a little distance are the barn and workshops. That fawn-colored building, beyond and to the right, perched on a rocky base and approached by terraces, is "the Eyrie": linen and laces of the laundry are disposed here: it contains a valuable library, and is sometimes vocal with the music of a soireé. Next, in sober burnt umber, with its four gables, is "the Cottage": here is a class-room, there is a fathering of little ones. Farthest, that white house, because erected by a descendant of the pilgrims, and accommodating sojourners, and being at a distance, is known as "the Pilgrim-House." All these are temporary homes. Feeling the want of a unitary edifice, to save time and prevent exposure, a situation is chosen for it, and the foundation dug, on a suitable declivity.

Agreeably to the principles of the Institution, there is, of course, for so many people, a variety of occupations, whose bases are agriculture, mechanics, economy and education. And the labors of these departments are distributed among groups designated by name, as "the Consistory," "the Dormitory," &c.: and their respective hours are appropriated with exactness, so that the machinery may not jar or a needful operation fail.

A little child smiles with greater delight at the skeleton of a horse rudely penciled on a slate than at a faultless image of the animal limned by the graver's art. Young imagination is pleased by

filling up the outline: in the perfect picture there is nothing left to do, and it is simply contemplated in fancy's repose.
  With the feeling of a child have I looked on this infant effort of associative thought, and conceived the possible excellence of its future development. And faith says here that one's conceptions are more imbued with a prophetic sense than with the dreaminess of the castle-builder. Originating in a wish to retire from the falsities of the world, and disclose the life of the individual soul, it has gathered gradual accretions around its little nucleus, heard and read and adopted suggestions from the genius of Fourier, and is striving, as its powers grow, and its acquaintance with the science extends, to assimilate to itself the teachings and practice of his theory. It is obviously but the incipiency of a great work. With few more than a hundred souls-- one fourth of the number required for the minimum organization of groups--it is but the chrysalis of a phalansterian institution. Yet the chrysalis is healthy and active. And as you consider the vitality of its cheerfulness, the pervading spirit of devotion to a great idea, bodied in solidity of attainments and garnished with graces of manner, your heart and hope foretell that this struggling creation will ere long strengthen and rise and float in beauty through the atmosphere of being.
  A mere worldling is not a competent judge of the merits and purposes of such an institution. A man who would look curiously on novel things, to talk of them again, or print them in his superficial travels, may see oddities and supposed discrepancies, as opticians used to teach us that objects are painted inverted on the network of the eye. A man who does not understand that he is a limb of corporate humanity, will not feel the pulse from its heart beating in his arteries. If you have no inkling of the science of unity, you cannot pronounce an enlightened sentence on its modes of education, powers of attraction and purpose of labor. God forms of men, through the centuries, instruments to shed brighter light upon the pathway of human destiny.
  When you have rolled about an hour and a half from Boston over the fine road to Brook Farm, entered its domain, alighted at "the Hive," and

given some consideration to its society, your attention is arrested by its simple, fraternal courtesy. Your sympathy is bewitched, and a prevalent cheerfulness rests on your spirit. I could prescribe myself no better exorcism of "the blues," than an hour, or day, or week of mingling in its ranks, and participation in its feeling. One has an intuition that rudeness would be overawed and discord ostracised by the presiding <u>genius loci</u>. All these germinant groups are apparently controlled by one sense of propriety and happiness. And there are among them persons from the age of speechless childhood up to three score years and ten, men from the undistinguished walks of life and those whose names are not "unknown to fame." What reconciles and blends these diversities? This harmony is now years old, bidding the false prophets of the past to eat their words.

Then you witness the phenomenon of the absence of servitude. You see yourself waited upon at table by persons whom the mass know to be their superiors--probably your own superiors: and the ready skill of intelligence, the motions of grace, dignity of bearing and smile of pleasure, gild vulgar labor with a charm which, at your plain meal, minds you of the ministries of angels. You begin to ask your common sense the question, What is there more menial in carrying a plate than in carving a duck--in changing a cover than in pouring out tea? It is for my equals, and therefore polite; it is voluntary, and therefore agreeable. . . . In another direction, a well-bred lady, or a scholarly barrister, is busied in the small and rough details of the culinary department, and doing it from aptitude or choice. A travelled visitant of courts tends the "toddling wee things" of the nursery, or stirs among the linen of the laundry, or tills and weeds a garden, and this with passion and a face radiant with rose-hue and smiles. Gentlemen whose pens contribute to the literature of the day, swing the scythe with a thewy arm, or drive a plough afield. To be sure, like the rest, they vary their occupations, and sometimes pay a visit to Mr. Parnassus, or court the melodious inspirations of St. Cecilia. But Association is showing the world how to tear down the gossamer fallacies of factitious society; and as, in mediaeval periods, learning was left to monks, and it was only fitting men of mark to fly the falcon, tilt, or fight: and the last four centuries have ennobled learning; so, the present age will dignify labor, and teach the training of an integral man.

Now, solve me this problem. Yon fawn-like girl, with the camelia on her cheek and dove-note in her lip, engages in the toils of the study or cares of the chamber, and through all her various relations, disturbs not a note of the reigning accord. Here is a gentlewoman ere while fed from the golden spoon of opulence, renouncing the cushion of luxury as readily as if its tassels were thistles, and its down were thorns. There is her junior, who declared herself ineffably indolent and the victim of ennui in this boastful, backward "civilization," voluntarily transformed into an assiduous, self-sacrificing devotee of domestic industry. There is the accomplished archon óf the establishment, amid a hundred things, unaffectedly and quietly yielding a moment's precedence to a little boy, who is vanquished by politeness. This person, with a face bearing the idiosyncrasy of India, is a recovered invalid from distant Manila. That one is a staunch Roman Catholic, a lover of true church, with force of character, evinced in his resolute and persevering self-denial of an evil habit. Whence this content, concord and devotion?

Actual employment is one solution. It is an extraordinary fact that men of consummate skill and women of genius in their art, of willing minds and faultless temper, cannot, in the incoherent, disorganized condition of society, obtain requisite occupation for their hands or heads. They desire it, and they are desired; but are crushed in the crowd, or cannot emerge from this social labyrinth into the light. And who knows whether, unheralded, they are worthy? Or how can they, again, insure their recompense? Six instances presented themselves casually to my personal observation in a single day. To weep tears of blood had been to them a useless sympathy. To grind one's teeth in agony, or growl a reproach over extant institutions, providing no general protection, heedless of the general welfare, had been worse than useless. After one upward glance of assured hope at an enthroned Providence, it seemed better, under Heaven, to study the means of extricating the

masses and refined sufferers from their common predicament.
    Actual and fit employment is often as impossible in one's own home. You may study till you "weary the flesh," stupify the brain and disease the lungs in sedentary immobility. You may invent expedients of solitary gymnastics, profitless to the world, talk impiously of "killing time," or die the daily death of listless lassitude. Under these circumstances, the physical and moral parts of men are undeveloped, the whole man has not appeared. Now, actual employment dispels despondency and puts ennui to flight. Actual employment of the material as well as spiritual man discloses the powers, improves the health and is an inlet of positive knowledge. Actual employment keeps a person too busy to crave the consolations of intemperance, or to indulge long in spleen, and of itself yields both stimulus and cheerfulness. And knowing that this employment is given to the degraded, uncherished being of a false society by a band of courteous brethren in whose fostering midst he moves, you discover a secret of its restorative magic, and the impulse of his pure resolution.
    Another solution of the problem is in their variety of labors. This variety at present is inadequate to fulfil the requirements of the theory. Brook Farm will be able to accommodate more residents when the contemplated building is erected, and then new and more various industries may be introduced. There should be so many in every phalanx, that each taste may find its several diversities of daily employment. Already the distribution of labors affords a charm. It is not as in the great world, where the cook cooks all day, and the tired sempstress gets a stitch in her side, and "the ploughman homeward plods his weary way," and Mr. Magister Syntax has talked himself into a bronchitis. The horse who runs a journey on a dead level will be more fatigued than he who runs up hill, down hill, and on a level. Instead of wearying one set of muscles, he has brought three sets into play. Soul and body both desire alternation, and when you furnish it, you perform a deed to reconcile a man to his estate.
    The sympathy with which you are infected here, amidst the ranks, is almost irresistible. It is a source of enthusiasm in labor. The words of an

orator are wasted on an individual in a solitary hall; in a crowd they leap like electricity from heart to heart, and then reflect an inspiration on the speaker's soul. A panic or an exultation spreads through a whole armed host. And so, if you make a visit to the residents of the Farm, you catch the contagion of industry. You may abide as a boarder, or visit as a guest. But one presently feels shabby in indulging the <u>dolce</u> <u>far</u> <u>niente</u> of "civilization" for here idleness is not among the insignia of nobility, refinement or wealth.

Yet another solution of the problem is in the inspiration of a grand idea. They see how many writhe beneath the lash of petty authority and contumelious office. Many feel the outrageous maladministration of law, and the tyranny of false opinion. Young orphanage may suffer, without reflection or research. Poverty, whose emaciate cheeks are wet by no tears, for its heart is dulled by wo and exhausted by want, may crave and fain enter a home of insured comfort upon any terms. But there are souls of plain men and sensible women who feel the perversion and wrong of society, and have caught the hope of "some better thing in store" for the race, and sublimated it into an inward prophecy, and are striving to work out its practical fulfillment. And there are souls of elevated men and accomplished women who witness social injustice, error and woes with anguish, who aspire to exterminate them, who believe the means revealed, who paint their ideal of man's dawning glory on a sky of prospect with the pencil of faith, who look through the vista of time on a panorama of industrial beauty and universal happiness, who write their hope and trust in glowing poesy and body it in living action. There are people of such spirit in Brook Farm and similar institutions in other States, where the germs of harmonic principles are just bursting into being, and promise to cover the material earth with verdure and bloom, and to load the spiritual atmosphere with fragrance and music. They are animated by this sacred hope, this grand idea; and it enables them to sacrifice the enervating pleasures of affluent homes amidst false relations, and endure temporarily rude privations coupled with the delights of truth, justice and charity, and forming the future basis of general wealth untarnished by the canker of selfishness and crime.

It is true that the originators of this association controlled its gradually accumulating elements by presenting the example and infusing the leaven of their own character, conduct and manners. A pure moral tone and urbane amenity of deportment ought to introduce the organization of every phalanx. It should not be undertaken without much forethought and serious resolve, without an understanding of its theory and an investigation of the living materials that compose it, without a desire not merely to acquire tangible riches, but to disclose the beauty of the soul. With such examples, it is astonishing to the uninstructed, how soon in association the contagion of self-sacrifice, truth, elevated morals and gentle manners is diffused. When Brook Farm is augmented and enabled to apportion the specific rewards to talent and capital, as it does to labor, we look to witness still higher improvements. Its success is already a moral triumph.

*A. B[loomer]. H[art]., "Brook Farm," Phalanx, 1 (27 July 1844): 220-221.

LETTER FROM CHARLES A. DANA

BROOK FARM, June 17, 1844.

Dear Allen:--Your Convention has the greatest attraction for me. I imagine that will assemble an amount of steady enthusiasm such as few occasions have ever called together. I should rejoice to be with you and to exchange greetings and words of encouragement with all earnest friends of social unity and true liberty. Especially would it give me pleasure to meet the ardent recruits that the hills and riversides of Maine are sending to our standard. In them, as far as I know them, is found the genuine spirit of peaceful warfare. I would fain, with the living voice, welcome them to our extending ranks, and from their fresh zeal, myself draw strength and inspiration for the work. But this is impossible. I must gladly seize your suggestion to give you, in the form of a letter, some of the actual results of Association. You will permit me to add a few thoughts, which in the present stage of the movement amongst us, seem to me to deserve consideration.

I confess that I speak of results with great hesitation. Cheering as they are, they still seem so poor and meagre, compared with the magnificent ideal which is in our minds, that they are hardly worth thinking of. When the future condition of Humanity lies before us, and we behold a United Race moving in beauty and intelligence to the fulfillment of its divine destiny, all present men and achievements sink into insignificance. But to be reassured and convinced that our efforts are not worthless or ineffectual, we need only to look back to civilization. Measured with it, the most defective of our associations is a paradise. The stale interests, empty excitements and paltry rewards which it hangs before us, are, at the best for a whole life, not worth an hour of the true human activity that the rudest form of the combined order produces. In all points of view the contrast is similar. In every aspect of Civilization we behold the falsehood, injustice, the oppression of the weak, the blind folly of the strong, increasing disorder and general unhappiness. In life it is the same tragedy to all, whether it wears in dullness and inanity, or is fooled off in empty shows, or as happens with a great part of mankind, is one prolonged scene of want, of misery, and of degradation. Its institutions nowhere guarantee the satisfaction of the simplest necessities of man, or embody the idea of brotherhood, of union, and of mutual help. No man feels that he is in the midst of his friends, but each with the same sorrowful distrust seeks his own selfish path. Sundered, hostile, miserable, destroying each other. Yet each filled with irrepressible longings for an unknown unity--such are men in civilized society. But even in the infant state of our practical enterprise this is greatly changed. Struggling as all our associations still are, with obstacles that might almost seem impossible, limited in numbers and in means, with hardly the germ of a Harmonic Organization, we have for ourselves at least settled the problem and experimentally confirmed our original conviction, that a better social state awaited Humanity in the course of the Divine Providence. And I am sure that no man not entirely prejudiced, could for any length of time witness even the imperfect operation of universal principles which we are able to obtain, without being convinced that Man was formed for social unity, and without regarding civilized disunity with horror and pity. I do not hesitate to say that we already have glimpses of that sublime Harmony for which Humanity is destined. Though it will arrive long after you and I have been withdrawn from this sphere of action, it is still an unspeakable happiness to labor for its advent. And in the fruit of our labors we shall leave to those who come after us the noblest inheritance in our power!

All our experience accords with the conclusions of science. The law of groups and series, the doctrine of Education, of Human Rights and of Social Economy as demonstrated by Fourier, have had in America experimental proofs to a greater or less degree. I regard them as established by practical trial, though the means of complete experiment have not been in our power, and though to outward observers great doubt may yet remain.

Of our own Association I may be allowed to speak with a personal affection. Indeed, no member of it, especially those who have been connected with it from the first, can help looking on with the deepest love and gratitude. Here our hopes are centred; here we have learned lessons that can neither be estimated nor forgotten; here our strength has been expended, and our life passed in freedom and in happiness. We have had heavy cares and responsibilities indeed, but still the genial gayety in which a really solemn and universal purpose is fitly prosecuted, has not been wanting. Were it all a little less earnest it would be a dream; it has such various and healthy enjoyments, such a summer gladness, is so free from false constraint, and from the austerity that is too apt to vitiate reforms. I might speak of particulars, but it is unnecessary. I will only say that whether we regard its objects, its circumstances, or its results, compared with life in Association the most fortunate life out of it seems worthless or intolerable.

For Fourier I learn daily a new reverence. His intellect is so symmetrical and balanced, so free from eccentricities and one-sidedness, that its greatness is not seen. It is only when we have become familiar with him that we can really be aware of his power. In his broad generalizations no necessary clearness is overlooked. By elucidating the Laws of Society and of the Universe, no least fact is ever left out of the account, but each is subjected to the same sure analysis. And in his grandest strains of scientific enthusiasm, when his head seems to tower among the stars as he utters his answers to the sublimest questions that the human mind can propose, we feel that he yet stands on solid footing and moves in those lofty regions calmly and naturally as their native inhabitant. Nor is his merit that of a discoverer merely. He has taught us not the science of Association alone, but the art also. His practical insight and judgment seem almost wonderful. I believe that he has foreseen most if not all the difficulties that will arise in the course of actual experiment, and scientifically provided for them. Surely we do not err in regarding him with gratitude as a chosen messenger of Providence.

I trust your Convention will not adjourn without at least looking towards positive action. Talk is good, but action is much better. The question just now most important in the movement will be likely to arise among you, that is--what is to be done? If our past experience has taught us anything, it is that success cannot be guaranteed to any Phalanx which does not start with a sufficient amount of scientific knowledge in its directors, with a large capital and with effective laborers. We must more than almost anything, avoid partial enterprises, which if they do not fail still cannot succeed. It is better to wait and bear the old burdens a little longer than to run the risks which must be encountered in such attempts. What, as Associationists, we most desire is to see an experiment upon such a scale as shall put scepticism at rest forever. To this end the friends of the cause must not dissipate their means and energies here and there, but concentrate them upon the point best fitted for the trial. Let them invest money in an amount sufficient to organize attractive industry without any needless delay. Let them select their best men and women to engage personally in the business, and the men most profoundly versed in the science be called to assist in its conduct. Then we shall see such results as the world has never dreamed of.

To me this seems plainly the shortest, nay more, the only road to our common end. Fifty partial associations may struggle on for years and not produce the effect which a well organized Phalanx would accomplish in as many months. Our object is not alone to get into association ourselves, but to bring the whole world into it, and this cannot be done till the vast amount of capital which, under Providence, civilization has been accumulating for this very purpose, is put at our command. To effect this nothing is necessary but the organization of Attractive Industry and the Harmony of the Passions. When these are once seen all men will hasten to lay aside their prejudices and their opposition, and will only desire too impatiently to participate in the benefits of the combined order. I know you agree with me in these views. I hope you will urge them upon the Convention. You will not misunderstand me to be so weak as to suppose that I am speaking in favor of

any particular location. I do not know which of
the Associations already established would be best
for the purpose. Devoted as I personally am to the
interests of the cause of Brook Farm, I should be
unwilling to have it chosen as the seat of the
grand essay, except on a careful comparison of
advantages it should be found most suitable. And
in selecting one of the existing Associations for a
complete trial, none of the others ought to be
forgotten. We are bound to maintain them all, and
each in its turn should be furnished with the means
of thorough organization, for each constitutes a
group of the grand Phalanx into which this nation,
now torn by so many conflicting interests and
poisoned by so many fatal evils, shall in Health
and Unity ere long be transformed.

Most faithfully yours,
CHARLES A. DANA

*Charles A. Dana, "Letter from Charles A. Dana,"
Phalanx, 1 (24 August 1844): 255-257.

FOURIERISM*

John A. Collins

The principles of Co-operative Industry, as laid down by Charles Fourier, are agitating the public mind not only in many of the European states, but are commanding the attention, claiming the sympathy and securing the cooperation of many of the most refined, intelligent and philanthropic men in the country. For myself, I differ, toto coelo, with Fourier, as to the principles of individual property, governments, religion, and morals. These I regard as subversive of human freedom, of a sound and healthy morality. Yet, notwithstanding this difference in opinion, I cannot but rejoice in the able expositions of the rottenness and inhumanity of our present social condition, which have been and are being made by representations of the several professions; by those who are the heirs to wealth, who fare sumptuously every day, and from those who rejoice to pick the crumbs as they fall from the tables of the rich. It is truly encouraging to witness the spirit of inquiry among the masses, touching the rights of labor and the encroachments of capital upon the infirm and pennyless. If this class of reformers have not the right principles as the base upon which to erect a new social superstructure, the philanthropic among them will not rest satisfied with their position and attainments, but will strive to embody their views in some new form that the great end, which they now seek may be obtained. With all my heart do I wish them success in so far as they embrace principles of action consonant with the present advanced condition of civilized society, and they are, by no means, few not insignificant. Civilization is on the eve of a mighty revolution. What is to be the phase which this new and progressive movement is to take, is an inquiry which experience alone can answer. Every experiment, embracing any new practical principles, should receive every possible encouragement. In their failure or success certain principles capable of being reduced to practice will be made apparent.

Whether successful or not they perform an important work in this great social revolution. The great mass of civilized society cannot be taken, in a day, from the deep slough of ignorance, superstition, jealousy and selfishness, and placed upon that platform of pecuniary and social equality which Fourier, even, contemplates. In the progress of the rise and history of society the work of one generation is but as a moment of time. It is comparatively easy to gain from the people, a theoretical assent or dissent from any given abstract principle, and to induce them to associate for the reformation of others, but is a matter, far more difficult to impress them with, in their intercourse one with another, a practical obedience to the principles of justice and of right, or of a personal reformation. Having been educated from our birth in the most narrow principles of selfishness and sensuality, it is no easy matter, however strong our wish or determined our resolutions, to overcome the constitutional weaknesses of our nature, to set aside fixed habits of education and to subject our passions to the rules of experience, of justice and of reason. I am constrained however, to believe that there are many at the present time, who, by their favorable organizations, and the peculiar circumstances which have surrounded them, are qualified to become efficient agents in giving a practical application to the principles of Communism, which when established, like the star of the East shall convene the magi from the East and West and North and the South, and like the stone cut out of the mountain, shall fill the whole earth with its intelligent, peaceful and benign influences.

But to the object of this article which was to give a brief abstract of an account of several Associations which appeared in the last Tribune. First and foremost is a long letter from Mr. Brisbane, in relation to the present condition and future prospects of "The Brook Farm Phalanx," located in West Roxbury, Massachusetts. I regret that the crowded state of our columns will not allow its publication entire, in the Communitist.

This Association has been in existance upwards of four years, if my memory serves me correctly. It was founded by George Ripley a distinguished Unitarian of Boston. Pained with the antagonisms and vices of the present social condition and feeling that no permanent good could be secured to the great mass of the people by the various benevolently intended, though superficial means, to ameliorate the suffering condition of mankind, cheered on by his wife who is truly an intelligent, refined and benevolent woman, Mr. Ripley united with a few whose wishes and convictions were similar to his own for the purpose of establishing a retreat from the snares of vice and the insane competition which surround him and also to embody and reduce to practice some new principles which might be of service to our suffering race. Gradually has it increased in experience, in strength and numbers. The Association now numbers about one hundred members. Attached to the Phalanx is a valuable school. This has been in the hours of its poverty a source not only of pecuniary assistance, but has given to it a deserved popularity. Without casting reflections upon other Associations or wishing to institute any invidious comparisons, Brook Farm is, probably, in the best condition and the most thoroughly organized and systematized and the most sure of immediate success of any Fourier society in this country. I greatly regret that they have not a more favorable soils upon which to work out their principles. It will be impossible for them ever to accomplish much by Agriculture. In Horticulture, Floriculture and raising fruit, and ornamental trees, something handsome may be done. The last year the Association has paid its interest, (which is considerable) supported its members and added to its improvements about $1400. Though sure of success, the Phalanx would be greatly benefitted, and very much needs from $15,000 to $20,000 to enable it to prosecute its arrangement with that economy and efficiency which is desirable. Besides being burdened with a skim milk soil, they have not the advantages of water power, but must supply this important deficit with steam. Being in the immediate proximity of a superior market, manufacturing may under an efficient system of arrangements, be carried on, to great advantage and thus the Phalanx may work out its own redemption from the slavery of poverty and dependence. If then any readers from the Communitist, who have money to loan on good security, or what is better,

to give away, I have no doubt they will find a
ready customer at Brook Farm, and will greatly aid
them in working out their experiment. The
Association has just received from the
Massachusetts Legislature an act of incorporation,
which will greatly facilitate ability for the
transaction of business.
There are already several large dwellings, a
large shop, and a large barn upon the domain. Add
to these, a large edifice 175 by 40 feet, which
forms one of the wings of the contemplated edifice
is in the process of construction and is to be
completed by the first of July next. The principle
mechanical occupations now carried on upon the
domain, are, carpentering, cabinet-making, and
manufacturing of brittania ware. The door, sash
and blind making by machinery and the printing
business are to commence immediately.
There is a fine nursery of fruit and
ornamental trees upon the domain. Something is
being done in Agriculture and gardening.

*[John A.] C[ollins]., "Fourierism," Communitist, 1
(23 April 1845): 91. Collins, founder of the
Skaneatales community, had visited Brook Farm in
July 1844, when he saw "about 115 persons on the
premises, and [the community] is in a flourishing
condition," and promised a more detailed report to
his readers later ("Brook Farm," Communitist, 1 [21
August 1844]: 26).

CELEBRATION OF FOURIER'S BIRTHDAY AT BROOK FARM*

The members of the Brook Farm Phalanx commemorated the birthday of Fourier by a festival of unusual interest. The disciples of Fourier have met for years past in various parts of the world, to commune together and offer up the homage of grateful hearts for his advent upon the earth, and these meetings have been signalized by an atmosphere of lofty and pure sentiment, brilliant wit, and soul-stirring eloquence, seldom if ever excelled on similar occasions; but they were simplistic meetings after all--the meetings merely of theorists, of receivers of a doctrine, who could pay but a simple tribute to the memory of Fourier,--the tribute of intellectual conviction; at Brook Farm, however, a practical Association, the meeting assumed a higher and more impressive character. It was a meeting not of theorists alone, convinced of the truth of the doctrine of Association, but of workers who illustrated them in practice; and their offering was a compound tribute to the memory of Fourier,-- the tribute of the mind and of the hands together. This was the feeling of those who had participated in former festivities, and it was one which deeply impressed all present.

An Association, indeed, seems the only fit place for the celebration of Fourier's birthday, where old and young, men and women, can join in the delightful service of rendering a respectful and affectionate tribute to his memory; there all can unite in offering up the incense of hearts overflowing with gratitude to him who consecrated his life to the holy purpose of elevating mankind to their destiny on earth, in admiring that exalted genius which has comprehended and revealed the sublimest truths of nature, and in invoking with hope made confident by partial experience, the speedy coming of that era of Harmony and Love and Peace which all the Prophets have announced, and which will be realized in Association.

The company assembled in the evening in the dining-hall of the Association, in which the taste and skill of the members had been displayed in numerous beautiful decorations and appropriate emblems. The ceilings and the walls were festooned with evergreen, and the tables in the centre and corners of the room ornamented with the richest and most fragrant flowers from the green-house of the Association. At one end of the hall stood the bust of FOURIER in plaster lately received from Paris; his brown wreathed with myrtle, and on the wall behind it, extending nearly across the room in large Roman letters of evergreen, was inscribed the name of FOURIER. Under the name the date of his birth, 1772. On each side of this inscription were the emblems of Industry and Hope,--the bee-hive and the anchor. At the opposite end of the room hung the banner of Association, composed of the primary colors, and bordered with white, the emblem of Unity. Over the banner, a plain tablet of azure was placed on which the words UNIVERSAL UNITY, were emblazoned in letters of silvery white. The Lyre, intertwined with flowers, as an emblem of harmony, the frame of which was white, and the strings of the seven prismatic colors, corresponding to the scale of the seven spiritual passions, occupied a conspicuous place on one side of the room; and opposite to it an inscription from the New Testament, containing the promise of the blessed Comforter as confirming the hopes which swell with rapture the breasts of those who have faith that Association will fulfil the glorious prophecies of inspiration, and bring down upon earth the kingdom of Heaven. Another tablet was inscribed with the fundamental law of Fourier, <u>Les Attractions sont proportionelle aux Destinees</u>. The tables offered a simple and elegant repast. The scene received an indescribable charm from the perfect social equality of all present, alike of the servers and the served, and the cordial friendship which animated every bosom and sparkled in every eye.

After an hour spent in social converse and enjoyment around the festive board, the President, Mr. Ripley, addressed the company in a short speech, calling their attention to the relation in which, as members of an Association, they stood with regard to Fourier, the discoverer of the laws of Universal Unity. Mr. Ripley gave a rapid sketch of the character of Fourier, his claims to the gratitude and reverence of the world, and the influence he was destined to exert upon the prospects of humanity. He then stated that he should read some select passages from the Scriptures, as being more appropriate to the spirit of the occasion than any language which he could command. These passages, selected from various portions of the Old and New Testament, presented an exalted view of the divine wisdom which was ever flowing into the hearts of the chosen leaders of the human race,--of the assurance of support from the Providence of God to every sincere and faithful effort for the elevation of man,--and of the sublime harmonies which the earth and its inhabitants are destined to enjoy in the progress of the ages.

When Mr. Ripley had concluded, there followed a beautiful chant by the choir, which enlived the evening by occasional strains of delightful music.

Mr. Brisbane then passed upon Fourier a glowing eulogium, and described in graphic and thrilling language the noble old man as he had personally known him.

Mr. Dana followed in some eloquent and inspiring remarks upon Universal Unity, happily alluding to the tablet on which the words were inscribed.

Speeches and sentiments of great brilliancy were delivered in the course of the evening by Messrs. Ripley, Dana, Orvis, Cabot, Westacott, Allen, Ryckman, and Dwight, members of the Phalanx, and Francis G. Shaw, Brisbane, and Macdaniel, guests.

Before the company separated, they united in singing Old Hundred. The scene altogether was one which will long dwell in our memory.

A GUEST.

*"A Guest," "Celebration of Fourier's Birth Day at Brook Farm," <u>Phalanx</u>, 1 (3 May 1845): 336-337.

FIRE AT BROOK FARM*

George Ripley

Our readers have no doubt been informed before this, of the severe calamity with which the Brook Farm Association has been visited, by the destruction of the large unitary edifice which it has been for some time erecting on its domain. Just as our last paper was going through the press, on Tuesday evening the 3d inst., the alarm of fire was given at about a quarter before nine, and it was found to proceed from the "Phalanstery"; in a few minutes, the flames were bursting through the doors and windows of the second story; the fire spread with almost incredible rapidity throughout the building; and in about an hour and a half the whole edifice was burned to the ground. The members of the Association were on the spot in a few moments, and made some attempts to save a quantity of lumber that was in the basement story; but so rapid was the progress of the fire, that this was found to be impossible, and they succeeded only in rescuing a couple of tool-chests that had been in use by the carpenters.

The neighboring dwelling-house called the "Eyry" was in imminent danger, while the fire was at its height, and nothing but the stillness of the night, and the vigilance and activity of those who were stationed on its roof preserved it from destruction. The vigorous efforts of our nearest neighbors, Mr. T. J. Orange, and Messrs. Thomas and George Palmer were of great service in protecting this building, as a part of our force were engaged in another direction, watching the workshops, barn, and principal dwelling house.

In a short time, our neighbors from the village of West Roxbury, a mile and a half distant arrived in great numbers with their Engine, which together with the Engines from Jamaica Plain, Newton, and Brookline, rendered valuable assistance in subduing the flaming ruins, although it was impossible to check the progress of the fire, until the building was completely destroyed. We are under the deepest obligations to the Fire

Companies, which came, some of them, five or six miles, through deep snow on cross roads, and did every thing in the power of skill or energy, to preserve our other buildings from ruin. Many of the Engines from Boston came four or five miles from the city, but finding the fire going down, returned without reaching the spot. The engines from Dedham, we understand, made an unsuccessful attempt to come to our aid, but were obliged to turn back on account of the condition of the roads. No efforts, however, would have probably been successful in arresting the progress of the flames. The building was divided into nearly a hundred rooms in the upper stories, most of which had been lathed for several months, without plaster, and being almost as dry as tinder the fire flashed through them with terrific rapidity.

There had been no work performed on this building during the winter months, and arrangements had just been made to complete four out of the fourteen distinct suites of apartments into which it was divided, by the the first of May. It was hoped that the remainder would be finished during the summer, and that by the first of October, the edifice would be prepared for the reception of a hundred and fifty persons, with ample accommodations for families, and spacious and convenient public halls and saloons. A portion of the second story had been set apart for a Church or Chapel, which was to be finished in a style of simplicity and elegance, by private subscription, and in which it was expected that religious services would be performed by our friend William H. Channing, whose presence with us, until obliged to retire on account of ill health, has been a source of unmingled satisfaction and benefit.

On the Saturday previous to the fire, a stove was put up in the basement story for the accommodation of the carpenters, who were to work on the inside; a fire was kindled in it on Tuesday morning, which burned till four o'clock in the afternoon; at half past eight in the evening, the building was visited by the night watch, who found every thing apparently safe; and at about a quarter before nine, a faint light was discovered in the second story, which was supposed at first to have proceeded from a lamp, but on entering, to ascertain the fact, the smoke at once showed that the interior was on fire. The alarm was immediately given, but almost before the people had time to assemble, the whole edifice was wrapped in flames. From a defect in the construction of the chimney, a spark from the stove pipe ahead probably communicated with the surrounding wood work; and from the combustible nature of the materials, the flames spread with a celerity that made every effort to arrest their violence without effect.

This edifice was commenced in the summer of 1844, and has been in progress from that time until November last, when the work was suspended for the winter, and resumed, as before stated, on the day in which it was consumed. It was built of wood, one hundred and seventy-five feet long, three stories high, with spacious attics, divided into pleasant and convenient rooms for single persons. The second and third stories were divided into fourteen houses, independent of each other, with a parlor and three sleeping rooms in each, connected by piazzas which ran the whole length of the building on both stories. The basement contained a large and commodious kitchen, a dining-hall capable of seating from three to four hundred persons, two public saloons, and a spacious hall or lecture room. Although by no means a model for the Phalanstery, or unitary edifice of a Phalanx, it was well adapted for our purposes at present, situated on a delightful eminence which commanded a most extensive and picturesque view, and affording accommodations and conveniences in the Combined Order, which in many respects, would gratify even a fastidious taste. The actual expenditure upon the building, including the labor performed by the Associates, amounted to about $7,000, and $3,000 more, it was estimated, would be sufficient for its completion. As it was not yet in use by the Association, and until the day of its destruction, not exposed to fire, no insurance had been effected. It was built by investments in our loan stock, and the loss falls upon the holders of partnership stock and the members of the Association.

It is some alleviation of the great calamity which we have sustained, that it came upon us at this time rather than at a later period. The house was not endeared to us by any grateful recollections; the tender and hallowed associations of home had not yet begun to cluster around it; and although we looked upon it with joy and hope as destined to occupy an important sphere in the social movement to which it was consecrated, its destruction does not rend asunder those sacred ties, which bind us to the dwellings that have thus far been the scene of our toils and of our satisfactions. We could not part with either of the houses in which we have lived at Brook Farm, without a sorrow like that which we should feel at the departure of a bosom friend. The destruction of our edifice makes no essential change in our pursuits. It leaves no family destitute of a house; it disturbs no domestic arrangements; it puts us to no immediate inconvenience. The morning after the disaster, if a stranger had not seen the pile of ruins, he would not have suspected that anything extraordinary had taken place. Our schools were attended as usual; our industry in full operation; and not a look or expression of despondency could have been perceived. The calamity is felt to be great; we do not attempt to conceal from ourselves the consequences; but it has been met with a calmness and high trust, which gives us a new proof of the power of Associated life to quicken the best elements of character, and to prepare men for every emergency.

We shall be pardoned for entering into these almost personal details, for we know that the numerous friends of Association, in every part of our land, will feel our misfortune, as if it were a private grief of their own. We have received nothing but expressions of the most generous sympathy from every quarter, even from those who might be supposed to take the least interest in our purposes; and we are sure that our friends in the cause of Social Unity will share with us the affliction that has visited a branch of their own fraternity.

We have no wish to keep out of sight the magnitude of our loss. In our present infant state, it is a severe trial of our strength. We cannot now calculate the ultimate effect. It may prove more than we are able to bear; or like other previous calamities, it may serve to bind us more closely to each other, and to the holy cause to which we are devoted. We await the result with calm hope, sustained by our faith in the Universal

Providence, whose social laws we have endeavored to ascertain and embody in our daily lives.

It may not be improper to state, as we are speaking of our own affairs more fully than we have felt at liberty to do before in the columns of our paper, that, whatever be our trials of an external character, we have every reason to rejoice in the internal condition of our Association. For the few last months, it has more nearly than ever approached the idea of a free social order. The greatest harmony prevails among us; not a discordant note is heard; a spirit of friendship, of brotherly kindness, of charity dwells with us and blesses us; our social resources have been greatly multiplied; and our devotion to the cause which has brought us together, receives more strength every day. Whatever may be in reserve for us, we have an infinite satisfaction in the true relations which have united us, and the assurance that our enterprise has sprung from a desire to obey the divine law. We feel assured that no outward disappointment or calamity can chill our zeal for the realization of a divine order of society, or abate our efforts in the sphere which may be pointed out in our best judgment as most favorable to the cause which we have at heart.

*[George Ripley], "Fire at Brook Farm," Harbinger, 3 (14 March 1846): 220-222.

BROOK FARM SCHOOL*

George Ripley

The Directors of the School connected with the Brook Farm Association have made arrangements for enlarging the establishment, and are now prepared to receive an additional number of pupils.

The course of study comprises instruction in the various branches usually taught in the High Schools and Academies of New-England, with particular attention to the modern European languages and literature.

Pupils of different ages and of both sexes are received; a constant maternal care exercised over the youngest; and the more advanced subject to the friendly counsel and assistance of the teachers, without the restraints of arbitrary discipline. Young men are fitted for College, or for commercial pursuits, or carried through a course of instruction, in the higher branches usually taught in the University.

Lessons are given in Music, Dancing, Drawing, and Painting, without any extra charge.

The School is under the immediate direction of Mr. and Mrs. RIPLEY, Mr. DWIGHT, and Mr. DANA, assisted by experienced teachers in the different departments; and every pupil of tender age is entrusted to the particular care of a lady of the establishment, who has charge of his wardrobe, personal habits, and physical education.

For young children, who are deprived of parental care, and for older pupils who wish to pursue a thorough and exact course of Study, without the usual confinement of a large Seminary, it is believed that this School affords advantages, that are rarely to be met with.

TERMS--$4 per week for board, washing, fuel, lights, and instruction in all branches.

Application may be made by mail to
GEORGE RIPLEY, Brook Farm,
West Roxbury, Mass.

* George Ripley, "Brook Farm School," <u>New-York Weekly Tribune</u>, 25 April 1846, p. 1.

HOW STANDS THE CAUSE?*

John Sullivan Dwight

. . . .
What has been the mission of Brook Farm, and is that mission yet accomplished? These are the questions which we wish to have considered. It is almost needless to review the history of this institution. Originally commenced without any purpose of Association on a large scale, without capital and in debt, its experience daily proved the need of organization like that in the mind of Fourier: then it partook of the first enthusiasm of the Associative movement to which we have referred above, and set to work with zeal to enlarge its industry and expand into a great industrial Phalanx. In this it failed: and it now is held in existence only by the considerable reduction in its members to which it has submitted, and by a modification of its internal arrangements, whereby every branch of business, and indeed every member, is made responsible for self-support, until there shall be nothing left that does not pecuniarily aid the institution. In this way so far as it goes, it must be sound; whether it will survive, however, remains to be seen. Of course we cannot enter here into all the details of its present arrangements and workings. But what is the motive which makes this life so clung to, in spite of so many discouragements and losses? It is the conviction of the important influence which it has always had upon the cause. How much of the impulse which has been given to the whole movement, by lectures, publications, discussions, conversations, has proceeded from this centre! It has been the nursery and school of Associationists, the social centre and strong-hold of those who are engaged in the great work of propagation. This it may yet be, and while we would do nothing to preclude any possibilities of enlarged and various industry, on associative principles, still we think that the peculiar providential mission of Brook Farm has been, to be the intellectual and moral centre of the movement. This has been the essential and

central fact of its existence; and all the rest
should always have been considered incidental. The
outward husk, the incidental part has failed; but
the essential _fact_ survives: the inspiring and
uniting influence which may still proceed from this
little school or centre, will be greater and better
than ever, provided only that its true character
and worth be generally recognized by all friends of
the cause. We do not ask for it any pecuniary aid;
we simply ask that it shall not be considered a
failure, because in one point of view it has
failed; we ask that its true importance to the
movement may be understood and recognized, and that
it be not judged by any false standard. If it
should be dissolved tomorrow, would not our plans
for propagation, to be at all efficient, instantly
demand the establishment of another such centre?
And could another be created in years which would
have the sacredness, the wealth of experience and
of cherished associations, and that binding power
between many souls, which this has?--At present the
only printed organ which we have, proceeds from
this place, and would cease with it; it is an
educational resort also to young and old, who
breathe here the hopeful spirit of humanity amid
all their lessons of literature and science; it has
sent forth nearly every lecturer, and been the
main-spring of nearly every meeting and convention
from which the cause has gained new impulse; it has
brought together manual industry with refined
scholarship and culture, and taught the two
elements to live and share together in equal honor,
and even in its lowest estate, amid its worst
embarrassments as a pecuniary and business
operation, there is a feeling, so long as it lasts,
that the cause of Association is not without "a
local habitation and a name": is not without its
holy land where pilgrimages may be made, with hope
of more than the imaginary influence of seeing the
spot where the dead Lord was laid, but of being
quickened by a living spirit, warmed to a new hope,
and filled with a clearer light, about the
destinies of society and the duty of each towards
so great a movement.

We can but hint at this idea, and there we
leave it for the present, to the earnest and candid
consideration of all who work and pray with us for
the coming of the great day of Unity.

*[John Sullivan Dwight], "How Stands the Cause?" Harbinger, 3 (7 November 1846): 348-351. Sections dealing with other communities have been omitted.

THE ANGELS OF THE PAST*

George Ripley

My buried days!--in bitter tears
    I sit beside your tomb,
And ghostly forms of vanished years
    Flit through my spirit's gloom.

In throngs around my soul they press,
    They fill my dreamy sight
With visions of past loveliness
    And shapes of lost delight.

Like angels of the Lord they move,
    Each on his mystic way,--
These blessed messengers of love,
    These heralds of the day.

And as they pass, the conscious air
    Is stirred to music round,
And a murmur of harmonious prayer
    Is breathed along the ground.

And sorrow dies from out my heart
    In exaltation sweet,
And the bands of life, which she did part,
    In blessed union meet.

The past and future o'er my head
    Their sacred grasp entwine
And the eyes of all the holy dead
    Around, before me, shine.

And I rise to life and duty;
    From nights of fear and death,
With a deeper sense of beauty
    And fuller strength of faith.

---

*G[eorge]. R[ipley]., "The Angels of the Past," Christian Examiner, 42 (May 1847): 343-344. This is probably Ripley's poetic reflections on the failure of Brook Farm.

BROOK FARM*

Margaret Fuller

SOCIALISM

In the preceding extracts will have been noticed frequent reference to the Association Movement, which, during the winter of 1840-41, was beginning to appear simultaneously at several points in New England. In Boston and its vicinity several friends, for whose characters Margaret felt the highest honor, and with many of whose views, theoretical and practical, she accorded, were earnestly considering the possiblity of making such industrial, social, and educational arrangements, as would simplify economics, combine leisure for study with healthful and honest toil, avert unjust collisions of caste, equalize refinements, awaken generous affections, diffuse courtesy, and sweeten and sanctify life as a whole. Chief among these was the Rev. George Ripley, who, convinced by his experience in a faithful ministry, that the need was urgent for a thorough application of the professed principles of Fraternity to actual relations, was about staking his all of fortune, reputation, position, and influence in an attempt to organize a joint-stock community at Brook Farm. How Margaret was inclined to regard this movement has already been indicated. While at heart sympathizing with the heroism that prompted it, in judgment she considered it premature. But true to her noble self, though regretting the seemingly gratuitous sacrifice of her friends, she gave them without stint the cheer of her encouragement and the light of her counsel. She visited them often; entering genially into their trials and pleasures, and missing no chance to drop good seed in every furrow upturned by the ploughshare or softened by the rain. In the secluded yet intensely animated circle of these co-workers I frequently met her during several succeeding years, and rejoice to bear testimony to the justice, magnanimity, wisdom, patience, and many-sided good-will, that governed her every thought and deed. The feelings with which she watched the progress of this experiment are thus exhibited in her journals:--

'My hopes might lead to Association, too,--an association, if not of efforts, yet of destinies. In such an one I live with several already, feeling that each one, by acting out his own, casts light upon a mutual destiny, and illustrates the thought of a master mind. It is a constellation, not a phalanx, to which I would belong.'
  'Why bind oneself to a central or any doctrine? How much nobler stands a man entirely unpledged, unbound! Association may be the great experiment of the age, still it is only an experiment. It is not worth while to lay such stress on it; let us try it, induce others to try it,--that is enough!

  It is amusing to see how the solitary characters tend to outwardness,--to association,-- while the social and sympathetic ones emphasize the value of solitude,--of concentration,--so that we hear from each the word which, from his structure, we least expect.'
  'On Friday I came to Brook Farm. The first day or two here is desolate. You seem to belong to nobody,--to have a right to speak to nobody; but very soon learn to take care of yourself, and then the freedom of the place is delightful.
  'It is fine to see how thoroughly Mr. and Mrs. R. act out, in their own persons, what they intend.
  'All Saturday I was off in the woods. In the evening we had a general conversation, opened by me, upon Education, in its largest sense, and on what we can do for ourselves and others. I took my usual ground: The aim is perfection; patience the road. The present object is to give ourselves and others a tolerable chance. Let us not be too ambitious in our hopes as to immediate results. Our lives should be considered as a tendency, an approximation only. Parents and teachers expect to do too much. They are not legislators, but only interpreters to the next generation. Soon, very soon, does the parent become merely the elder brother of his child;--a little wiser, it is to be hoped. ------- differed from me as to some things I said about the gradations of experience,--that "to be brought prematurely near perfect beings

would chill and discourage." He thought it would cheer and console. He spoke well,--with a youthful nobleness. -------- said "that the most "perfect person would be the most impersonal"--philosophical bull that, I trow--"and, consequently, would impede us least from God." Mr. R. spoke admirably on the nature of loyalty. The people showed a good deal of the sans-culotte tendency in their manners,-- throwing themselves on the floor, yawning, and going out when they had heard enough. Yet, as the majority differ from me, to begin with,--that being the reason this subject was chosen,--they showed, on the whole, more respect and interest than I had expected. As I am accustomed to deference, however, and need it for the boldness and animation which my part requires, I did not speak with as much force as usual. Still, I should like to have to face all this; it would have the same good effects that the Athenian assemblies had on the minds obliged to encounter them.

'Sunday. A glorious day;--the woods full of perfume. I was out all the morning. In the afternoon, Mrs. R. and I had a talk. I said my position would be too uncertain here, as I could not work. -------- said:--"They would all like to work for a person of genius. They would not like to have this service claimed from them, but would like to render it of their own accord." "Yes," I told her; "but where would be my repose, when they were always to be judging whether I was worth it or not. It would be the same position the clergyman is in, or the wandering beggar with his harp. Each day you must prove yourself anew. You are not in immediate relations with material things."

'We talked of the principles of the community. I said I had not a right to come, because all the confidence in it I had was as an experiment worth trying and that it was a part of the great wave of inspired thought. ------- declared they none of them had confidence beyond this; but they seem to me to have. Then I said, "that though I entirely agreed about the dignity of labor, and had always wished for the present change, yet I did not agree with the principle of paying for services by time; [1] neither did I believe in the hope of excluding evil, for that was a growth of nature, and one condition of the development of good." We had valuable discussion on these points.

'All Monday morning in the woods again. Afternoon, out with the drawing party; I felt the evils of want of conventional refinement, in the impudence with which one of the girls treated me. She has since thought of it with regret, I notice; and, by every day's observation of me, will see that she ought not to have done it.'

'In the evening, a husking in the barn. Men, women, and children, all engaged. It was a most picturesque scene, only not quite light enough to bring it out fully. I staid and helped about half an hour, then took a long walk beneath the stars.'

'Wednesday. I have been too much absorbed to-day by others, and it has made me almost sick. Mrs. ------- came to see me, and we had an excellent talk, which occupied nearly all the morning. Then Mrs. ------- wanted to see me, but after a few minutes I found I could not bear it, and lay down to rest. Then -------- came. Poor man;--his feelings and work are wearing on him. He looks really ill now. Then -------- and I went to walk in the woods. I was deeply interested in all she told me. If I were to write down all she and four other married women have confided to me, these three days past, it would make a cento, on one subject, in five parts. Certainly there should be some great design in my life; its attractions are so invariable.'

'In the evening, a conversation on Impulse. The reason for choosing this subject is the great tendency there to advocate spontaneousness, at the expense of reflection. It was a much better conversation than the one before. None yawned, for none came, this time, from mere curiosity. There were about thirty-five present, which is a large enough circle. Many engaged in the talk. I defended nature, as I always do;--the spirit ascending through, not superseding, nature. But in the scale of Sense, Intellect, Spirit, I advocated tonight the claims of Intellect, because those present were rather disposed to postpone them. On the nature of Beauty we had good talk. ------- spoke well. She seemed in a much more reverent humor than the other night, and enjoyed the large plans of the universe which were unrolled.

-------, seated on the floor, with the light falling from behind on his long gold locks, made, with sweet, serene aspect, and composed tones, a good exposé of his way of viewing things.'

'Saturday. Well, good-by, Brook Farm. I know more about this place than I did when I came; but the only way to be qualified for a judge of such an experiment would be to become an active, though unimpassioned, associate in trying it. Some good things are proven, and as for individuals, they are gainers. Has not ------- vied, in her deeds of love, with "my Cid," and the holy Ottilia? That girl who was so rude to me stood waiting, with a timid air, to bid me good-by. Truly, a soft answer turneth away wrath.

'I have found myself here in the amusing position of a conservative. Even so is it with Mr. R. There are too many young people in proportion to the others. I heard myself saying, with a grave air, "Play out the play, gentles." Thus, from generation to generation, rises and falls the wave.'

Again, a year afterward, she writes:--

'Here I have passed a very pleasant week. The tone of the society is much sweeter than when I was here a year ago. There is a pervading spirit of mutual tolerance and gentleness, with great sincerity. There is no longer a passion for grotesque freaks of liberty, but a disposition, rather, to study and enjoy the liberty of law. The great development of mind and character observable in several instances, persuades me that this state of things affords a fine studio for the soul-sculptor. To a casual observer it may seem as if there was not enough of character here to interest, because there are no figures sufficiently distinguished to be worth painting for the crowd; but there is enough of individuality in free play to yield instruction; and one might have, from a few months' residence here, enough of the human drama to feed thought for a long time.'

*[Ralph Waldo Emerson, William Henry Channing, and James Freeman Clarke], Memoirs of Margaret Fuller Ossoli (Boston: Phillips, Sampson, 1852), 2:72-79. Channing wrote and edited the section on Brook Farm.
    1. This was a transitional arrangement only. [Channing's note]

HAWTHORNE, BROOK FARM, AND TRANSCENDENTALISM*

George William Curtis

In his preface to the "Marble Faun," as before in that to the "Blithedale Romance," Hawthorne complained that there was no romantic element in American life; or, as he expressed it: "There is as yet no such Faery-Land so like the real world that, in a suitable remoteness, one can not well tell the difference, but with an atmosphere of strange enchantment, beheld through which the inhabitants have a propriety of their own." This he says in the "Blithedale" preface, and then adds that, to obviate this difficulty and supply a proper scene for his figures, "the author has ventured to make free with his old and affectionately remembered home at Brook Farm as being certainly the most romantic episode of his own life--essentially a day-dream, and yet a fact--and thus offering an available foothold between fiction and reality." Probably a genuine Brook Farmer doubts whether Hawthorne remembered the place and his life there very affectionately, in the usual sense of that word; and although in sending the book to one of them, at least, he said that it was not to be considered a picture of actual life or character--"Do not read it as if it had any thing to do with Brook Farm (which essentially it has not), but merely for its own story and characters"--yet it is plain that it is a very faithful picture of the kind of impression that the enterprise made upon him.

Strangely enough, Hawthorne is likely to be the chief future authority upon "the romantic episode" of Brook Farm. Those who had it at heart more than he, whose faith and hope and energy were all devoted to its development, and many of whom have every ability to make a permanent record, have never done so, and it is already so much a thing of the past that it will probably never be done. But the memory of the place and of the time has been recently pleasantly refreshed by the lecture of Mr. Emerson and the "Note-Book" of Hawthorne. Mr. Emerson, whose mind and heart are ever hospitable, was one of the chief, indeed the chiefest figure in this country of the famous intellectual Renaissance of twenty-five years ago, which, as is generally the case, is historically known by its nickname of Transcendentalism--a spiritual fermentation from which some of the best modern influences in this country have proceeded.

In his late lecture upon the general subject Mr. Emerson says that the mental excitement began to take practical form nearly thirty years ago, when Dr. Channing counseled with George Ripley upon the practicability of bringing thoughtful and cultivated people together and forming a society that should be satisfactory. That good attempt, says Emerson, with a sly smile, ended in an oyster supper with excellent wines. But a little later it was revived under better auspices, and as Brook Farm made a name which will not be forgotten. Mr. Emerson was never a resident, but he was sometimes a visitor and guest, and the more ardent minds of the romantic colony were always much under his influence. With his sensitively humorous eye he seizes upon some of the ludicrous aspects of the scene, and reports them with arch gravity. "The ladies again," he says, "Took cold on washing-days, and it was ordained that the gentlemen shepherds should hang out the clothes, which they punctually did; but a great anachronism followed in the evening, for when they began to dance the clothes-pins dropped plentifully from their pockets." And again: "One hears the frequent statement of the country members that one man was plowing all day and another was looking out of the window all day--perhaps drawing his picture--and they both received the same wages."

In Hawthorne's just-published "Note-Book" he records a great deal of his daily experience at Brook Farm. But he was never truly at home there. Hawthorne lived in the very centre of the Transcendental revival, and he was the friend of many of its leaders, but he was never touched by its spirit. He seems to have been as little affected by the great intellectual influences of his time as Charles Lamb in England. The custom-house had become intolerable to him. He was obliged to do something. The enterprise at Brook Farm seemed to him to promise Arcadia. But he forgot that the kingdom of heaven is within you, and when he went to the tranquil banks of the Charles he found himself in a barn-yard shoveling manure, and not at all in Arcadia. "Before breakfast I went out to the barn and began to crop hay for the cattle, and with such 'righteous vehemence,' as Mr. Ripley says, did I labor, that in the space of ten minutes I broke the machine. Then I brought wood and replenished the fires; and finally went down to breakfast and ate up a huge mound of buckwheat cakes. After breakfast Mr. Ripley put a four-pronged instrument into my hands, which he gave me to understand was called a pitchfork, and he and Mr. Farley being armed with similar weapons, we all three commenced a gallant attack upon a heap of manure."

Hawthorne was a sturdy and resolute man, and any heap of manure that he attacked must yield; but he had not come to Arcadia to sweat and blister his hands, and his blank and amused disappointment is evident. He had a subtle and pervasive humor, but no spirits. He sees the pleasantness of the place and the beauty of the crops, having knowledge of them and a new interest in them; and he has a quiet conscience because he feels that he is really doing some of the manual work of the world; but he is always a spectator, a critic. He went to Brook Farm as he might have gone to an anchorite's cell; but the fervor that warms and adorns the cold, bare rock he does not have, and the mere consciousness of well-doing is a chilly abstraction. "I do not believe that I should be patient here if I were not engaged in a righteous and heaven-blessed way of life. . . . . . I fear it is time for me--sod-compelling as I am--to take the field again. . . . . . Even my custom-house experience was not such a thralldom and weariness; my mind and heart were free. Oh, labor is the curse of the world, and nobody can meddle with it without becoming proportionally brutified!" Very soon, of course, the pilgrim to Arcadia escapes from the manure-yard, and declares as he runs that it was not he, it was a spectre of him, who milked and raked and hoed and toiled in the sun. Hawthorne remained at Brook Farm but a few months, and after he left never returned thither, even for a visit.

The "Blithedale Romance" shows that he was not unmindful of its poetic aspect; but his genius was stirring in him, and he felt that he could not work hard with his hands and write also. So he went off, and never came back; and although he may have remembered certain persons kindly, his memory of the place and of his life there could not have been very affectionate. Probably there were other diaries kept at Brook Farm; certainly there were many letters written thence, in which still lie, and will forever lie, buried the material for its history. But it is likely to become a tradition only, and upon its finer side more and more unreal, because of such sketches as those of Hawthorne. The most comical part of the whole was its impression--that is, such impression as it made, and without exaggerating its extent or importance-- upon the steady old conservatism of Boston, which was of the most inflexible and antediluvian type. The enterprise was the more appalling because it seemed somehow to be a natural product of the spirit of society there. The hen of the tri-mountain had herself hatched this inexpressible duckling. Dr. Channing, indeed, was the honored intellectual chief; the culture of Boston had owed much to the liberal theology; old Dr. Beecher had battered that theology in vain; but the liberality of Boston was like the British Whiggery of the last century. It was more intelligent and more patrician than Toryism itself.

Mr. Emerson, as we said, was practically the head, or at least the accepted representative, of the new movement. His discourses before the Phi Beta Kappa Society at Harvard College, his address to the divinity students, and his noble Dartmouth oration, followed by his lectures in Boston and his "Nature," had set the barn-yard--not offensively to retain the metaphor of the hen--into the most resonant cackle. Into the midst came Theodore Parker's South Boston sermon, and there was universal thunder. The pulpits which Dr. Beecher had assaulted, and which had watched him most serenely, when they heard Parker thought that the very foundations of things were going. The most distinguished chanticleers went to Mr. Emerson's lectures, and when asked if they understood him, shook their stately combs and replied, with caustic superiority, "No; but our daughters do." And when the experiment began at Brook Farm there was no doubt in conservative circles that for their sins this offshoot of Bedlam was permitted in the neighborhood. What it was, what it was meant to be, were equally inexplicable. Are they fools, knaves, madmen, or mere sentimentalists? Is this Coleridge and Southey again, with their Pantisocracy and Susquehanna Paradise? Is it a vast nursery of infidelity; and is it true that "the abbé or religieux" sacrifices white oxen to Jupiter in the back parlor? What may not be true, since it is within Theodore Parker's parish, and his house, crammed with books and modest under the singing pines, is only a mile away?

These extraordinary and vague and hostile impressions were not relieved by the appearance of such votaries of the new shrine as appeared in the staid streets and halls of the city. There is always a certain amount of oddity latent in society which rushes to such an enterprise as a natural vent; and in youth itself there is a similar latent and boundless protest against the friction and apparent unreason of the existing order. At the time of the Brook Farm enterprise this was every where observable. The freedom of the anti-slavery reform and its discussions had developed the "come-outers," who bore testimony in all times and places against church and state. Mr. Emerson mentions an apostle of the gospel of love and no money, who preached zealously but never gathered a large church of believers. Then there were the protestants against the sin of flesh-eating, refining into curious metaphysics upon milk, eggs, and oysters. To purloin milk from the udder was to injure the maternal affections of the cow; to eat eggs was Feejee cannibalism, and the destruction of the tender germ of life; to swallow an oyster was to mask murder. A still selecter circle denounced the chains that shackled the tongue, and the false delicacy that clothed the body. Profanity, they said, is not the use of forcible and picturesque words; it is the abuse of such to express base passions and emotions. So indecency can not be affirmed of the model of all grace, the human body. The fig-leaf is the sign of the fall. Man returning to Paradise will leave it behind. The priests of this faith, therefore, felt themselves called upon to rebuke true profanity and indecency by sitting at their front-doors upon Sunday mornings with no other clothing than that of the pre-fig-leaf period, tranquilly but loudly

conversing in the most stupendous oaths, by way of conversational chiar-oscuro, while a deluded world went shuddering by to church.
These were harmless freaks and individual fantasies. But the time was like the time of witchcraft. The air magnified and multiplied every appearance, and exceptions and idiosyncrasies and ludicrous follies were regarded as the rule, and as the logical masquerade of this foul fiend Transcendentalism, which was evidently unappeaseable, and was about to devour manners, morals, religion, and common-sense. If Father Lamson or Abby Folsom were borne by main force from an anti-slavery meeting, and the non-resistants pleaded that those protestants had as good right to speak as any body, and that what was called their senseless babble was probably inspired wisdom, if people were only heavenly-minded enough to understand it, it was but another sign of the impending anarchy. And what was to be said--for you could not call them old dotards--when the younger protestants of the time came walking through the sober streets of Boston and seated themselves in concert-halls and lecture-rooms with hair parted in the middle and falling upon their shoulders, and clad in garments such as no known human being ever wore before--garments which seemed to be a compromise between the blouse of the Paris workmen and the *peignoir* of a possible sister? For tailoring underwent the same revision to which the whole philosophy of life was subjected, and one ardent youth, asserting that the human form itself suggested the proper shape of garments, caused trowsers to be constructed that closely fitted the leg, and bore his testimony to the truth in coarse crash breeches.
    These were the ludicrous aspects of the intellectual and moral fermentation or agitation that was called Transcendentalism. And these were foolishly accepted by many as its chief and only signs. It was supposed that the folly was complete at Brook Farm, and it was indescribably ludicrous to observe reverend Doctors and other Dons coming out to gaze upon the extraordinary spectacle, and going about as dainty ladies hold their skirts and daintily step from stone to stone in a muddy street, lest they be soiled. The Dons seemed to doubt whether the merest contact had not smirched

them. But droll in itself, it was a thousandfold droller when Theodore Parker came through the woods and described it. With his head set low upon his gladiatorial shoulders, and his nasal voice in subtle and exquisite mimicry reproducing what was truly laughable, yet all with infinite bonhomie and with a genuine superiority to small malice, he was a humorous as he was learned, and as excellent a mime as he was noble and fervent and humane a preacher. On Sundays a party always went from the Farm to Mr. Parker's little country church. He was there exactly what he was afterward when he preached to thousands of eager people in the Boston Music Hall; the same plain, simple, rustic, racy man. His congregation were his personal friends. They loved him and admired him and were proud of him; and his geniality and tender sympathy, his ample knowledge of things as well as of books, his jovial manliness and sturdy independence, drew to him all ages and sexes and conditions.

The society at Brook Farm was composed of every kind of person. There were the ripest scholars, men and women of the most aesthetic culture and accomplishment, young farmers, seamstresses, mechanics, preachers--the industrious, the lazy, the conceited, the sentimental. But they were associated in such a spirit and under such conditions that, with some extravagance, the best of every body appeared, and there was a kind of high esprit de corps --at least in the earlier or golden age of the colony. There was plenty of steady, essential, hard work, for the founding of an earthly Paradise upon a rough New England farm is no pastime. But with the best intention, and much practical knowledge and industry and devotion, there was in the nature of the case an inevitable lack of method, and the economical failure was almost a foregone conclusion. But there were never such witty potato patches and such sparkling cornfields before or since. The weeds were scratched out of the ground to the music of Tennyson or Browning, and the nooning was an hour as gay and bright as any brilliant midnight at Ambrose's. But in the midst of all was one figure, the practical farmer, an honest neighbor who was not drawn to the enterprise by any spiritual attraction, but was hired at good wages to superintend the work, and who always seemed to be regarding the whole affair with the most good-natured wonder as a prodigious masquerade. Indeed, the description which Hawthorne gives of him at a real masquerade of the farmers in the woods depicts his attitude toward Brook Farm itself: "And apart, with a shrewd Yankee observation of the scene, stands our friend Orange, a thick-set, sturdy figure, enjoying the fun well enough, yet rather laughing with a perception of its nonsensicalness than at all entering into the spirit of the thing." That, indeed, was very much the attitude of Hawthorne himself toward Brook Farm and many other aspects of human life.

But beneath all the glancing colors, the lights and shadows of its surface, it was a simple, honest, practical effort for wiser forms of life than those in which we find ourselves. The criticism of science, the sneer of literature, the complaint of experience, is that man is a miserably half-developed being, the proof of which is in the condition of human society, in which the few enjoy and the many toil. But the enjoyment cloys and disappoints, and the very want of labor poisons the enjoyment. Man is made body and soul. The health of each requires reasonable exercise. If every man did his share of the muscular work of the world no other man would be overwhelmed by it. The man who does not work imposes the necessity of harder toil upon him who does. Thereby the first steals from the last the opportunity of mental culture--and at last we reach a world of pariahs and patricians, with all the inconceivable sorrow and suffering that surround us. Bound fast by the brazen age, we can see that the way back to the age of gold lies through justice, which will substitute cooperation for competition.

That some such generous and noble thought inspired this effort at practical Christianity is most probable. The Brook Farmers did not interpret the words "the poor ye have always with ye" to mean "ye must always keep some of you poor." They found the practical Christian, in him who said to his neighbor, "Friend, come up higher." But apart from any precise and defined intention, it was certainly a very alluring prospect--that of life in a pleasant country, taking exercise in useful toil, and surrounded with the most interesting and accomplished people. Compared with other efforts upon which time and money and industry are lavished, measured by Colorado and Nevada speculations, by California gold-washing, by oil-boring, and by the stock exchange, Brook Farm was certainly a very reasonable and practical enterprise, worthy of the hope and aid of generous men and women. The friendships that were formed there were enduring. The devotion to noble endeavor, the sympathy with all that is most useful to men, the kind patience and constant charity that were fostered there, have been no more lost than grain dropped upon the field. It is to the Transcendentalism that seemed to so many good souls both wicked and absurd that some of the best influences of American life today are due. The spirit that was concentrated at Brook Farm is diffused, but it is not lost. As an organized effort, after many downward changes, it failed; but those who remember the Hive, the Eyrie, the Cottage; when Margaret Fuller came and talked, radiant with bright humor; when Emerson and Parker and Hedge joined the circle for a night or a day; when those who may not be publicly named brought beauty and wit and social sympathy to the feast; when the practical possibilities of life seemed fairer, and life and character were touched ineffaceably with good influence, cherish a pleasant vision which no fate can harm, and remember with ceaseless gratitude the blithe days at Brook Farm.

*[George William Curtis], "Editor's Easy Chair," Harper's New Monthly Magazine, 38 (January 1869): 268-271. Emerson's lecture on Brook Farm had been reported in the National Anti-Slavery Standard, 31 October 1868, p. 2.

MY FIRST VISIT TO BROOK FARM*

Georgiana Bruce Kirby

We had all heard of the "Community"--as it was called, in spite of itself. It had been a favorite topic for some time with the radicals in Boston. It was through my cousin "Tom," who was there at first "rusticating," and later, as a sympathizer and student of social science--as he declared--that I was so fortunate as to get an invitation to spend a week at Brook Farm; and it was quite an exciting time for me--for it was not every one, even among those friendly to the movement, who had an opportunity to take a look at the fact itself.

I was tolerably well informed on what was called the "associative" principle; for my cousin, in his casual visits to town, was used to argue the matter in dead earnest; but I confess, that to me, young, and full of romance, my cousin's conversation, when we were alone together--the pictures he drew of Arcadian simplicity, cordiality, and studiousness--to which he gave such warmth of coloring--interested me much more than any discussion of principles. I had grown through these casual conversations, to take a vivid, personal interest in the every-day existence of some half-dozen members of the Community; while the others--amounting to seventy, it seemed--equally good, equally remarkable, no doubt, loomed undefined in the dimmer distance.

There was Hero--she of the speaking eyes--who was graceful in her gracelessness; and whose every mood, be it grave or gay, mischievous or compassionate, made her equally attractive; and whose irreverent <u>badinage</u> became transmuted, by a swift gleam from those eyes, into the most innocent and infectious fun. She was ignorant of admiring observers as the daisy in the meadow; and to her sweet humility the gates of heaven stood open.

And Leander--the youth who arrived at the Farm with such a bad reputation, and in one year had proved himself pure gold. He it was who owned the boat that now and then carried the dearest friends down the Charles River to Cow Island; and he had built the evergreen bower in the pine-woods, for Hero.

There was Sybil--the ubiquitous--full of resource, with wonderful epistolary powers. She had worked for Anti-Slavery Fairs, and stood by Garrison in the late mob. Now, she appeared to me a pale girl at her midnight vigils; and, again, a natural, domestic woman, walking the earth firmly, while she looked upward to the skies. Formerly, Tom spoke much of this young person, as one who had assisted him in arriving at a solution of many questions--as a person of acknowledged intellectual position; but lately, his interest in her had seemed to flag.

The Pacha, "our little Madonna," and Mrs. Grant Smith, with others, I imagined myself on intimate terms with.

Such gay stories as Tom told about the fun he had, helping the girls with their work--so jolly they were over the scrubbing and dish-washing. It was particularly pleasant to lend a hand in the evening, when there was no need of hurry. "Nice girls!" He had blacked their boots with real gusto several times, for the dance.

He cleaned the fish on Fridays--when, for the sake of a few Catholics, fish was the diet. "You should see me, Salome, with shirt-sleeves tucked up, and an apron on, scraping away at it, in the kitchen-sink."

At any time it was worth while to listen to the talk out there. You never heard the words "fashion," or "beau," no shallow, purposeless words, such as you were often bored to death with elsewhere.

They got so tired sometimes! The work was too heavy; but that would all be rectified when things were better established. If only the rich people could have their eyes opened to the worth of "association!"

I had learned, also, that a continuous correspondence was kept up between the young people. I had hints of certain mysterious notes, of great intrinsic value, that were constantly passing to and fro. Accidentally, I had read a line or two of one of these fragmentary missives; and it was a great temptation, which only a sense of honor could overrule, to read on, from the transcendental beginning to the transcendental end.

On one point mistake was impossible: Tom was certainly growing in manly beauty. The expression of his face was toned down; finer lines were noticeable around the mouth; and he carried himself more with the air of one who had taken his destiny into his own hands, and asked no favors. Was all this due to the climate of West Roxbury; or, was it the subtile influence of transcendental companionship?

The day came: the Friday in the late September, when the West Roxbury omnibus set down myself and one other person--an Andover student on furlough he proved to be--at the original farm-house, which I afterward learned was the "Hive," near the door of which two curly-headed boys were playing with a lazy Newfoundland dog.

I was immediately welcomed by friendly, smiling faces, and addressed, in the most familiar tone, by two young women.

"So glad you've come, dear!"

"How much she resembles Theodore!"

"Perfectly delighted to meet you, at last!" and Hero took possession of my carpet-bag, and hurried off with it.

"Your cousin Theodore has just gone to the assistance of Marcus, who was hauling a heavy load of potatoes, when the oxen became unmanageable, and no shouting or goading would move them in the right direction. He has a singular power over animals, you know: they mind him at a word."

"What," I exclaimed, laughing, "Tom manage oxen! How droll! But what makes you call him Theodore?"

"Dear me! Yes; we ought to explain. You see, dear, your cousin was so altogether charming, so natural, and so in sympathy with our ideas; and we were so thankful to have him here, that we could not think of calling him 'Tom,' and 'Theodore'--gift of God--was so appropriate: it seemed, really, the only proper thing to do. There is a middle letter, 'T,' in his name, I believe?"

"That stands for Trotman. His mother was a Trotman."

Soon the blowing of the horn warned us of the supper-hour, and we hastened down the irregular, uncarpeted stairs, to the refectory.

After greeting Tom, who had waited for me in the narrow entry, we entered the large, low dining-room, with its long, pine tables, and benches to match--now cheerfully illumined with the evening lamp. Fifty persons ate in this room; and as I made my way to the place assigned me, piloted by my gay and confident acquaintance, a welcome beamed on me from every side.

I descried the companion of my ride, seated at the opposite table, and attended to by the highest official.

Such faces as lit up this old, dull room! Take thirty mature persons--most of them under thirty--many of them the product of fine civilization for generations; sift out of this number any that could be classed as sordid, sensual, or materialistic; sprinkle in twenty children of fair parentage; inspire each, young and old, with the divine idea of Democracy--and then, imagine the picture.

There sat the genial honest farmer, beside the pale scholar; a mother, who looked motherly enough to be the mother of all the world, beside the younger Pericles; twin children, (demure sprites); a quaint, smiling Dominie-elect; a Diana; a hard-shell Baptist, (recommended by Emerson as unequaled with the axe, or in argument for his sect) hale at seventy; long-haired youths, with eyes full of sentiment; such was the company--and those who saw it will not look upon its like again.

There was much lively conversation. The head person was making puns between each mouthful, which caused great hilarity.

The meal occupied less time than usual, I was told, because one of the members, who had been to visit a new society--the "North American Phalanx," somewhere in New Jersey--had returned the evening before, and, tonight, was to report progress, in the large parlors of the Pilgrim Hall, (a fourth house built for the especial accommodation of some sterling converts from old Plymouth) and the meeting would commence at half-past seven.

The returned Brook-Farmer had also brought with him two strangers--candidates for admission to the society, I believe; but owing to a something cold and unspiritual in their appearance, they were at once looked upon with disfavor, amounting to dislike.

It was highly gratifying to me to see how great a favorite my cousin was, in this "goodlie

companie," and I was quite proud to have so wellestablished and notable a relative, to introduce me. He intercepted a tall youth, with crisp, chestnut curls, and a lurking humor in his eyes, dressed in the usual blouse and turned-back shirtcollar, saying: "Indoctrinate her into the Church, Leander--or, at least, make a proselyte of her; Portia will help, while she adjusts her flock of pitchers," and he passed into the kitchen, where I afterward saw him handling the plates in a masterful manner--the plates that Sybil was washing at the great sink--conversing, the while, in low tones. Her brow was fairer, as her cheek was flushed; and her deep, violet eyes reflected their brilliancy. That evening she was handsome.
 Never had I seen work so rapidly and deftly disposed of before. Even now the straggling crowd were hurrying up the winding road to the place of meeting.
 The parlors were already well filled, as Hero and myself entered. I was surprised to see, among the crowd of Brook-Farmers, Miss Margaret Fuller and Wm. H. Channing (the Apostle). Miss F. had supped in her room, and Mr. Channing had walked over from Theodore Parker's to hear the report.
 Sybil--who took a place near me, and held my hand, with a curious, half-pitying expression on her face that puzzled me--pointed out to me, by name, John Cheever, the radical Irishman, who though nominally of the plebeian class, read nothing beyond Shakespeare, Homer, and the Bible; and Phillips, a bronzed, thick-set sailor, turned gardener; also, various heads of departments, and the more notable youths and maidens.
 The speaker shortly proceeded to state that the new Association was made up mostly of mechanics--many of them Germans--that they were industrious, enterprising, and hopeful, and, financially, on a good, solid basis, etc., etc.
 Presently, one of the strangers I have alluded to asked, in thin, nasal tones, "What class of people they were, morally?"
 The speaker looked his perplexity.
 "I mean, are they respectable, moral people-- for instance, do they swear?"
 In turning toward the questioner, my attention was attracted to a young woman, who, with head bent forward and brow contracted, demanded eagerly:
 "Do you consider all swearing profane?"

"Certainly," he answered, in the same chill, soulless voice; "what good person thinks otherwise?"

"There is profane swearing, no doubt," she said, trembling, and excited in her earnestness. "There is profane swearing, where the heart is filled with vindictive passion--with malice; but most of the swearing indulged by young people and uncultivated people is only so much emphasis to back up their sentences with."

The entire attention of the audience was now directed to this young person, whose name, I learned, was "Portia." Others ventured a few remarks, while she pushed her argument to a conclusion:

"Swearing shows that those who indulge in it are wanting in intelligent respect for their own statements; or are doubtful if they will be accepted as true by those they address. I do not deny that it is in extremely bad taste; that it is vulgar and disagreeable; and yet, a great deal of informal swearing is indulged in by the really reverent and kind-hearted. These mechanics Mr. B. is describing, do, in all probability, swear a little every day; and I'm sure God loves them just as well as he does us."

The discussion was more diffuse than I have shown--in fact, took up about twenty minutes, altogether; and I fancied an uneasy feeling of disapproval on the faces of a few elders, who would scarcely be able to determine the limits of so much youthful impulse.

On coming out into the clear moonlight, we were joined by Portia, and, presently, by the sailor, Phillips. The latter, with much feeling, thanked Portia for the part she had taken.

"I am sure, Miss, it's not language that's so wicked; it's the way one feels in the heart. I declare, if you had not got up to answer that miserable croaker, I should have dared to do it myself. I was thinking, all the time you were talking, of once when I was at sea--leagues from land in the Pacific; and we fell in with a water-logged ship, with nine starving men on her. They hailed to us, and we hove to. Then they begged to be taken on board. Now, our Captain was one of your pious sort. (My last Captain did not swear, but then he was a jolly bird.) Well, when the

Mate, with his hands on the ropes ready to lower the boat, heard the Captain's cold-blooded decision, 'Tell them we can't take them; we have only provisions enough to take ourselves to port;' why, the Mate swore an oath--I should not dare to repeat it to you, Miss; in a bad cause, it were enough to sink a ship--and wishing that he might be hung, besides, at the yard-arm, if he did not fetch those poor souls on board. And down went the boat, in spite of the Captain, and on board they came; and we all arrived safe and sound in port. Now, Miss, I ask you, who swore--the Mate or the Captain?"

At breakfast, next morning, Miss Fuller said she entirely agreed with Portia's definition of the habit; but it was improper to interfere with the object of the meeting. She laughingly described one of her own brothers, who, being told not to say "By George," as it was a sort of swearing, came next day, entreating to be allowed to say, "By Halifax," as he could not get along without something of the sort.

This day--being Saturday--there was but little leisure to give to visitors. A deal of scrubbing and cooking was going on, preparatory to the Sabbath; so I was permitted to wander about, observing, and enjoying the freedom accorded me.

In the kitchen: brown-bread, pork and beans, in earthen jars, and tins-full of rice-pudding were in the hands of skillful cuisiniéres.

In the kitchen, too, Cynthia and Portia were engaged, paring huge pans of potatoes; the former singing the while, in a full and clear, but uncultivated voice, stirring Methodist hymns, for the benefit of the latter, who, having stepped at a bound from Episcopacy to rationalism, was a stranger to this spirit, yet threw herself heartily into the chorus:

"Oh, I'm bound for the Kingdom;
Will you go to glory with me?
Oh, hallelujah! Praise ye the Lord!"

Sybil, with mop and pail, was purifying the painted chamber-floors. Tom was at recitations; returning just in time to take the mop out of her hand, and attend to his room himself.

In the dining-room, Margaret was ironing Community-collars, and, with book stuck open with two forks, committed German poems to memory. Leander, stretched on one of the benches, repeated the words after her:

"Zerraufte sie ihr Raabenhaar,
Und warf sich hin zur Erde,
Mit wuthiger Geberde."

"If ever you are disappointed in love, Mrs. Madge, and want any help about tearing out your raven hair, send for me: I could do it in true transcendental style for you."
"What do you mean by the word transcendental?" I inquired.
"It's well you asked me. I am the only one who has given the word sufficient attention," he said, quickly. "it means, my dear, obscure, vague, ambiguous, hidden, nebulous, enigmatical, sealed, mystical, impenetrable, incomprehensible, mysterious, inscrutable, inconceivable, etc. It's really dangerous to live in such a place as this, you will find."
"Don't mind his nonsense," said Margaret, rather gravely, and aside. "This rattle-brain way he has is all that is left of his former unruly character. He's at heart a noble fellow. Transcendental we interpret as above mere reason, freely, religiously, intuitive, spiritual; at one with Nature."
"Why need you explain to her?" joined in Sybil, who, with empty pail beside her, had for some time been leaning on her mop. "She is one of the elect, herself; she must respect her own thought more, and take the pains to examine it more closely, and she will see <u>she</u> is a transcendentalist."

I remember well one instance of the questioning spirit. Hero and Portia had set the tables for the noon meal. Large, steaming joints of corned-beef, with cabbage, were already on the table, which the girls surveyed with any thing but admiration. Suddenly it occurred to them to cater to the higher sense, by gathering a few of the flowers which still withstood neglect, on the terraces that sloped to the brook, just below the house. Acting on the impulse, they ran quickly across the road and down, near the old tree; and in less than three minutes had the flowers arranged in some champagne-glasses. The question now arose: Before whom should they be placed? Hero insisted, with great warmth, that Professor Olden, Mr. and Mrs. Grant Smith, and Julian F., who had always been accustomed to elegant surroundings, should find familiar blessing and refreshment in their near presence. They, she averred, were starving from want of the aesthetic element.

Portia, on the contrary, persisted they should be placed near Cynthia, Harlan, and Thane--all good, honest souls, struggling up through the practical to the ideal. It was our first duty to awaken in them a sense of the beautiful.

Hero was silent; the speaking eyes dropped; the slender vases were before Harlan et al. There was a bustle of feet, a murmur of voices, and odor of various viands, and all were seated, when Portia met Hero's glance, and those luminous orbs betrayed a mischievous triumph. The flowers were before the Professor; and the elegant Mrs. Grant Smith held one of the glasses in her hand, admiring the delicate, purple tint of the asters.

* *

I often, toward sunset, found Sybil in Tom's apartment, which was alike sleeping-room and parlor. Now, she was deep in "Sartor-Resartus," claiming his sympathy with this last gospel; or she read from Ellery Channing:

"What if none will look at thee
Sighing for the honey-bee,
Or great moth with heavenly wings,
Or the nightingale that sings:
Curious spider, thou'rt to me
Of a noble family."

Or, they were mutually indignant over the great master's essay on "Love," and the still more dubious lines,

"Who drinks of Cupid's nectar-cup,
"Loveth downward, and not up."

This last was stark treason to the divine passion, if no inner meaning could be discovered; and it would take priestly handling to evade the manifest intention of the text.

I was getting anxious about my ingenuous cousin, for, to all appearance, Sybil was self-poised, with conscious power; while his soul lay entranced in her keeping--fully surrendered. Was she aware of the fact? I asked myself, over and over again. He was "so altogether admirable," she had once said to me. Had she misled him by her devotion to his spiritual interests? Had she unconsciously made him the subject of her peculiar magnetism? After all, I might be mistaken.

The morrow came, as usual. The Sabbath, made for man, was kept here with perfect freedom. Some walked two and a half miles to hear Theodore Parker preach in his little church at West Roxbury; some went to Catholic services in Boston; some sought solitude in the pine-woods; others, special companionship at home: but no one was hindered or disturbed by another. There was an air of quietness over all; and each, in his way, profited by it.

The refectory, on Sunday, was particularly attractive. Pure white linen gives any man a more cheerful appearance; but when to this was added bright tartan blouses, (those plaids that depend on just a fleck of contrasting color) black velvet, and grass-green merino, mixed up with graver hues, and the braid and frogs of the Hungarians--the effect was very good.

The smooth and carefully braided hair of the girls and women, with their fresh muslins and calicoes, and, above all, the peaceful leisure of this one day, gave to all an air of refinement and repose. The trio sat at the end of one table with heads bent forward, communicating with engrossed, exclusive air.

At supper, it was whispered that the younger Pericles would sing at the "Eyrie"--one of the new houses--upon which several young men volunteered to assist with the dishes. My services, also, were cordially accepted. It was strange how much at home I was already. Without formal introduction, I fell into the way of addressing those about me, as others did, by the given name; though I certainly could not venture to accost the quaint Dominie--the best Greek scholar in Massachusetts; familiar, too, with the <u>arcana</u> of Nature--as "Commodore," a new name, conferred by Hero. So entirely was I swept along in the current, that I scarcely noticed how seldom Tom and I were in the neighborhood of each other. Sent into the kitchen for dry towels, I found him, as before, deftly seconding Sybil, and I realized in a momentary glamour of the atmosphere in which they stood that reminded me of a sentence in a note I had received in the morning, signed "Your friend--perhaps," that ran thus:

"We wish not only to pour the oil of Christian living over the bruised and exhausted form of humanity; to lay the corner-stone of universal brotherhood (and with no Masonic trowel, but the common one used by unwilling slaves so long): we must also be able to spiritualize the dish-washing and scrubbing."

And now we ascended, in the moonlight, the winding path of the "Eyrie," where the younger Pericles was already singing. Stray individuals, just freed from similar duties, preceded or followed us on the same errand. We went up the steps of the building with caution, lest a note of the melody that floated through the open French windows should be lost to us. It was with surprise that, entering the high room, we found not only the chairs and sofas occupied, but the floor well covered with seated listeners, whose stillness left the singer ignorant of their presence.

I did not at first recognize the operatic air, so modified, and retarded, and shorn of its usual ornamentation. A sad and touching theme now, with a refrain that called for noble endurance, in one borne down by suffering.

The accompaniment consisted of simple chords and _arpeggios_, quite subordinate to the theme. Presently another voice joined in, making sweet harmony. They sang of love and death, and such things; and a lullaby, in which you saw the angels watching the babe and mother.

Thus the evening lengthened, and the moon waned. Turning round with a sudden shiver, I discerned in a dusky corner my cousin, lost in a dream of bliss, holding Sybil's hand.

Low praises and half-spoken thanks were murmured toward the young Pericles, who truly was both poem and poet before ever he sang that night. Then the brethren and sisters separated for their various homes.

The next day all were busy as bees in a hive. Feeling ashamed of idleness in the midst of so much industry, I begged to have some substantial duty assigned me. Without remonstrance, I was forthwith conducted to the mild Lady Superior, who, with slender, unaccustomed fingers, was stitching together the ticking for a straw bed--a primitive article of furniture, called for by every fresh arrival. "In this case," said the lady, "The novice will have to forego window-curtains; the sheets have exhausted the bolt of cloth." I heard, next day, that the young man had been nearly crazed by the direct rays of the moon, which made a circuit of the four windows in his room.

The Lady Superior was gracious and fluent; but, as the Spiritualists would say, I found myself in "another sphere," and I stitched away in friendly silence. When I ventured to remark on the affinity--a perfectly respectable word, in those days--that existed between so many of the young people, she replied, with unpleasant decision:

"I am sick of the word 'affinity!' 'Analogy' is glorious; but I tire of the intense moods of these undisciplined girls." And I was sorely puzzled when she remarked to the Professor: "Sophie Deane is coming to-morrow to spend a few days with me. It will be such a relief, for she doesn't know the meaning of the word 'idea'--never was troubled with one--but she has strictly conventional manners. What a rest it will be!"

And I will here acknowledge that I was struck, from the first--and not disagreeably--with a novel phraseology common at the Community. The word "somewhat," for instance, pleased me as delightfully indefinite, and I adopted it at once into my vocabulary. The words "consciousness" and "unconsciousness," "intuitive," "analogous," I got along with pretty well; but I was floored by "subjective and objective," and it is doubtful if I am to-day on my feet regarding them. Neither could my slow, English mind comprehend Madame Guyon, or Law's "Spirit of Love"--works which were like common bread and butter to most at Brook Farm.

I also observed a general feeling (among the pietistic party) of contempt for the body. They looked on it as an enemy--"a demonition bore," Hero said. "I get so impatient of the body and its miserable limitations," said a youth, whose eyes were the admiration of the juveniles. "If we could only slip our bark how much more could be accomplished." Meanwhile, I sewed assiduously with the Lady Superior, until such time as the dinner-horn sounded, when, together, we walked to the Hive.

"You need not speak, dear: I can read it all in your face. The juices are all dried out of you. Next thing, she will press you in a herbarium," whispered Sybil. "I declare, you begin to look like a ribbon-grass already. Never mind, after dinner I have a dear, little note from the Commodore to read to you. You will have to adore him, as we do."

THE NOTE

"As you say, dearest Sybil--(I am sure you understand the very brotherly nature of my affection for you, which I am only too happy in believing you return, out of your generous and pure soul) as you say, our circle is incomplete, for want of old people: a grandfather and grandmother, with white hair, and the benignity that indicates the near-by sweetness of death. We should not be content, dearest friend, until we can attach this element from the world--until our experiment, as some blindly call it, is justified of age, as well as of saintly and jubilant youth, like yourselves. (Why should I not utter what is so true to me?)

"It is universal love--appreciative, suggestive, tolerant love--that binds your fair circle together. You do not, like the vulgar artist, paint the eyes darker, the skin fairer, the contour more symmetrical; but with genius born of humility, you perceive the ideal, the possibilities of each, and insist that every one shall carry about with him a vivid memory of his highest moments.

"Will not your sweet friend, Salome, be persuaded to join us? It would be a grateful task, could I assist her in the study of astronomy, to which I see she turns with earnestness. She brings with her always a breeze from the woods.

"Your old, but ever-new friend,
                                       THE DOMINIE."

So the days passed, divided into recitations, housework, notes, and meetings (for, on every emergency, either a note was written, or a public meeting called): a meeting sometimes of women; sometimes of men; usually of both.

I meditated a great deal on the fitness or unfitness of a union between my cousin and Sybil. There was something in the latter that perplexed me, and arrested my sympathy; while yet I entertained for her only a sentimental reverence. Usually, I detected and defined characters easily, and to be moved from my first impressions, was to open my arms to grief. Sybil, however, I had prejudged favorably. Should I, on my arrival, have gazed into the alluring depths of her violet eyes, or at her pale, restrained, unsatisfactory mouth; at her silken hair, or her curiously unsymmetrical person? It was too late to answer the question: from the first, too late for Tom.

I had been dwelling on the matter one afternoon, when he came in, carrying a superb collection of autumn wild-flowers--for her, of course. The large family were already at supper. The day had seemed to busy to permit a moment for note-writing; yet he carefully turned up his plate, sure of finding the one he, with a slow movement, placed in his vest-pocket. I was aware of a sudden chill. Was it he, or myself, that trembled? He rose to close a door, and did not return. After supper, I missed him till the tables were cleared: then his shadow, with listless air, passed with Sybil the outer door.

An hour later, wandering in quiet through the dimly lighted, deserted little parlor, I found him, with haggard countenance, dreary and all unnerved, sitting on the sofa. I shook from head to foot as I entreated him to speak, to explain what was the matter.

"She has refused me! My God, Salome, she has refused me!" he said, throwing his arms heavily around me.

"My brain is on fire"--shivering as if with cold. "I'll go to my room. The place is so terribly desolate."

It was my nature to follow my friend. I was in entire rapport with the sufferer, and only retained enough strength and self-possession to take advantage of any change in him. Young and inexperienced as I was, there was something fearful in this abandonment of grief, this despair of youth--the first rebellion against destiny.

I watched, dreading the night, the morrow. What if fever should set in, or worse!

Leander, good fellow, hearing that his chum had a chill, came offering service, and bringing what he called a relic of bigotry and virtue, in the shape of a night-lamp belonging to Sybil. Declining the assistance, I accepted the gilt sapling, wound with delicate, ivy leaves, from the bent bough of which hung the purely tinted glass with taper alight. In those tedious and sorrowful hours, when all was so still that the slightest sound was ominous of evil, with nothing to do but to note the irregular and wiry character of a pulse and bathe a fevered brow, the lamp--a waif from a former elegant home--was a source of relief to my wearied mind. It was so prettily designed; the moths and beetles that connected the deeply veined leaves that balanced the whole were so instinct with life, that I almost felt them to be company for me. And I allude to this because it was just such odds and ends of previous conditions, contrasted with the otherwise barren furniture, which suggested a return to the Middle Ages.

In the morning early, a light step at the door and a cautious tap; and in silence Sybil handed in some slight refreshment and some cooling drink. Her face expressed self-forgetfulness, self-sacrifice: I could almost imagine she wore a savage girdle that was eating into her flesh when her mystical eyes met mine. Yet I could not smile lovingly on her, with Tom in that limpsy condition. If he ever was quite himself again, I might enter into another treaty with her.

He turned listlessly over as I closed the door, and motioning the gruel out of sight, called me to the bedside.

"Salome," he asked, in a blank tone, "what do you find worth living for?"

"Why, dear"--arranging his disheveled curls--"yesterday, I should have told you I lived for the pleasure of it: just breathing the air was good enough. then to walk is so splendid; and I like to sleep. I can not deny that I enjoy eating, too. you also will live, and be happy yet."

"Never! You don't know any thing about it, and I trust you never may!"

"You needn't wish that," I said. "I'd rather have your experience than none. I'm quite tired of loving and suffering vicariously. I wish I could die of a broken heart."

I was glad to hear him talk. The Methodists are right in saying that "open confession is good for the soul." By speech the weight, little by little, is lifted.

Just then the kind Dominie knocked hesitatingly at the door, and handed me a note. It contained merely a hinted sympathy, with the request that Theodore would allow him to assume the care of the furance till he recovered from his indisposition. And yet there was a something more implied which dispelled my sleepiness. I bathed my face and smoothed my hair, and spoke with more courage and hope to my poor cousin. I made him look at me while I ate, that at least he might keep up the memory of how it was done.

Presently the door opened, and Sybil handed me a sprig of jasmine, with the whispered request that it might be placed where it would meet his eye; also, a note for Tom.

She lingered so in her assiduous inquiries after his health and mental state; there was such a tender pity in her eyes, that I began to doubt the real nature of the case. Closing the door softly behind me, I drew her away from it, and then asked resolutely:

"Do you love my cousin?"

"Most certainly," she replied, "I love him. The rich promise of his tropical nature drew me to him from the first. I was so much interested in his development that I gave him my every spare moment. In return he read to me while I sewed, and was most kind in his attentions."

"Will you marry him, then?" I continued.

"My dear child, you do not understand. I could not install myself teacher for life! He is not twenty; I am twenty-six. How could I anticipate such a result? Do not fear. He will overlive it. Every one of any account, you know, has such an experience." Then sadly: "I have had myself. It makes one free of the universe. Spiritual power never exists previous to it, nor companionship."

"But I know nothing of personal love, and you want me to come and live here," I returned.

"It was in you when you were born, my dear. You are an exception. If it were not so, how could you be such a pillar of strength to your cousin? You have lifted half his burden already."

I pushed away the compliment impatiently, and left her, while she was still speaking, for I was sure my cousin called, or groaned. Still holding the jasmine, I handed him the delicate missive, which, on seeing the direction--"To my Brother"--he crumpled angrily in his hand and dashed to the floor, throwing himself back hopelessly on his pillow. "Sybil, Sybil!" he moaned.

At the sound she glided in, and with a look of pity laid her hand on his brow. He met her with such a longing, yearning, entreating expression, that to withstand it she needed a heart of stone.

Taking his outstretched hands in hers, she answered the look.

"Theodore, it is impossible. You must use your reason, dear child. Should I run away from my true mate? Could I be blind to the fact if it were a verity? Don't we gravitate to those we belong to when nothing material intervenes? You represent youth to me, not manhood. I love you as a younger brother."

At the word "youth" he sprang up.

"Yes, oh God! Where is now my youth? Give me back my youth! Why do I suffer? Oh, Sybil, since the first month I came here, when I walked, and studied, and danced with you, it has been heaven. The stone-wall between here and the Eyrie contained innumerable poems; the very oxen were spiritualized. The dull mist, that others complained of, held wonderful pictures for me. Now the life is sucked out of every thing: all is leaden. You have lifted me up to heaven only to cast me down to hell, because of my 'youth.'"

"The years will repay you," she said, softly. "Instead of a golden mist, you shall perceive the Divine Spirit everywhere. You will love and be loved by her, who even now awaits you. You will be ashamed of this want of faith."

He turned from her. I quietly left the room, and descended the stairs to where healthy, happy people were moving about, self-forgetful, intent. How had personal love come to them, I wondered. I determined to seek the solitude of the pine-woods, and take counsel there. If there had been wrong, I could not unravel it. Change was desirable, I knew. Why not follow it up to Harvard?
* *

"What a wise, motherly soul you are, Salome! I may thank you that I have not become a complete wreck. Where did you get your pluck and decision from, cousin? I'm afraid it's very cowardly, though, abandoning the field in this way. Perhaps I ought to stay and fight it out."

"If you're burned, I don't mean you shall sit in the fire and sing your death-song; and you can't die of a broken heart, with an iron constitution. Bear with the blues, Tom; I have a presentiment you've lots of work to do in this world."

So we left in the morning on the omnibus, after bidding farewell to the Lady Superior and other principal members, with a promise on my part to return. The Dominie, with coal-hod in hand, presented me, with hesitancy, a note, and I reluctantly accepted a kiss from Sybil, and gave a most cordial one to the mischievous Hero. The vehicle wheeled round, and was rattling over the bridge.

Engrossed in my own multitudinous thoughts, I had not noticed that the Andover student sat opposite to us, and appeared more desirous of claiming acquaintance than when we passed and repassed each other going between the different domiciles; and he was obliged to force his remarks on my attention just before the omnibus arrived at the terminus. This was his question:

"Would you be kind enough to tell me what I have been carrying in the tin-box, between the Hive and the Eyrie, every day?"

"Meals, of course," I answered. He bowed his thanks, and, smiling an amused smile, handed me out of the vehicle.

* [Georgiana Bruce Kirby], "My First Visit to Brook Farm," Overland Monthly, 5 (July 1870): 9-19. In her Years of Experience (New York: Putnams, 1887), Kirby notes that she has here assigned pseudonyms to real people and has often created composite characters.

REMINISCENCES OF BROOK FARM*

Georgiana Bruce Kirby

I.

It was yet early spring, the weather uncertain and gloomy, nature attired in her most unseemly garments, when, having luggage which could not go by the omnibus, I found myself and effects in the West Roxbury stage, which was under bonds to deliver me at a certain station in that village, half a mile from Brook Farm. Here I received the most explicit directions for the rest of my journey, and wended my way, solitary, but in no cheerless mood. It was a peaceful country half-mile, between straggling woods and pastures; the low gray stone fence cropping out here and there, and then disappearing amid heaps of brush-wood and vines. The wind went soughing through the trees, snapping off now and then a dead branch, which crackling fell to the ground. The deadest of dead leaves, but lately released from under the snow, whirled and danced on before me; but there was no melancholy in the scene for me. I was free; I was returning to my own again; in my heart the climate was fairest June; and I hummed, as I stepped briskly on,--

"Pipe low, ye winds,
And glad the summer day."

There were no perplexing forks to the road, to mislead the pre-occupied traveller; and it was to this happy circumstance, rather than to any merit of my own, that I found myself approaching the old farm-house for which I was destined, instead, as might well have been the case, some strange, unfriendly homestead, miles away. I held anticipation in check; but there was no subduing the exhilaration of the hour; for I was on the bridge, metaphorical and literal, that was to conduct me to a new era. From this bridge, that spanned the brook after which the place was named, I could see the long, bare arms of the old cottonwood tree, which in summer overshadowed the hive, swaying restlessly to the breeze; and the brown terraces below, where the girls had picked the asters and nasturtiums with which to decorate the tables when I was on a visit there the previous autumn. The few persons whose duties took them abroad in that locality, I failed to recognize; but Carlo, the lazy Newfoundland dog, I was well acquainted with; and he announced my arrival by a low, satisfied bark.

I have said, that, on this particular day, earth and sky wore a chilly, unfriendly air; but the girls' voice in the kitchen, as I entered unobserved, brought back the wealth and color of the autumnal days which had crowned my first welcome. What hearty, boisterous congratulations from the younger handmaidens! what subdued, earnest greeting from Sybil and Margaret! The walls of the large kitchen, even the huge stove, smiled and beamed with cordiality for me. I accepted it all, and returned in kind.

Sybil, who was always the one to assume responsibility, conducted me into the little parlor, saying, as she relieved me of superfluous garments,--

"You will notice some changes, dear,--some new faces. Only one gone besides Theodore; and he did not really belong with us. Among the new-comers is a young man, who, in many ways, is quite remarkable; but he is just now absent on a visit to Milton, where a certain 'Martha' holds him; the personification of mental and physical health, she is reported to be. His name is Adonis; and dear Pericles is his bosom friend, and very much under his influence,--consciously under his influence," she added with religious emphasis, "which makes all the difference in the world, you know. It would be impossible for Pericles, who is as keenly positive as Sir Philip Sidney, to be unconsciously under any one's influence."

So I thought, remembering the pliant form and many-sided character of the young Hercules.

"You remember the Plainlys," she continued, "Jemima and Harry? The whole family are here now, and we are as crowded as ever; but a wing--you doubtless observed it as you came along--is being built as rapidly as may be; and, when that is completed, we can stretch ourselves out once more.

Poor Dora Plainly, the mother, finds division of labor quite another thing from cooking, dressmaking, washing, ironing, and bearing children, all alone. She takes charge of the first meal, and the puddings and pies at dinner, and sews a good deal, but still, as she says, feels the burden removed entirely from her weary shoulders. The younger children blossom round us like roses. We have been obliged, you see, to arrange a table for eight in this parlor. We of the inner circle eat in this room--Hero, Leander, Janet, Pericles, the Dominie, Adonis, yourself, and myself. I insisted on reserving a place for you."

I thanked her, more than grateful for her delicate consideration.

How, as she talked, I knew the old spell was creeping over me! I had held my judgment in abeyance concerning her dealings with my cousin, intending to study her more closely, and to keep myself apart from her influence till my mind was made up on broader grounds. Now her violet eyes took possession of me; her pressing, chastened manner, so gentle yet persistent, wound itself around me; while her pale, restrained mouth, contrasted with the thoughtful brow shaded by the silky hair, was inexplicable as ever.

At dinner I took in the situation anew. There was more in the gracious kindliness of manner than in any conversation that took place during the repast; and, if simply the presence was the criterion of worth, no other argument could be needed here. There was indeed, as I afterwards learned, a siren in the opposite room, and a Jesuit in the carpenter's shop; but these gave just that necessary spice to the otherwise pure and simple whole which would insure striking effects. At any rate, the Jesuit was not mistaken for John, nor the siren for Una.

I found that duties had already been assigned me, subject to my veto, one part of which was to teach the smallest class of children for two or three hours a day. This I declined; for it was an unsettled question with me how far we had any right to oblige a small child to learn that for which he often had a natural, and, as I believed, a healthy repugnance, viz., the primer, and to sit still. It was finally agreed on, that I should take charge of the boys' bedrooms at the eyrie, help with the ironing on the afternoons of three days in the week, and in the mornings help to prepare vegetables, &c., in the kitchen.

The next consideration, and that of paramount importance with the girls, was my proposed course of study. A moral-philosophy class, under the able direction of the professor [George Ripley], with Victor Cousin for text-book, was just under way. Of course I joined it; and very interesting it proved, after the more circumscribed and stereotyped reasoning of the pulpit,--this science of the soul, affirming that evil is not a principle, a tangible entity, opposed to good, but inharmonious, unbalanced good, for which we might therefore hope to make conditions that should induce harmony. The professor was well versed in eclectic philosophy, and his exposition of the different systems was delightfully clear. Victor Cousin may have since entered a cloister, but the door he opened for perplexed souls remains still open.

Democracy, and the highest mental and spiritual culture, were evidently the animating ideas at the Community. Had the world denied you opportunity for study? Here your soul's needs should be attended to at once. Did you desire chirography, or Sanscrit, it was all one. Hence, in the course of time, there were classes in German, French, and European history, in Italian, Greek, and mathematics. Two Hibernian sisters were learning to write; and Hero, untroubled by theories, bravely consented to sandwich the primer between German fairy tales and children's melodies for the little ones.

The presence of so many young men, who were there expressly for their school education, obliged, it is true, the formation of many of these classes,--youths from Manila, Havana, Florida, and Cambridge; but Italian, German, moral philosophy, and the English classics were requirements of the "Community" proper.

I was also induced to join the class in European history, over which the lady superior [Mrs. Ripley] gracefully presided; and I took some pains to persuade Cynthia to enlarge her mental boundaries along with me. It soon became apparent, however, that "the wholesome nymph," as Hero had christened her, lacked the element of growth in her nature, and could advance no farther than the idea of democracy. She could not divest herself of her accessories, the saucepans and skewers, over which she reigned queen in the kitchen, but held them all, abstractly speaking, carefully in her lap during the lesson. This greatly disturbed some of us; for we reasoned, that, in this case, we were getting the benefit of her disciplined and valuable practical skill without returning adequate compensation.

At the time of my arrival at the farm, came also a young man [Charles A. Dana] from Harvard, full of Greek and German, full of masculine energy and enthusiasm. His handsome brown eyes had been overtaxed at college, yet he could teach if not study; and a German class was the first move of Don Carlos. It consisted of not more than seven; and a royal time we had of it, from Follen's Reader to Schiller's "Song of the Bell," Pegasus, Wilhelm Tell, Goethe's "Hermann and Dorothea," "Faust," "Dichtung and Wahrheit." What wonderful sentiment and conception we found in these creations! Dictionaries were scarce, oil-lamps dull, hours too short, and the student often over-weary from labor; but what hinderance could these obstacles offer to the fervent zeal of youthful converts? I was to have studied arithmetic. What nourishment could I find in that, or in American history, which included one revolution, and that retaining slavery and the slave-trade? No romance except that found among fugitive slaves; Washington and Mrs. Martha Washington worn decidedly threadbare. Better study Rhine legends, and live a poem for later chroniclers to write down. But I anticipate.

I had been assigned a sleeping apartment at the eyrie (the quadrangular edifice on the hill, some three minutes' walk from the hive), and Hero had accepted me for a room-mate. A pretty French window in our room overlooked the peaceful solitude of the near pine woods, with just a glimpse of Charles River in the distance. To me this seemed one of the mansions of the blest.

From the first day, my companion, with her usual innocent daring, took all my external affairs into her hands; while I, only too gladly, yielded to her dictation.

"Tell me exactly how much money you have brought with you, that I may see you do not lose it, or give it away, or spend it extravagantly.

The idea of your being trusted with money! I heard of your buying three half-mourning dresses, because the style was so quiet. I am the 'community' within the Community. It was fore-ordained before the beginning of the world that you should be guided by me. How dare you wear your best shoes every day?"

So she ran on, pleased and amused at the docile acquiescence of one five years her senior. It gave me a sense of relief to be thus taken charge of after carrying about the painful consciousness of my own responsiblity for nearly two years. To rest with Hero's loving arm around me, to wake to the divine serenity of that early morning air, gave the soul strength for the conflicts of after years. Nourished by it, the sweetest enthusiasms took root, and collected store of vitalizing material.

It was easy to understand now what an amount of moral and intellectual force was wasted in the world through the distrust that keeps caution ever active. Here men and women, forgetting suspicion, met each other with a frank friendliness. It was a quiet abandonment to the spirit of fraternity and the higher institutions. Not that these people were angels; they were only the best of their kind, and inspired with a noble idea.

It was a joint-stock association; yet it could not be told by observation who had invested more, and who less, and who simply himself. At first I was convinced that the young Pericles must be a large shareholder: he had the large, unconstrained mien that should belong to a person occupying that position. I was persuaded of my error when I saw him anxiously examine his well-worn black-velvet tunic, which he intimated must last two months longer, or he would have to resume his old-world coat.

It was easier to discriminate between members of the association, boarders, half-boarders, and scholars, by the air of leisure or of business habitual with each. I knew, without being told, that Erasmus [Charles King Newcomb], whose apartment adjoined ours, was a full boarder, from his habit of reading Greek long after the rest of the household had retired, and then reciting the Church Litany at intervals through the rest of the night. The walls were not so thick but in the still hours his invocations were audible to us.

He was a young man, with large, devout eyes, an introverted expression, a want of firmness in his gait, and a profusion of black curls so badly cared for that I often felt the temptation to forcibly secure him in a chair, and treat his head to a thorough brushing. Besides being a lover of Greek, Erasmus was a worshipper of Nature. Touching the Catholic Church at certain points, he diverged again to what that church would call blasphemy. He was at the "Community" for the sake of the greater freedom which our unconventional manner of living permitted, and that he might dwell more with realities. His room, not large, was adorned by rare specimens of the stately bulrush, strange moss-covered branches, and ferns and maiden-hair of exquisite delicacy and beauty. On the walls were engravings of Jesus, of Ignatius Loyola, and Francis Xavier, framed with wreaths of the creeping pine. It was not often that we held speech together; for he was retiring, reverent, and illuminated; and I, healthy and impetuous, and, besides, inclined to resent the suggestion that I wished to invade his personality. If he did ever condescend to address me, I was sure to retain of what he said a few condensed texts of unusual depth and appositeness. About this time Fanny Ellsler appeared in Boston; and one day I ventured to ask him if he had seen her dance.

"Salome," he replied reproachfully, the religious eyes steadily facing my levity, "how can you, how dare you, ask me such a question? You shock me beyond measure. Don't you know what she is?--a vile creature."

I felt deeply reproved and humiliated; and, in view of my degraded mental state, begged the loan of "St. Augustine's Life," which lay on the table at the foot of the rough wooden cross. It was only a small fragment of the literature of which he consumed so much; but it might help to put me en rapport with his more exalted vision.

The next day took Erasmus to Boston, where he remained a week; and after his return, while attending to his room, I was astonished to see a picture of Fanny Ellsler pinned up between Loyola and Xavier, and carefully framed like the others.

"Did you see her, after all?" I asked with hesitation.

"Yes, Salome; and she is divine!" he answered, momentarily raising his prayerful eyes to mine. "I thank God for such an illustration of universal grace and spirituality. You ought to see her."

When Hero and I had read "Augustine's Life," and got all we could out of it, I returned it, with a note explaining my want of sympathy with the great man, who, by his life, proclaimed religion and natural affection at variance. Friendship is by some one defined as "congeniality in one or two great principles of thought." My young friend and myself had an irrepressible faith in human nature; in fact, we were constantly surprised at the world's getting along as well as it had under such difficult circumstances. We agreed in loving the people who passed us in the streets, and in feeling certain that they cordially returned the sentiment. Self renunciation, in the narrow sense, self-crucifixion, protracted remorse, was, we thought, just so much waste of power and time, and gave evidence of an unhealthy mental condition. The belief which united us separated us, to some extent, from Sybil, Erasmus, and Torquemada, who leaned to the other extreme.

On the opposite side of the house were the apartments of Adonis, Pericles, and several of the younger students. It was to the cheerful room of Adonis, which was furnished in superior style, since it could boast of a rocking-chair and clock, that Portia, on spare hours of certain afternoons, took her sewing, and at supper, afterwards, gave us fragments of Christopher North, out of the "Noctes Ambrosianae," whole chapters of which Pericles had read to her, "doubly suffusing them with his own humor in the rendering," as she joyfully assured us. Or she had heard a modest manuscript poem of his own, or one by Ellery Channing or Monckton Milnes; and she went about repeating,--

"And then she looked down on me
With a look that placed a crown on me."

We were all happy in her good fortune; for it was a great thing to be able to economize our time in this way. How well worth while it was to set the large parlor in order, that receptive numbers might listen to Pericles' singing! His method of applying modern ideas to life, at this point in his career, was to adapt to beautiful old melodies words worthy of them. The most touching verses of Shelley, of Byron, and Barry Cornwall were put in place of the shallow ditties of lovesick shepherdesses, pirates' serenades, and Arab ravings; and so admirably did the modern thought fit itself to the ancient strain, so fully were singer and listeners _en_ _rapport_, that really profound effects were produced, and the most valuable part of the education, that which kept the soul awake and plastic to all heavenly influences, was secured.

I must describe his friend Adonis, who sometimes added his pure tenor voice to the rich bass of Pericles. I first contemplated him in the partially dug-out cellar at the "eyrie," where he had taken on himself the office of stoker at the furnace. I was bumping my head against the rafters, and making shipwreck on the treacherous rocks below, in my search for the oilcan and feeder of the establishment, when my eyes lighted on his lithe, well-proportioned figure, and his beautiful rather than handsome face, as he leaned beside the furnace, graceful, self-conscious, benignant. Seeing me, he advanced, his long, wavy ringlets a haze of gold, before he closed the door of the stove, to conduct me over less dangerous shoals to that part of the cave appropriated to the very few household utensils. This, then, was he who had served some artist as a study when he was painting a picture of Jesus, and who had kept his serenity when stoned by boys on the wharf, for daring to be eccentric and leave his hair unclipped. All the next day, and for many other days, I went about in a reverie, trying to harmonize and digest these facts. Yes, he had certainly the same smooth, symmetrical, fair face which the Byzantine artists chose to fasten on the Great Teacher. But could that strong, loving soul, working at a carpenter's bench, for years struggling with the most solemn life-problems, alone, misunderstood, yet himself in sympathy with the unintellectual, the sick, and the sinful, have worn a smooth, merely beautiful face? To say nothing of the Syrian complexion, his eyes must have expressed prescience, profound sadness, religious earnestness, and they looked from under beetle brows. His mouth had other lines and curves than the full, luxurious ones of easy civilization in the nineteenth century. His figure, too, to represent his rugged, difficult experience, would be more stalwart, and less symmetrical than that of the elegant Adonis, who should have been stoned

"In some good cause,--not in his own,"

to permit of the slightest parallel being drawn. Here I rested. Adonis was not to blame for being beautiful. Besides, he made a charming feature in the landscape; and, as such, I decided to accept him with admiration and thankfulness. Seated at meat, gliding gracefully through the dance, working in the field, he was a picture pleasing to the eye, not intended for rough usage.

Hitherto, I have said nothing of the friendly relation which was gradually established between myself and the learned young dominie (I say young; but he was one of those people who we are sure was born at about thirty-four, and will never get any older). It was he, who, on the occasion of my first visit, had so kindly signified, in a note to Sybil, his desire to teach me something; and it was under the mild, steady rays of this friendship, that I grew in mental health, and kept my heart at home and at peace. Sometimes, indeed, I was a very little jealous of Hero's charming audacity, of Sybil's fluency in tête-à-tête, and of the bewitching style and manners of the Siren. It is so hard for youth to tolerate variety in friendship; but I felt myself so much richer than ever before in the enjoyment of this unobtrusive, tender, human providence, I was so fully occupied with my studies, and my labors in the household, that I managed to silence envy, and at the same time to consolidate and deepen my intimacy with the two girls.

In my top bureau-drawer, beside the pretty copy of Heine's poems he had given me, lay a pile of his treasured notes, their free-flowing, honest chirography a satisfaction to contemplate. Sometimes a heavier letter, cautiously loaned for a limited period, lay near them,--a letter freighted with the far-reaching thoughts of some man or woman of genius; for these missives came not unfrequently from east, west, north, and south, bringing an atmosphere of prayer or prophecy, of insight or far-sight, directed to one or another of the larger lights among us, who received them reverently, and saw to it that the sacred lore was not scattered indiscriminately, too fast, or too far. It was a rare privilege to have access to so much of the characteristic and interior thought of that most prolific time.

Apart from our invigorating life in the classes I have mentioned, I was conscious of an ever-increasing delight in the discovery of the wonderful powers and capabilities of my own language, which both the speech and writing of the more highly-educated of our number opened before me. I myself, in a bungling sort of style, could baste together a jacket and trowsers for a stray idea; but how different this from the specially adapted, perfectly adequate clothing used by thoughtful, scholarly persons, to express their well-defined thoughts!

Conscious of all our happy privileges, it was not strange that we should look back to the old order of society with a pity not wholly free from contempt. How remote it was, how unstable its foundations, how unconscious of the coming change, of the external re-organization, which must follow conversion to the cooperative principle! About twenty years, we girls thought, would suffice to convince the whole civilized world of the folly of the competitive system. From this state of mind, it followed that any proposition to visit or correspond with uninterested outsiders, was listened to with supreme indifference.

The professor's valuable library was ranged on either side of the wide entry that extended through the old Hive. One glass door opened from this entry into the dining-room, and another into a meadow. Here, snatching an hour from his out-door labors, the professor might sometimes be seen, spectacles on nose, absorbed in a book. On one of these occasions as, full of happy buoyancy, I passed through this entry, I was moved to confide my satisfaction to the master of moral philosophy. At first he did not hear me; then I spoke louder, leaning from the stairs,--

"Professor, Professor, I am <u>perfectly</u> happy." It had seemed to me abundantly worth while that somebody who had helped to bring it about should be informed of this fact; but he only glanced up, with an absent expression, and said,--

"Ah, indeed!"

And I experienced a sensible disappointment.

A little later in the spring, word was brought us of a company of sweet singers, three brothers and a sister, from New Hampshire, who were beginning to attract attention by their simple musical entertainments, and who desired to visit us. They were then at a town a few miles up the river, and a boat was sent to fetch them. Abby Hutchinson was then a pretty brunette of thirteen, very picturesque in her bodice of scarlet velvet. The brothers were genial young Americans, all alike pledged to social reform. The perfect unison attained by the four voices constituted the peculiar charm of their singing; and they produced such marked impression on the public by this, even through the most unmusical music, that we could only wonder why they did not attempt that which would do their powers more justice.

Once during this summer an invitation was received by the Community to attend an anti-slavery gathering at Dedham; and large numbers accepted the call, going in farm-wagons, and returning by moonlight, full of question and argument. It was predicted by some of the anti-slavery friends, that, if we should "hitch on to their car," we should reach our desired goal more surely; but it so happened, that, of all the various kinds of people at the farm, there were at this time only two who were zealously committed to this great cause. Not that any were pro-slavery; but they did not see the real significance and importance of the movement. They were more friendly than otherwise, and too refined to be capable of the silly prejudice against mere color. When L. and others of the proscribed visited us during the following summer, they must have felt that they were treated simply and naturally, as fairer persons of the same average intelligence.

This suggestion, that we should ally ourselves with the anti-slavery party, leads me to speak of the special origin of these co-operative associations; for ours was by no means the only one. Speaking superficially, they were the outcome of a series of private conferences held in Boston, at which the well-known and greatly-beloved Universalist minister, Rev. Adin Ballou, and the Unitarian ministers, Rev. George Ripley, Theodore Parker, Samuel Robbins, Orestes Brownson, John S.

Dwight, and Warren Burton, gave themselves to the consideration of a possible reorganization of society on unselfish principles. Each of these gentlemen at the time presided over some religious body; but they had one and all come to the conclusion that it was up-hill work preaching Christianity, or the doctrine of brotherly love, while the entire social fabric was based on the selfish theory of "Every man for himself," and "Sauve qui peut." It was evident, they thought, to any well-constituted mind, that the good of one was the good of all, and vice versa; yet this great fact was wholly ignored in the present organization of society. It was set forth at these conferences, that,--

The degradation of labor undermines physical health, and diminishes mental power; while, with the largest class, anxiety for to-morrow takes the color and joy out of to-day. That,--

The glory and beauty of art, which should be made to clothe the commonest things as well as the grandest, investing each with a dignity of its own, is wholly wanting under the present system. That,--

Economy alone, and apart from any higher considerations, demands a revision of our present methods. That,--

Every child born into the world should, of right, be guaranteed the best of care and culture. That,--

Conditions produce character, and we should therefore institute conditions.

Mr. Ballou thought that success in practical reform would be furthered by an avowal of belief on the part of those uniting. They should sign themselves abolitionists, woman's rights, anti-orthodox, opposed to war and to the use of intoxicating drinks.

Mr. Ripley, on the contrary, would avoid the slightest appearance of mental chains, and depend wholly on the spirit of fraternity. In consequence, a friendly separation took place, Mr. Ballou heading a body of substantial reformers, who established themselves at Hopedale, Mass.; while Mr. Ripley and his friends proceeded to West Roxbury, and a third party was soon fixed at Northampton. All these organizations rejected communism as unfavorable to individuality, if not a disorder in nature. They desired honest co-operation, in which skill and capital should get their just deserts, to the end that skill might be stimulated and encouraged; so that if, for example, a man wanted to saunter down the Rhine next year, he might do it by working more or foregoing more this year.

I began by saying, that, superficially speaking, the associative movement was the result of certain conferences held in Boston. Really, it was an outgrowth of the advanced thought of a few educated men, whose natures had been liberated and enlarged through access to the modern German school of philosophy; and who, unlike the leaders in that school, endeavored to apply these modern ideas to life. This philosophy was at swords' point with the grim spirit of Puritanism, which sought to cover creation with a blight, and unwillingly saw the flowers spring up in the sunshine of the open meadows, and whose antediluvian Calvin had pronounced labor a curse.

The various "communities" which sprang up in New York, Ohio, and elsewhere, and falling apart left no valuable results behind, originated in quite another source.

From causes which I have heretofore enumerated, it fell out that we were held by the country folk round about to be a "stuck-up," unneighborly set.

We had considerable debate with our consciences about our nearest neighbor, Oland, who did all our butchering. Not one of our number would agree to kill any animal larger than a chicken; and the moral question arose, Why, if the deliberate killing of animals would degrade our souls, did we encourage Oland to degrade his? If it was brutalizing to the character to kill an ox, ought we to eat steak? And yet, how it was relished! Then, again, was the craving for animal food a natural or an acquired instinct? No one could tell. Very few were willing to test the matter by abstaining from meat a sufficient time to be sure that the normal condition had been regained. One thing we did agree on; and that was, that the least we could do, after blunting the sensibilities of Oland père, was to visit the other members of the family. Accordingly, at a time when Don Carlos was absent in New York, feeding his optic nerves on the precious metals, Hero and I decided to make acquaintance with some of the nearest farmers' families, and to take Oland in place of German. The first day, we called on three kind-hearted, weather-beaten housewives, whose spirit-level was soft-soap, rag-mats, tallow-dips, and patchwork quilts. We tried to shy round the soap, to fence off the mats, in vain; and, fagged out by our attempts to take the enemy by surprise, we returned home sadder and wiser women. That night, after supper, our circle had a long talk on the subject of woman's proper duty in the matter of visiting.

"How far," asked Margaret, "ought we to give ourselves to the task of assuaging the self-love of Mrs. Nickleby's relatives? Ought we to attempt to galvanize into temporary life and warmth all the putty and bass-wood within a given circuit,--that is, if we ourselves happen to be fully charged?"

"It is fortunate for us that we men are absolved from such endless waste of time," observed Erasmus, surprised into joining the conversation from the indignant vehemence of the usually undemonstrative Margaret,--"unless, indeed, a fellow happen to be religious teacher, with a good share of the feminine in his composition. Then he generally dies young, or becomes hopelessly bankrupt, through excessive drain on his capital!"

"After this," said Hero, "I never mean to visit where I can neither help nor be helped in some lasting way."

"You will then have plenty of time to prepare for your work," continued Erasmus. "Women fritter away much precious time in what they call social life. Social life is nearly worthless, unless it include intellectual and spiritual life. When I consider the large social power possessed by women, I always regret their content with displaying it on such a superficial plane."

"But men have always told us they did not like women who could think at first hand."

"I beg to remind you," he replied with emphasis, "that, no matter what we have said, we have always acted on the opposite principle."

In the early part of this summer, Theodore Parker came over often to read to the professor portions of his "Discourse on Religion," which he was then giving in sermons to his congregation at his church in West Roxbury. The dominie, with Hero, Portia, and myself, went frequently to hear him, meeting at the church others who had walked the whole distance from Boston for the purpose. We carried with us our lunch, which we ate in the pulpit at the close of the service. We were anxious to persuade ourselves that there was nothing sacred in the wood-work of the desk itself. The dominie shook his head, smiling reproachfully at us from below, and declaring that he wished to retain the superstition about the wood, since he had once occupied the pulpit himself. When the lunch was disposed of, the good-natured sexton was generous enough to blow the organ bellows, while I played "Black-eyed Susan," and "Roland the Brave," the only airs I could remember.

It was during this summer that there was much excitement in Boston on account of the escaped slaver Latimer, whose master had hunted him up, and at length secured him in the city jail. Mrs. Follen said that a cordon of women ought to surround the jail, and prevent his restoration to slavery. A meeting was called by the abolitionists for the purpose of arousing opposition to the disgraceful proceedings, and to this meeting some of us went. Fanueil Hall was packed, floor and galleries, very largely with the respectability of Boston and Cambridge, which was with the slave-master. How the crowd below surged towards the platform, yelling like infuriated animals, hissing like fiends, and then staggered back again! I well remember Redmond (the colored orator) taunted them with his stinging satire till, mad with rage, they would have torn him limb from limb, had not his friends seen the crisis approaching, and hustled him speedily out of a door at the back of the stage.

We were in the gallery, where every few moments a systematic rush and plunge would nearly send us over the low barrier at the edge. I see Phillips now, with his commanding figure and regal eye, waiting for the lull; then, with firmly-planted foot, repeating word for word his condemnation of the baseness. At such times he uttered sentences that burnt into the brain; and to see him was to understand what is the power of the human will. One moment the spell worked, and his silver-clear cadences rang like martial music through the hall. But soon succeeded hideous yells, and other evidence of savage monomania, as if no just impression had been made. A few years later I met two young men who were present on the above occasion; and they told me that they had roared themselves hoarse in the attempt to drown Phillips' voice; then--they could not clearly explain the phenomenon--they went home converted, and had since worked diligently for the slave.

This summer, also, brought me the acquaintance of Sibylla. "A greater than Bettine," she had been heralded in whispers. She was indeed an artist of no mean calibre, both with the pencil and with word-painting; an American princess of fortune; a self-elected Bohemian, giving her three legal guardians infinite trouble and anxiety by the extreme eccentricity of her orbit, which she preferred should be as difficult of calculation as that of a comet. Respectable conventionalism was her abhorrence. She swept, with an imposing train of admirers, through the winter arc of the New-England year, and then disappeared for longer or shorter periods. She was in a distant, unfrequented region in Maine, domiciled with her old nurse, spending her days on the ocean, rowing her own boat, bareheaded and ungloved, that she might lose no iota of the varied good of the long summer days; or, pulling in her oars, she floated with the tide, reading Plato or Shelley, or the fugitive manuscript leaves of the then unknown to us Elizabeth Barrett. Or she penetrated fearlessly into the shadiest solitude of the forest, and there wrote to her most insignificant slaves those wondrously fascinating epistles that wrought more powerfully on their imaginations than even the bewildering charm of her presence. Months of such exposure sent her back to society skin-brown as any Bohemian, but with the roots of her spirit cool and fibrous, and rich in the sustaining qualities which only solitude can confer on her favored children.

Or she was in a rude Western city, in the studio of an artist, whom the world as yet had not done itself the honor to recognize; where, in linen blouse, she sat day after day, copying with Pre-Raphaelite exactness the models for a group of Hours. Returning, she took possession, spite of guardianship, of an ancient building, which she converted into a Moorish dwelling, with arched ceilings, arched recesses, arched entrances, and windows of filigree stone; not an angle above or around to tire the eye that sought rest in curves. In this she kept an art-school for a few of her younger protégées, and finished by sketching them in a crayon drama, which needed no key to decipher the story.

Sibylla, when I first saw her, was making her exit from one of the narrow doors of our low dining-room; and in her gliding movements, and the alluring expression of her gray eyes, I read ample confirmation of the romantic story. As she bent low, courtesying herself out of the door, I noticed a curious expression on the faces of many, as if, notwithstanding they remained behind, in spirit they had departed with her. When through my dreams that night I caught echoes of a delicious melody, made up of two parts, and again heard light footsteps on the opposite stairs, I knew they were those of Pericles and Adonis, who had fitly celebrated her coming by a serenade in the moonlight.

Immediately after breakfast, however, having occasion to fetch milk from the barn, I discovered Sibylla perched on the hay, reading Greek with Erasmus; and I wished more than ever to brush his hair for him, and put on his best tunic, that he might, by being above criticism, do justice to the hour.

We now heard of an Englishman, L[ane]., who entertained ideas more inherently radical than our own, and whom we were shortly to welcome among us. He, with one Wright, had been keeping a school on the educative principle, at Ham, in Surrey. The old system, which we still clung to, poured every thing into the memory, and kept pouring, without reference to natural capacity, or powers of digestion and assimilation. The new plan was precisely the opposite of this; viz., to evolve all out of the child's mind by appealing to intuition and reason. Mere knowledge, it was asserted, was valueless; the mind should be early accustomed to observe closely, and to consider principles which flowed into it through the intuitive faculty. Papers on this and other topics, written in a tersely nervous style, had appeared in certain English journals; and it was reported that Mr. Emerson, who had corresponded with this writer, had said that it was worth a journey across the

Atlantic to sit at his feet. Mr. E. did not put his belief to the test; but the expounders of the "eductive" system came over to Concord, and later to Brook Farm, where their dogmatic manner of announcing the new truth gave offence and arrested sympathy. Besides their peculiar educational theory, they were averse to the eating of flesh and the drinking of the weakest tea; thought we ought to discontinue the use of cotton, because the demand for it encouraged slavery; and of wool, because we had no right to deprive the sheep of his natural clothing. This reduced the philosopher to linen, a most ineffectual defence against a New-England winter.

It was from these gentlemen that we first learned what was the power of the mother over the intellect, heart, and conscience of her unborn child. Woman had generally been credited with a share in the disposition of her offspring, but the intellect was supposed to depend on the father; genius must be traced to some grandfather, or grand-uncle,--anywhere but to the mother, whose every thought and emotion had circulated through her child, in unbroken sequence, during the entire period of its antenatal existence. She might be an immature, characterless girl: it was of no importance; the children were the father's; represented him, took his name. Vicious, selfish, weak-minded children were either so of their own deliberate choice, or by some mysterious decree of Providence; the parents, least of all the mother, were in no wise responsible, and could in no degree have modified the facts. All this error, Mr. L. assured us, would pass away with the old order of things, and parents would be held strictly to account for their inefficient, sickly, unlovable children; the mother especially, who had the balance of power in her hands, would be held to greater responsibility than even the father.

This was the greatest news yet; for if, by the study of and obedience to law, the next generation might be secured in higher moral and intellectual endowment, we could predicate the "rise and progress," and avert the decline, of nations. The newly-discovered truth approved itself, as Swedenborg would say, to our interior consciousness; and it is to the seed sown by these reformers that can be traced the very general harvest of intelligence, noticeable all over our country, on the subject of inherited tendencies. It was a pity that the iron temper in which so much valuable information was communicated and enforced wrought unfavorably to the propounders of it. Dogmatism was quite foreign to the spirit of the life at Brook Farm, and controversial discussion unknown; so we viewed, with something like amazement, the unnecessarily aggressive attitude assumed by our guests.

Even that model of courtesy and tolerance, the Concord seer, so ran the report, found himself traversing the streets of Concord in a perplexed mood, three days before Thanksgiving, debating with himself the question of inviting or not inviting his new friend to the festive board. To invite Mr. L. to America, and exclude him from his Thanksgiving table, would be both inhospitable and ungentlemanly; but then he was sure to spoil the dinner and destroy the appetite of his guests by assailing the turkey as the flesh of a dead animal, and by inviting attention to the fungi baked in the fermented bread, and to the alcohol in the wine which could never assimilate with the blood and tissues. The feast of reason and the flow of soul would be effectually interrupted, and the day of rejoicing be turned into a day of cheerlessness and disappointment. Under these circumstances, judgment was rendered in the negative.

Very unlike Mr. L. was our next notable visitor, Mr. Alcott. The quintessence of gentleness, his teachings resembled the flow of a clear, placid stream. He held one conversation on the law of insight which I was not quite up to; for I sympathized with Harlan, who interrupted once or twice with, "Mr. Alcott, if you would only be a little more practical!" to which Mr. A., with unruffled sweetness, replied,--"Yes, we will endeavor to be more practical"; and then proceeded in what was to me the same vague strain as before. Erasmus said he was "steeped in Brahminism to the lips"; and Sibylla compared him to the odors of the lotus-flower, and to good dreams, saying we needed more of this sort of flavor to our external, unaestetic lives. After this conversation, we cut all the pies "from the centre to the periphery," and a few of us were moved to make trial of a vegetable diet.

II.

On the dreariest of winter days, when the sleet and biting wind detained at the Hive the few women who had ventured down the hill to dinner, and caused quite a bustle in the kitchen, putting up meals for those who staid behind, came the omnibus with no less a person than C. P. C[ranch]., the preacher, poet, musician, and lastly, painter. How a simple, affluent soul puts one at ease! The circumscribed and impoverished alone call out apology. The furniture of the parlor at the Hive was beginning to look extremely shabby; but I doubt if any one noticed the fact, when that evening C. P. C. sang to the notes of his guitar,--

> "Here's a health to ane I lo'e dear," &c.
> "Take thou, where thou dost glide,
> This deep-dyed rose, O river!"

melting to tears the more susceptible of the sympathetic audience. In our crowded apartments that night, no one, weatherbound or otherwise, questioned but we were most favored of fortune in being permitted to enter the sphere of such exquisite melody. No after quartettes on the violin, in which he took part; no weird passages from the "Erl King," with mysterious, awe-inspiring piano accompaniment; no charming caricatures (from his note-book) of "The Experiences of the Childe Christopher Down East," or of the Harvard Mill in the process of grinding out ministers, could efface the glowing memories of the ballad sung on this first evening in the shabby little parlor.

On a less inclement day, and at length protected by a warm cloak which she had long needed but could not afford to purchase, Miss Fuller again made her appearance. She had been previously described to me as one in whom the woman, saint, and scholar were united; and my great reverence for a person at once so remarkable, and so in need of rest and leisure, made me keep at a very careful distance. Only at a later day, when brought accidentally face to face with her in the pine woods, did I allow myself, at her request, to engross a moment of her valuable time. But ever after this interview, when she was to honor us with a visit, I claimed the privilege of giving up my room to her, first preparing it for her presence by the burning of pastils begged from Camilla. I took great pleasure also in serving her breakfast in her room, using for coffee the one decorated china breakfast-cup owned by the establishment.

It was on one of these occasions, when Hero was absent, that I sought shelter with Sybil in her very limited quarters at the Hive; and there was no end of congratulation on the part of the latter, on the event which threw us together again for a whole week. The labors of the day over, in company we reviewed certain packages of notes, which, ranged in their separate order, in the lavender-scented upper drawer of the bureau, called perhaps for a more enlightened interpretation. These, with weightier matters, occupied us till a late hour of the evening; the more important affairs being two marriages which had taken place within as many months,--one of "Goody-Two-Shoes with the Virtuous Basket-Maker," as Mrs. Grant Smith satirically expressed it; and another which, although formed out of the remnants of previous engagements, promised more than ordinary happiness. Our satisfaction in the prospects of the last couple still held our thought, when we passed the ivory gate, and entered the land of dreams.

I was sunk in profoundest slumber, separated from any and every theory of the universe, when Sybil, in tones of alarm, sought to arouse me, exclaiming, entreating,--

"Oh, it was too fearful! Do wake up, and help me to recover from the horror of it."

She was sitting up in bed, shuddering in the pitchy darkness. As soon as I was able to comprehend, she explained that she had dreamed of the young lieutenant, the protégé of the Siren; he who of late had relieved for her the tedium of the unfriendly days by sleigh-rides and other courtesies, but whose regiment we had learned was ordered South. This young man had appeared to her in great mental agony, with an open paper, or letter, in his hand, on which the word "impossible" was alone legible. Pointing to this word, he asked her to read it aloud, which she had done, when he immediately seized a pistol (which she had not previously noticed) from a table, and shot himself through the temple. She was sure the blood and brains were spattered over her. I quieted and assured her to the best of my ability, till the fearful impression was partially dissipated, and we both slept again; when she had a second time aroused me, saying the dream had been repeated, with a sequel, in which the father of the lieutenant was in the Siren's parlor, using very loud and condemnatory language,--charging her with the murder of his son. At the same moment the clock in the dining-room struck ten, and he passed out of the front door, when it appeared that he was not the young man's father, but his step-father.

Although I was somewhat acquainted with Sybil's faculty of prophetic dreaming, as her dreams were not always presentiments this occurrence made no lasting impression on me, being obliterated besides by the after-sleep. She, too, in the confusion of early rising and the preparation of breakfast, had lost sight of it. It returned very forcibly, however, as she was about to ascend the front stairs, and while the clock in the dining-room was striking ten; since she then, to her great astonishment, heard violent language, together with sounds of weeping and remonstrance, proceeding from an adjoining room; at the same moment an elderly gentleman came out of the room in question, and, without noticing either of us, made a rapid exit from the front door, slamming it fiercely behind him.

This extraordinary proceeding amazed us both. Sybil indeed seemed dumbfounded, although she admitted presently that the stranger who had made all this commotion was much larger and stouter than the step-father in her dream. I ventured cautiously to open wider the door of the room, where the Siren lay on her couch deluged in tears, but pleading innocence.

"I had no idea he would be so foolish as to shoot himself," she explained, as with her handkerchief to her eyes she swayed back and forward, sitting on the pretty chintz-covered sofa.

"How could I help his loving me? I could not make myself into a fright, or an imbecile." (She was indeed a second Venus de Medici.)

Portia, who had been sent in by Sybil to fill the place she refused to occupy herself, asked the weeping Venus if she were quite clear in her conscience that she had not trifled with the young man's affections; to which she replied that "she believed love always deepened the nature; the laws governing it were very little understood, and, until they were understood, how could she hold herself responsible for that which she could not anticipate?"

Still she rocked herself to and fro, bewailing more the harsh charges made by the father, than the unnatural death of the son, with whose heart she had so selfishly, so recklessly, amused herself. She was charming, even in her present mood of shallow regretfulness,--very charming while spiritually opaque, if I may use such a term. "With us, but not of us," Portia wrote her the following day; and to which she replied, accompanying the note with a lace collar, that "she was aware of that fact, and loved Portia all the more for her frankness in telling her so."

Three months later, the Siren, laying off the widow's weeds which so well became her blonde hair and complexion, married a respectable middle-aged man, a druggist in Boston, and, dropping the character of "avenger of her sex," made a small circle of her husband's relatives into enthusiastic admirers and warm defenders of their new kinswoman.

I pause here to suggest that no sensible reader will expect or desire that I should give a detailed account of how many sloppy days there were now in the wash-room, or of the approaching signs of exhaustion on the faces of those members who worked eight and ten hours a day, and studied hard besides; or how scanty our wardrobes finally became; or that sometimes, but not often, the rice-puddings were too dry. By a decree of the gracious Providence we are obliged to forget what has been disagreeable in the past, and far be it from me to attempt to contravene this law. Neither do I reiterate, "we scrubbed, we washed, we sewed; we planted and weeded and reaped." This must be taken for granted. Work amid such companions had no power to enslave the mind. Indeed, it is a poor workman anywhere who in thought cannot rise above his anvil, his carpenter's bench, or his plough. I describe the persons and incidents which impressed me most strongly,--persons who to-day stand to the eyes of many in a more resplendent light than historical picture to worshipful artist in the Louvre; incidents, however poorly described here, so unique that they should not be allowed to pass away with those concerned in them.

The prevailing aspect of the life at Brook Farm varied constantly, and no three months resembled the preceding three months, or could at all be compared to the same period of the previous year in special interests; and so engrossing was the last phase, so swiftly did the panorama roll by, that there was danger of undervaluing the past, and permitting oblivion to cover what should have been chronicled. Under such fructifying and generous influences, with the younger and more elastic natures a wonderful change took place in a year or two; and to this change every feature bore testimony. Cruder qualities were refined, and the finer ones in this genial atmosphere pushed through the surrounding crust, to light and freer life, till often, without any distinct evidence of artistic power, you were yet justified in accrediting many of these youths with genius. For what is it to have genius? To have the inner eye opened, and to be able to discriminate between appearance and reality? or to see from an angle that reveals brighter lights and deeper shadows than others see? or is it courage which puts aside precedents, and writes axioms of its own? Whatever it may consist in, there is no difficulty in drawing the line that divides it from obtuse and respectable mediocrity. It was the conscious want of this one drop of elixir in her blood that made Jemima so unwilling to recognize merit in others, and so continually dissatisfied with outward circumstances.

"I'm sure I can see nothing so admirable in Pericles. At heart he's just as much of an aristocrat as any of his set in the world. What has he sacrificed to the cause?" Or--

"I don't see that Thane has a streak of genius in him, as you insist. Whenever I'm near him he's always talking quite stupidly. Then if you could have seen him, last Thursday, as good as force his poor little wife into her room, and positively forbid her walking to Boston, when she had set her heart on going. You call it 'balance,' and 'tone,' and a kindly decision of character. I call it masculine tyranny, a domineering spirit!" Or--

"Well, I hope we shall be able to afford a bonnet or two, between us, soon. I've seen four or five of the girls in Sybil's check straw this winter. You may say no one goes to Boston oftener than once in three months. What is they don't? What is a person without proper accessories? For my part, I think one's self-respect fades with one's clothes; and ours are getting very seedy."

"Isn't that perfectly pitiable? poor thing!" said Portia, who, passing, had guessed at the burden of the tale. "Self-respect, indeed! I feel as if we were all kings and princes, drinking from the same bowl with the gods, and living in the light that gilded Parnassus."

"Queens and princesses, too, you mean, of course?" I suggested.

"Yes, indeed!" she replied. "I don't know but there's more of the pure blood in the feminine half of the community. You know, yesterday, when the question was openly mooted, who should take care of Pedro,--that is, of his leprosy,--seven women sprang to meet the disagreeable necessity, and only one man,--Thane. But, speaking of Jemima, it really takes the better part of a day to get rid of the wet blanket she crowds around you, and see again the soul of things, as well as to be gladdened by their shimmer and shine. It is doubtless wise to be negative in the presence of the angels; but when Jemima approaches we have to gird on the armor of positiveness, or consent to part with faith and hope."

In strong contrast to this young woman was Sybil; who, if any thing, was inclined to over-estimate the excellence of others, and who was overpowered with self-condemnation on discovering that in thought alone she had done injustice to John.

"It does not signify that he was in the chrysalis state, and has now burst his shell and come into the full use of his wings. I ought to have divined the latent qualities, instead of pasing him day after day, withholding recognition of his possibilities. It was cruelly ungenerous of me. I deserve to suffer, and I do." And I've no doubt but she indulged herself in the luxury of composing a penitential psalm to suit the circumstances.

At Brook Farm, as elsewhere, the course of love (I will not say _true_ love) would not run smooth. I had noticed for some time past that Hero was a little irritable, and unusually silent and quiet; but, as the mood of a friend was held sacred and inviolable, I abstained from interference, until the silence grew to sadness, and the quiet to evident depression of mind and body. We were making the beds together one day, when a glance at her troubled, pale face decided me.

"There is something wrong, dear," I said. "Can I help or advise you in any way? Isn't Leander all right? He seems very gentlemanly and devoted." ["Tuck the under sheet well in at the top, dear."]

"O Loma! what am I to do ? I'm perfectly miserable. Yes: Leander is all right, and all wrong too. The trouble is, I can't love him; and he insists on being so attentive, and won't take the least hint; and I haven't the courage to tell him the truth. There's no more union between us than between Russia and Poland."

"But I thought you had been greatly moved by his manner of pleading his cause; that, in fact, he had <u>magnetized</u> you into loving him?"

"Yes: that state of things lasted about two days. That was the most ridiculous theory of mine," she replied, with a gesture of impatience. "The idea of animal magnetism making a union between minds and hearts! There never was a more fatal delusion than that. I have an aunt who was magnetized, I see now, into marrying a man she had not a particle of respect for. Of course, the fact that a man or woman had an agreeable external atmosphere, as we say, would be well enough if the deeper affinities existed. The latter must be perceived first, however. I shall never make such a blunder a second time,--if I have the chance."

"You will certainly undeceive Leander without delay? Poor fellow!" I said.

"Yes; that's what I feel. Poor fellow! I ought to have held on to my first impressions. He has not the least ability to enter the sphere of another,--no capacity for intimacy. Nothing that holds one. He has character, but not intellect. His thought is so circumscribed, so wanting in variety. And yet what an honorable, upright, handsome creature he is!" And she sighed deeply, in anticipation of the work before her.

It was an awkward affair, as such <u>dénoûments</u> must always be. To Leander it proved a <u>severe and</u> unexpected blow, leaving him in that unstrung, despairing, unsettled condition, which, for a man, is in itself a temptation. Portia took him under her motherly wing, and I think proved some slight stay to his weary soul; but we were all more at rest when he was called to do active duty, as supercargo of one of his father's China-bound ships.

The Charles River, but lately released from its icy bondage, flowed cold and gray and still, under the motionless, sad clouds, and told no tales of last summer's parties to the island, or of the chorus of voices which in the warm twilight had made the water-lilies blossom out more abundantly. Could those hours be repeated? I half doubted. My charming Hero was called to take up her abode once more under the home-roof at the Meadows. Diana had been five months gone. The domine had been all winter meditating a change, since our attitude to the world did not wholly approve itself to his conscience, and he was not sure that he could cordially give in his adhesion to the "idea." At any rate, he preferred to take a calmer view of us from a distance; so, having explained his position in his peculiar, modest way, he one day appeared in a long overcoat, with an umbrella, and a small parcel tied in a blue-silk handkerchief, and bade us a tender farewell. That summer he was to spend in dear old Plymouth, raising vegetables for the market, in company with his handsome young friend Agricola.

I should have related that some days prior to his departure he came to Hero and myself, and begged us, should he ever return to the community, to change our manner of addressing him, our whole demeanor, so far as it referred to him. "We always looked at him and spoke to him as if he were a saint, incapable of baseness of any sort; whereas he was one of the meanest and worst of men, capable of the most savage crimes. It would grieve him sorely if, by showing himself to us in a true light, he thereby forfeited the friendships he so highly prized. The bare mention of such a calamity brought tears to his eyes; but he would no longer sail under false colors: the deferential attitude we assumed only increased his miserable sense of unworthiness." This self-impeachment was in itself so very singular, considering the remarkable conscientiousness of our friend, that I suppose we looked our incredulity, when he further offered to prove what he had said of his own depravity, if Portia, who was included in the charge, could be present. There was no difficulty in finding the latter; and she joined us, facing him with that absolute trust and confidence to which the domine objected.

He now, with a solemn sadness, opened up the facts. We had, he said, in a thousand ways let him know that we thought him incapable of malice; but the truth was, that he had held murder to his heart for months and months. There had been times (pausing to remember, lest he should understate), nine or ten, he was sure, when, had he seen Don Carlos struggling amid the waves, drowning slowly before his eyes, and he could, by extending so much as a finger, have saved him, he would not have done it. No: he should have secretly rejoiced in his terrible situation, and have seen him disappear forever, conscious only of a fiend-like exultation; because--because he had been in advance of him in securing us girls in a German class, when it had been his, the dominie's, most earnest desire to teach us that language himself."

Ah! but it was a fine, a delicate satisfaction to know ourselves thus held in estimation by a man so wise and true; for it could not be that the value inhered in the scholarship mainly. We naturally enough waived aside this portion of the evidence of his extreme depravity, excusing ourselves on the ground, that in our minds we were convinced that, however unexpectedly to himself, he would at the last moment, had the trial occurred, have extended the required help. He was positive to the contrary, and went on adducing more of the same kind of evidence, to all of which we gave grave and respectful hearing, but found it insufficient to warrant us in bringing in a true bill. For once we were divided, three against one; and separated, assuring the beloved domine that in so high regard did we hold him, that if with our own eyes we had seen him do the deed he dreamed of, we should refuse to believe the evidence of our own senses. The mingled air of content and dejection, of failure and success, on the face of the domine at this point, would have made a curious study for a painter. Relieved, no doubt, by his own honest confession, I never saw him brighter or more genial than he was during the remaining days of his stay with us.

The Lady Superior also disappeared about this time for a two-weeks' vacation, and was heartily missed by the group in the washroom, over which she was "chief," and by the demure twins, whose sole guardian she was. The last-mentioned, freed from the restraint imposed by the only person to whom they acknowledged allegiance, actualized (this world we held to have a peculiar transcendental significance) their innocent wishes by getting up a small private party, which included impromptu charades, in their bedroom. The supérieure, having left seventy of us behind, wrote from the centre of "first circles" in Boston and Cambridge:--
"I am overwhelmed with social life here, and feel the change is good for me. I have seen Diana several times, and am each time more impressed with her growing purpose and healthy sentiment. She regrets the fate that holds her apart from us; yet I would not take her from her brother, whose balance-wheel she, for the present, appears to be.
"I think of my little girls with a degree of solicitude, though Margaret writes that they give evidence of the self-governing power.
"I am not unmindful of my much-endeared associates and occupations of the washroom, and shall shortly return to them with renewed zest. Sybilla promises to accompany me, and will remain with us till her 'Moorish studio' is completed."
The religious question, which had hitherto, intolerant spirit! concerned itself with the divine or human nature of Jesus, now assumed another attitude, and in secret voice, through the partially converted few, demanded your allegiance to the Roman Church. Young Jerome, Sybil, and Mrs. Grant Smith began to have the demure air of persons who have submitted to authority. Slowly the fact of their partial conversion leaked out, and the mystery of their mental condition was an inscrutable one to Portia and myself. Was it, we asked, that the speculative intellect needed rest, and was willing to find it in inanition? Or was it a love of extremes, which caught glimpses of novel excitement in this only other remarkable move left them? Or had the sensuous or imaginative temperament nothing in common with our crude attempt to live the golden rule? In one, and one only, of our number, did an undue love of power account for his making such a somersault.

Erasmus, far from being included in the late movement, regretted that any influence of his had contributed to its strength.

"Apart from its psalms and anthems and dramatic rites, it is unworthy the consideration of rational souls," he wrote to Sybil, when it was too late. "The horrible fanaticism of the lives of its devotees cannot be distinguished from that of Hindoo fakirs, Turkish dervishess, and barking Methodists. I regret that I ever cherished the images of such originals; for, since I have learned better the world of men, I have wholly distrusted its canonized saints. How can any pure-hearted and clear-headed person believe God's truth could pass uncontaminated through those brutal and licentious popes, John, the extortioner; Sixtus, who filled Italy with blood that his sons might be wealthy; Innocent, whose crimes grew into proverbs; and Alexander, the assassin, the fratricide, the sensualist. Sit among the daisies, Sybil, and with the blue sky above you, and the free breezes fanning your temples, try to make the dogmas of the church harmonize with nature if you can. Undoubtedly, poetry and heroism is possible, no matter what the intellectual belief; but there is little chance for either in darkness and slavery. 'The Lives of the Saints' gave me a fit of indigestion: can you say you have read and enjoyed the volumes?"

It was even so. Now we heard of the 'Nuns of Port Royal,' and 'The Exiles of Arcadia'; then we were offered solid volumes of controversy; but Carlyle, which we were used to take as a tonic, and Tennyson, in which we found a cordial, with George Fox, Law, and Mme. Guyon, were dismissed to the shades. Rough wooden crosses, and pictures of the Madonna, began to appear, and I suspected rosaries rattling under the aprons; that is, in the case of these few, for the community at large went on, working and studying, loving and planning, quite ignorant of the new theory that placed them outside the divine order, cut off from the principal sources of grace and truth.

Sometimes, but not often, the new spirit showed itself in brief argument, like the following, opened unintentionally by the reticent Jerome:--

"How touching it must be to see the church-doors in Italy and France open all the week, and rich and poor turning in at any hour, to ask a blessing or offer thanks!"

"We say our prayers at home, because we live mostly at home," replied Portia. "In southern France and Italy they work, eat, and sleep in public, and, of course, pray in public. They are well paid for what we should call a comfortless custom, in the health attained through the ever fresh air and the life-giving sun."

"The ever fresh air!" It was Sybilla's low, musical voice that spoke. "The ever fresh air in the towns is frequently but an ever repeated variety of vile smells! Just there," --and she rose to point out a spot in a lovely little bit of Venetian scenery which hung on the wall,--"just there, where the light is most tender, the stench is the vilest. There is the magnificent architecture, of course, which has no other effect on the people than to keep them in awe of the priests who rule. For cleanliness, ventilation, and sincerity, you must look to Protestantism, which now-a-days winks drowsily at science, and says, sotto voce, 'Go ahead.'"

"But you will not deny," said Sybil, "that the worship of the Virgin must have a refining effect on the heart of a man, inclining him to more tenderness and reverence for woman?"

"No one can say this idea has failed of a sufficient test," she answered; "then look at the licentiousness of Catholic countries, where the peasant woman is a beast of burden, where marriage has no sacredness. What influence has the Madonna on an Irishman who is a slave to his master and a tyrant to his wife? Ah! you should go where I have been, in France and Italy, and see the beast in its own den and amid its native forests; here its savage nature has to be a little disguised."

"And yet," said Portia, "Look at our Madonna; dear little soul, how pure and unselfish she is! She wanted me to go to confession with her the other day; and I'd half a mind to borrow her confessor, and try the effect. She said it kept her at peace till the next time. It would not be difficult to confess to Mr. Emerson, but he would be shocked at the proposition to take charge of even one soul. I should like to have Margaret Fuller for a spiritual adviser; but how could a man understand a woman's trials and temptations, especially those of wifehood and motherhood, and he a celibate? The only time I went to church with the Madonna, a thick-necked sensual-looking priest discoursed on chastity, reviewing the three orders,--marriage (the lowest); celibate orders, next above; and, towering above monks and nuns, the priesthood. So Torquemada will be placed above his great-hearted mother! Modest of them, isn't it?"

"You alluded to the Madonna, and the benefit she derived from confession," continued Sibylla. "I should judge from her appearance that she had an inactive mind; and to such a nature obedience is sweet, while the <u>habit</u> of obedience makes it a weak necessity, and absolves her entirely from the duty of thinking for herself, or regulating her life by her own judgment."

"Protestantism has to me a cold, unpoetic, unimaginative character," said the beardless Hiram,--the sentimental youth whose skill and capital were vested in his handsome eyes,--"whereas the Mother Church is rich in associations, and appeals to human nature on so many sides. What respect can we feel for either one of the two or three hundred sects, and fragments of sects, into which Protestantism is divided?" Never were his eyes so luminous, his manner so self-satisfied. Gazing upwards with one eye, he with the other held on to the plate of cake, lest Jemima and Molly, who were hurrying in, clearing off the tables, should deprive him of his just rights.

"It is the thousand little sects of Christendom which confounds the Church, as you call it," replied Portia. "It is a sort of skipping about that she cannot put her finger on; and freedom, divided into a thousand pieces, re-appears more vigorous, more invulnerable than ever. She will be <u>one</u>, only when human science, social science, shall make practical Christianity possible; when organized fraternity shall have swept from the earth ignorance, poverty, crime."

"It is an old adage that 'the proof of the pudding is in the eating,'" said the excellent Harlan, as he stuck his fork into a piece of cold mutton (he had been delayed at some outdoor job, and was now eating supper alone). "In Switzerland you can tell when you have passed from a Catholic canton to a Protestant canton, by the greater neatness and thrift everywhere visible. There will be no danger, thank Heaven! to be apprehended in this country from the Scarlet Woman, as long as our public schools are kept at the point of excellence. As long as our boys and girls learn natural philosophy and physiology, just that inkling of law is sufficient to knock away, and in a manner that admits of no replacing, the underpinning of superstition. That is why the Catholic leaders detest our public-school system. It undermines as fast as they build up,--not religion, the union of humility, aspiration, and love, but superstition, which makes ready tools for the despots. If the Romish Church could strangle our public schools, she would then be on the high-road to success, in spite of the unfortunate illustrations offered by Spain and Italy."

Harlan spoke in his usual composed manner, without bitterness; Portia, on the contrary, with excited vehemence; while Sibylla concealed beneath a graceful courtesy her horror of this cruelest form of oppression.

It was a year of more before every necessary step had been taken, and five of the original transcendentalists kneeled before the altar to surrender the last iota of their spiritual independence, when the most zealous abolitionist of the number dropped the good work out of her hands, as if it had been evil only, and proceeded with prayer and penitence in its stead. As I observed before, except among these few, catholicism was a dead letter. Just now Fourier and finance were sufficiently engrossing topics for the more responsible members; while Emerson and German, and the transfiguration of the scouring pail and hod, occupied the thoughts of the younger ones.

News of a new method of curing disease, by means of water, reached us from Graefenberg this summer, and we were not slow in testing the merits of the umschlag and "pack." Unfortunately the lay of the land did not permit of a douche. The Schrutt system, or starving cure, also a late importation from "Vaterland," found less favor with us.

Delightful letters from the domine at Plymouth kept us posted respecting the newly-fledged Free-soil party, as well as the success to be attained in market gardening. Private word from another source explained,--"The customers, with significant nods, declare that for the first time in their lives they are trading with a green-grocer who knows his place, and always trundles his wheelbarrow of vegetables to the back door."

"You, Loma, must certainly come down with Heloise," wrote our friend a little later in the season. "The sea-breezes and the sight of the rock on which my forefathers landed, would refresh your over-worked soul and body. Plymouth is like an old European seaport, full of personal romantic history,--fresh, brave, delicious to an English person, who has starved on the new bread of Yankeedom, who is half dead from same-sickness, caused by an absence of the picturesque."

But the fates ordained otherwise. I could not go. Hero, as I have said, was no longer with us, except in spirit, and Portia now shared with me the quiet and the view of the little chamber at the Eyrie. Excepting that I constantly missed the speaking hazel eyes, and the loving <u>badinage</u> of my first New England friend, I had nothing to complain of; as, between Portia and myself, there was much that was congenial also, and my work, which had been re-arranged for me, threw us much together.

I ought to describe her, but there was nothing especially noticeable about her but her eyes. A person decidedly below medium height, compactly built, heavy masses of auburn hair, a pure forehead, nose too pronounced, mouth rather unfinished, the contour of the face indicating great persistency and force of character. Three generations back, her ancestors, on the father's side, were inhaling the strong wind and fog of the Zuydor Zee. This was how I accounted for her eyes. They were an epitome of the Dutch Republic. You could read, in the glint and intensity of their steel-blue, whole chapters of hand-to-hand fighting on the dykes. They contained all the dignity and unswerving purpose of William the Silent, the agony poured out on the people by Duke Alba. You never see more than one such pair of eyes in a lifetime. I had seen her mother on one occasion. She had all Portia's energy and fore, with the refinement and spirituality left out. There was unmistakable relationship between them; while the mother's expression suggested the picture of a she-bear, fighting for her cubs.

"Poor mother!" she said, explaining the incongruity and the resemblance at once. "I can pity and sympathize with her now; but when I was younger, I met severity with defiance. You would not believe it; but mother comes of a good family, and was quite aspiring as a girl, but marrying young, and finding father inefficient, the struggle began,--the struggle for bread, with constantly enforced maternity, made her gradually loosen her hold on her ideal. I fancy I can trace in my younger brothers and sisters the different points at which she dropped first this aspiration and then that, until, alas! where in my youngest brother every trace of an ideal disappears. Mother had wonderful physical powers; and so, instead of giving way bodily, and sinking into an early grave, as would have been the case with most women, she grew impatient, rough, severe. Father was in sentiment a reformer, and gave half of the little he made to antislavery. He believed only in retaining the one slave the law allows every man, if he feel so inclined. It was this inconsistency that made mother furious." But to return:--

Erasmus, who was singularly sensitive to the presence of others, at length found Portia occupying the seat exactly opposite him at the table. For a few days he braced himself to withstand what he called "an unwarrantable appeal for assistance," and finally shuffled out of his place, and fell into a vacant seat at another table, apologizing thus for this desertion of the old set:--

"Why does she disclose all that agony, and make that reproachful, dumb appeal with her eyes? I feel personally wronged. Whatever burdens she may have borne, whatever bitter cups she may have been obliged to drink, no special responsibility attaches to me, and I won't endure it any longer."

"Bless your heart!" I said, laughing. "The Dutch Republic and the inharmonious conditions in her childhood have given her that expression of eye. She is the most self-reliant of us all, and only suffers when dwelling on the suffering of others,--of the masses."

But he was not to be moved by explanations. He was glad others were unconscious of the "profound exactions" made by those eyes; for himself he should resist to the death.

Perhaps Portia did divulge unintentionally in this way the deeper life which we all conceal, but as a rule she attracted instead of repelling. She had the natural faculty for winning the confidence of all simple souls, men and women alike; and where sympathy or council was needed, in affairs involving lover, friend, or intruder, she was more often appealed to than the supérieure, or any older person. The supérieure, gentle, refined, and cultivated as she was, yet lacked nature, and was wholly incompetent to advise or influence, in important emergencies, vigorous, natural young persons, not on her plane of thought. Her love was not glowing enough to fuse the wilfulness of the one she overlooked, or make clear and orderly the confused thought; or, if injustice had been done, she was unable to appeal to the self-respect which lay behind the present error. While you were in her state of mind, she graciously accepted you; when you were groping in the dark, or tempest-tossed on other shores, she helplessly abandoned you to your fate. Possessing more than average social power, in all fair weather her sails appeared bright and hopeful, with the rest in the prettily-fringed harbor of the new territory. When danger threatened, if you could not see with her, she withdrew. And thus it was that Portia, who could, without the least difficulty, comprehend the very spirit of your circumstances, was to many of the lads and young girls a spiritual mother and counsellor, when few suspected the fact. I alone knew how much strength she parted with in thus responding to the demands made on her sympathy. It was somewhat puzzling to me that such a girl as Portia had kept free of personal love up to the age of twenty-three. She, like myself, had only loved vicariously; and sometimes I did wish that I were a man, in order that I might propose to her at once, and thus show the high estimate I had of her.

"Ah!" she would reply regretfully, "I cannot help believing there is some necessary quality left out of my composition. I cannot fall in love. Now, if you were a man, I should look through and through you, and there would be an end of it. I somehow always have to view men--young men especially--in the light of excuse. It is such a loss to me."

Then we plunged again into the work, into the study and the sympathizing, until at last so much over-doing produced its effects, and it seemed doubtful if, in my case, health would not fail me entirely. In order to avert so great a calamity, it was proposed that I should go with Camilla and Mrs. Grant Smith, who had planned to test the water-cure at a limited establishment of their own, some three miles distant, where a fall of twenty feet had been secured for the <u>douche</u>, and plunge-baths had been built large enough to swim in. I gladly entered into the agreement; only the separation from Portia troubled me. She, however, set about making my preparations at once, and promised to keep me informed of all matters, esoteric and exoteric, at the Farm, and the re-union could be looked forward to as not so far distant.

For the present, then, our business, the business of the three absentees, was to sleep, walk, and bathe,--to bathe, walk, and sleep; and on myself the new régime acted most favorably. Messengers from the Community came often, with notes and "extra necessities"; but we were under orders to direct our steps always away from "that dangerously exciting place." It will therefore be necessary now to depend for a while on Portia's notes and personal narration.

"This summer of '42 [she wrote] will be the most splendid to recall. Think of Dolores [a <u>prima donna</u> since, and dead], sitting on those huge gray bowlders near the Eyrie, and pouring her soul out in song, with Pericles adding his undertone. Angels might listen enraptured. The music she sings is often free of the high notes, which always destroy the effectiveness of those that preceded them. (I hope we all understand now, that the upper notes contain no pathos, and the straining up to them makes the listener gasp for breath.)

  "'Hark! softly, hark,
  Beloved, hark!'

I shall hear that air, those tones, all through the centuries.

"We danced last night. The boys, Fabian and Gregorio, begged that they might have that pleasure before Dolores left. Adonis never made to ethereal

a picture as when gliding through the dance with
Dolores, and yet afterwards I was led to doubt if
they are engaged. We were talking, Adonis and I,
of the thunder-storm (which I know refreshed you as
it did me); and I expressed my great satisfaction
in these commotions of nature, and equally in the
varied phases of human nature. He listened with
eager attention while I anathematized the will-less
condition he and Sybil admire so much, and declared
my intention to go on loving and disliking,
approving and condemning, making and demanding
sacrifices, enjoying a storm even more than a calm,
humbling myself in the dust, but not staying there,
rising instead triumphantly to claim my birthright
of crown and sceptre. I think he would willingly
have had me rave on an hour longer; but I am
careful of my health, and had to retire early. At
breakfast I found this note under my plate; and as
it seems no more belonging to me than the meteor to
the earth, I send it for your consideration and
decisive word."

THE NOTE.

DEAR PORTIA,--How I love you! Will you not at
last receive the tenderness pent up in my heart so
long? We are engaged to love each other, as are
all with unspeakable devotion. This great fount of
air, which lays its cool moist hand upon our infant
foreheads, baptizes us to love; this holy moonlight
breathes the marriage vow; this horizon of sunset
green and gold is our wedding-ring. Is there purer
joy than to stand clapsed together in its centre,
with our eyes upon that holy spirit which blesses
and confirms us? Silent and serene,--silent and
serene; what is this vast sea of love on which we
all float?
   The silence of a thousand years,--so
accumulated, so profound; the serenity which can be
known, but never told. The moon of other worlds
treadeth with white feet these lulled waves. The
shadow of eternity broodeth here. This boundless
silence seems to utter "God."
   Will you not admit, dearest Portia, that there
is something unspeakably deep in these moments, on
which all other moments wait as handmaids and
worshippers? Can we look up to them without a
certain shame that we slide away so easily and far

from their bright eyrie? They are not hopeful, nor resigned, nor prayerful. Every thing that looks <u>towards</u> good shrinks away, and is <u>not</u>, beside the actual <u>presence</u> of all-good. We love and know. Love and wisdom,--who hath ever scaled their summit? Who hath faltered before loftier peaks?

Our course may be figured as a floating ascension, where the force which carried us to one height, though diminished for a time, is now accumulating to bear us up still higher. Certainly the fragrance of these ecstasies, these flowery oases, as you call them, sweeten the air and the moods of the intervening wastes.

Nay, Portia, do not cease to write your swift and central thoughts. It startled me, it made my heart sink, when I apprehended any refusal of communication. Were it only one intuition so vital, so intimate, I would wait patiently a thousand years if assured the title my sympathy gives me would be met confidingly. Why shut yourself to me because your instinct has not opened your nature to others?

Does the face of Nature <u>never</u> chide our excitement, my dear Portia? I was thrilled with the turbulence of a holy ecstasy, when a glance upon the landscape brought that rebuking face of calm and wise superiority,--that hand which does all things perfectly, without hasting, without resting, full before me. Do we not feel this same omnipotent serenity behind Nature's storms, a serenity which is our goal and Nature's?

Your brother,

ADONIS.

III.

Sibylla, gliding Sibylla, had disappeared, after a six-weeks' stay among us. She had been graciously pleased to favor me with a small share of her confidence, and I felt proportionately elated and happy,--with reason; for is there any greater good fortune than to have really known noble and beautiful persons? After her return home, she sent me "Bettine's Correspondence with the Canoness Günderode" (just translated by Miss Fuller), and a disembowelled Coleridge. "Pardon my courage," she wrote, "in sending you little more than the covers of the book: I find it contains the 'Ode to Dejection' you wished to recall; so I do

not wait to get a new whole volume. For my rambles
on the shore of Lake Superior, I cut out each day
the leaves I wished to read, and so avoided
burdening myself with the remainder."

Besides such distinguished visitors as
Sibylla, with Mr. Emerson, Miss Fuller, and those I
have previously mentioned, a few outsiders,
connected, in one way or other with the first
settlers, availed themselves of the opportunity
occasionally to take a look at us; and the more
superficial and artificial of these could hardly
conceal their amusement at the fanaticism exhibited
by well-bred women scrubbing floors, and scraping
plates, and by scholars and gentlemen hoeing
potatoes and cleaning out stables; and particularly
at the general air of cheerful engrossment apparent
throughout. The bride of Rückhalt, the artist,
could scarcely be numbered among these mild
disdainers, although she left behind her, in the
respectable city, any grain of trust her heart had
ever held for us. Rückhalt had helped to launch
the enterprise by dropping all of his few precious
dollars into the treasury, while owing to a morbid
reserve, an utter incapacity for freedom in social
intercourse, he was unable to give, as he had
intended, his proper self, with the product of his
late pictures. His shade, or double, moved about
among us for a few months; but the artist himself
lived wide apart from us, isolated, but no longer
shy or constrained; he had lately dwelt in a
secluded upper chamber in Twilight Court, Boston,
where he was preparing his famous creations,--
Remorse; Fruitless; Frozen to Death;--which in
conception and execution placed him at the head of
American painters. His pale bride unwillingly left
his side for so long as two days, in order to make
up her mind, from actual observation , if it were
best for him to sever his connection with us, by
having his name erased from the books when it was
not possible to extract the dollars from the empty
exchequer. Touched by her frail appearance, Hero
and myself offered to resign our little room for
her use, and having done so, while crowding
ourselves into inconvenient cribs and corners, felt
no end of pity for the wife of the poor artist. In
the afternoon, returning to the chamber for some
necessary garment, it was but natural for me to
stoop over the bed, where she lay quite worn out
with the short journey, and impress a kiss on her

pallid cheek. But she turned away with evident signs of disgust; and in the evening I overheard her ask Mrs. Grant Smith, "What about that girl, the servant, with the Jewish name; Huldah or Salome, was it?" and I recognized at once the demon of caste, whose very existence I had forgotten.

The report of our doings and intentions brought also people from far and near, requesting admission to the society; sometimes a whole family would arrive without having previously warned us of their approach, and of course had to return as they came; for the accommodations were always extremely limited, and admitted of no sudden expansion.

Among all the members, there was not sufficient capital to embark such an enterprise fairly; and in our business department we suffered from having to compete with the world outside, where hands worked doubly cheap, in order to provide the support, not only of those who pay in brain-work, but for that portion of society which uses neither brain nor hands to purpose,--the (in every sense) non-producers. A few wealthy persons, in sympathy with the new gospel, risked, from time to time, more or less, in aid of the movement; and we were hopefully awaiting the time when intelligent capitalists and skilled artisans, converted to the cooperative idea, should, by the establishment of manufactories, place our enterprise out of the reach of any possible danger. At present, the scholars and the dairy were our main dependence.

At one time it seemed likely that a new method for raising calves, advocated in the agricultural journals, would further our interests. The young calves, it was urged, could be brought up on hay-tea, without the aid of physiological chemistry on the mother's part. Thus the demands of the human conscience and the pocket would be harmonized, and the tremulous, plaintive lowing of the cow, together with the ineffectual struggles of her defrauded offspring, would become concerns of the dead past; since the most nutritious of hay-tea could be provided at merely nominal expense.

The professor was to test the thing; and he proceeded at once to the task. He brought into the kitchen, on several successive days, a huge discarded coffee-pot, jammed full of hay, on which he poured boiling water, and then placed it on the stove, that the more potent virtues of the herbage might be set free. It was noticeable, that, pending the experiment, he entered the kitchen, not with his customary disengaged air, but having the aspect of one, previously innocent, who had at length become entangled with criminals. He looked neither to the right hand nor the left, aware, I've no doubt, of the indignant glances cast on him by Sibylla and Margaret, who prophesied a failure of all our efforts, as they watched the not animated movements of the calf in the pasture.

"How can we expect to prosper," muttered the former, with repressed horror, "if we violate the maternal instinct in that way?" and she took evident satisfaction in observing that each day the calf belied the theory by growing weaker.

"The cow is, under this experience, progressing towards the old order we name 'civilization,' which calls for self-abnegation and the wisdom of accepting calmly the inevitable," said the ironical Don Carlos, as he passed through the kitchen, and took in the situation. As he spoke, the little fellow was seen from the window to keel over and give up the ghost; thus in less than a week putting the theory to rout.

It was now the fall of the year; and, my small stock of money being nearly exhausted, it became necessary to consider anew the situation. Before, however, there had been time for much anxiety, word was brought me, that, if I wished to remain, and take my chances with the Association, I should be cordially accepted as a "member." And now began my first delightful experience of "Woman's Rights": for in the meetings of the Association no distinction was made on account of sex; and a proposition could be put, discussed, and voted on, with entire freedom, by women and men alike. This new sense of power and responsibility widened my horizons, and included all the benefits I was prepared to take advantage of. It was the keystone to the arch, the value of which I had scarcely appreciated before possessing it.

Seldom is an aspiration, or even an ambition, fulfilled according to its original form and dimensions, because of the ever-varying changes constantly taking place on the surface of character, if not at its depths. Having earned our money, we apply for our loaf, and are surprised, it is not unlikely, at the shape, the color, or at the larger or smaller proportion of it. How few of us understand that in any case we have fully our money's worth! I had prayed for arithmetic and history, and the companionship of my equals; and I had found opportunity for unlimited culture, and a company of advanced thinkers,--large-hearted, pure-minded, religious, and cosmopolitan. I was held in loving esteem by a goodly number of both young and old (forty years made the limit of the longest experience). Work had its own zest; study adorned all that lay below it; intimate friendships filled the spaces between. If the loaf were too large, of necessity I could not appropriate the whole. I did indeed seem to be receiving my own with compound interest.

As one of the very few actual members of the Association, I could appreciate better the difficult position occupied by the heads of the departments. For every thing that went wrong they were responsible, while that which succeeded was attributed to the working of the divine idea. A quite critical phase of affairs was presented, when the table was for a short time supplied with second-best butter. This could not in the least be tolerated. If the association principle did not include the very sweetest and best of butter, it was worse than a failure, and we might as well return to cold-blooded competition at once.

At this distance of time, I understand also how great a degree of solicitude and apprehension must have been felt by the Professor and the Lady Superior concerning the almost unrestrained companionship of so many young people of both sexes. They could not know, as we did, how really noble and pure were the relationships between them. Perhaps they did rely somewhat on the fact of their mutual occupation in the higher studies, though they knew little of their common aspiration after truth. We were, besides, absorbed in books,--in Carlyle first, then in Swedenborg, Tennyson, Sterling, and Walter Savage Landor. I do not include Emerson; because he, with his "Self-Reliance," "Heroism," and the "Over-Soul," seemed an integral part of the movement itself. Such activity of the interior and higher faculties consumed the vitality which might otherwise have wrought confusion and unseemliness. There were love-affairs, of course; but they flowed generally in an atmosphere of religious sentiment.

It was thus with Hero and Leander. After the former had refused her lover, on the ground that he was not sufficiently her senior, she devoted herself so exclusively to his welfare and happiness that a second proposal naturally followed. This, she declared, was in the true order of nature, "Because, you see, he put me in communication with him through the terrible earnestness he displayed on that occasion, while it yet took time for me to change my mind." The intercourse that subsequently took place, was, as I could plainly see, of the most innocent and beautiful character, and, beyond that, tinged with the light of a new-born reverence.

The first proposition had taken place while Hero was washing the breakfast cups in the dining-room; and the knowledge of this recalled the case of my "cousin" Tom, who had been moved, contrary to all precedent, to hand Sibyl his petition while assisting her with the dishes at the great sink in the kitchen. Now, it was not unusual when the weather was bad, for a convocation to be held in the parlor at the Hive for the informal discussion of any subject chosen by the majority. Such a season occurred during my first visit, when the question proposed was,--

"Is labor in itself ideal? or, being unattractive in character, do we in effect clothe it with the spirit we bring to it?"

Margaret and Leander insisted that it was in itself divine, as was proven by the invigorating effect it had on character. It was _doing_, -- faithful, patient repetition of material duty, of service, or production, that proved and disciplined the _will_ and the reason. Such pleasure, such unfailing satisfactions, attended the most needed occupations, that surely the work must be in itself ideal!

"The garment we have expended our time and skill upon finished," said the former, "what a gratified sense of power we are conscious of! The apartment put thoroughly in order, what a delightful compensation one glance round it affords! The dinner, requiring such a combination of skill, at last on the table, a just pride is quite permissible!"

"That too much labor disgusts the mind, as well as degrades the body, is no argument against the character of the labor itself," continued Portia. "The odor of violets may be prolonged to disgust, and the finest music presently produce exasperation. So deeply imbedded in the very constitution of our being is the idea that labor is a curse, that we have woven the false sentiment into our laws, customs, and literature; and we are scarcely fit judges of its character. It is only the bravest thinking and doing, like our own, that will ever root out the error. In the old order of society, the great mass of cultivated people lack health and vigorous individuality, because they have not had the stimulus of necessity to this inexpensive but admirable means of training."

"It is Puritanism that has declared labor a curse and hideous," reiterated Erasmus. "I do not care how far back the statement was made, it has on its face the die of some antediluvian Calvin."

"We have turned aside from our subject," said Mrs. Grant Smith. "The question was, not the uses, but the character, of labor. No one can see more plainly than myself the injustice done labor, in civilization, where the laborer has been cut off from the best culture and been virtually whipped to his task. Chattel slavery is labor slavery, only a trifle less disguised. Yet I must differ from you all, in finding any thing aesthetic in the ordinary forms of labor,--say scrubbing, washing, preparing vegetables, &c., &c. Who," she asked smiling, and in a tone that defied disproval, "who would ever think of proposing to a girl while she was washing the dishes?"

It vexed me that I could not rise and summarily disprove the infallible dictum by adducing my cousin, who, at that moment, lay tempest-tost on his bed, because of the answer he had received to his interrogation.

This winter brought to the farm a cordial sympathizer and earnest laborer, J. S. D[wight]., and with him all sorts of talk about the meaning and uses of music, and much delicate improvisation. Soon there was a class of little ones (I see them now with their arms clasped about each other, crowding up to the instrument, where the gentle, genial master accompanied), singing from the first "Boston School-Singing Book," (Has there been so sweet a collection since?) and later, a larger class, who attacked the glees in "Kingsley's Choir," and presently Mozart's 7th and 12th masses. How modestly J. S. D, in a late number of "The Atlantic" speaks of the "Mass Clubs" which "sprang up" about this time, not only at Brook Farm, but in Boston, and of the writing and lecturing on the great masters, as if he himself had not been the sole instigator and indefatigable worker, assisted, no doubt, measurably, by the articles of Miss Fuller! First, it was necessary to create a larger want for something better than the Swiss Bell-Ringers and mangled psalmody: then he set himself to work to <u>cause to be assembled</u> the talent that would supply, while it increased, the demand. It will never be known by what studied and persistent manipulation a sufficiently large public was brought to believe that Beethoven's symphonies and Mozart's masses were divine creations, and, as such, their performance should be called for by all lovers of fine music. When at length an audience, such as would justify an orchestra of eighty instruments in rehearsing some of the noblest productions of Beethoven, Haydn, and Mozart, was secured by means of subscription-tickets, a new era in the Boston musical world was inaugurated,-- notwithstanding that at the outset it became necessary, through the papers, to apprise the younger portion of the said audience, that great composers never indulged in conversation while their compositions were being rendered. But these concerts were given, I think, the following winter; and I must return.

    The Professor, J. S. D., and Don Carlos now began to give considerable attention to the formulas of the social system propounded by the untranslated Fourier. We heard a good deal of "attractions being proportioned to destinies," and of "groups and series"; and, as far as we went, there certainly seemed much incontrovertible truth and much sound practical sense in the details and the general sweep of his plan; yet, for all this, those friends with whom I was most nearly united failed to be moved by the humane Frenchman's scheme. It suggested perfectly-made machinery, which, if it could be put together might work admirably,--go of itself. But there it was: we could never get over the 'if'; and we doubted-- could the Phalanstery be erected, complete in all its appointments, even to the "Badges of Honor," and the most delectable cooking--would the soul be content abide inside the arrangement?

"No inconsiderable man, this Fourier," wrote the Dominie from his barren little chamber at the Hive to our more home-like bower at the Eyrie, after listening to some reading from the author in question, "a rare and original mind; a picture of life very fascinating and attractive to poor flesh and blood; but our nobler part protests at much which a genuine descendant of the Puritans must always find it hard to swallow."

"I am greatly drawn of late to a close study of Fourier," wrote the Lady Superior to Sibylla. "His science of association recommends itself more and more to my feelings and conscience; and I am constrained to accept him as a man of genius, a discoverer; though I believe that in many things his system is to be modified by the spirit of our time and nation. The unfolding of the groups and series is as beautiful to me as the opening of the buds and leaves in spring, and will give a grace and charm to the actual, never imagined before."

But the only application of Fourier's principles made by us at this time was in the matter of waiting on the tables. Hitherto the desire experienced by each to wait on every other had resulted in some confusion; yet it seemed so selfish to eat while others, as hungry, stood to serve, that we had been unwilling to think of any other plan. It had even been found necessary to call a meeting to settle the question of griddle-cakes, or no griddle-cakes; since those eating their breakfasts declared they could not enjoy that delectable food while oppressed by the thought of two or three friends, with empty stomachs, leaning over the stove cooking it. It is true that the vote taken on this occasion was in favor of that diet, the most disciplined cuisinières insisting that the sight of the golden-brown cakes made the trouble a pleasure; but this obligation referred at most only to one day in seven, and certain self-sacrificing women would make more or less confusion, during the other twenty, out of the twenty-one meals. Now Don Carlos managed to organize a group of servitors, comprising four of the most elegant youths in the community,--the son of a Louisiana planter, a young Spanish hidalgo from Manilla, a rudimentary free-soiler from Hingham, and, if I remember rightly, the brother of Gen. B[arlow].; and these, with one accord, elected their handsome and beloved tutor chief. It is scarcely necessary to observe that the business was henceforth attended to with such a courtly grace, such ease and promptness, that the change was welcomed by every one; although it did seem at first very much as if we were all acting a play. The group with their chief took their dinner, which had been kept warm for them, afterwards, and were waited on with distinguished consideration; yet I confess I never could become entirely reconciled to the new arrangement.

It was now winter; and, instead of boating, the scholars took to skating: those from the tropics, who had never before stood on ice, could not have enough of the fascinating sport. Sometimes, but not often, a party, including the older members of the community, with sleds and skates, would make the moonlight on the river social. In the crisp starlight, wearing an improvised bloomer-suit, I took my first lessons in the art from Portia; and, returning over the desolate snow-covered fields, we exchanged records, and from that time became more and more intimate. One Sunday, seeking health and solitude at the same time, we decided to steal off unobserved to the river, passing by way of the solemn cathedral of the woods, the more fully to enjoy the religious serenity of the sabbath. A gracious silence flowed all around us, unbroken by insect or bird; and, having thus far succeeded in our plans, we were a little chagrined, on reaching the frozen stream, to see, just in advance of us, Erasmus, with his friend William. So, after fastening on our skates, we lingered, in order that they might distance us, when, following slowly, a deep bend in the river brought a church-spire into view; and forthwith we saw Erasmus fall on his knees, and clasp his hands together as if in prayer, and, after a few moments, rise, take off his skates, and, fording his way through the unbroken snow of the bank, approach in the direction of the not distant church.

"He will certainly not go in there with that old checked blouse on, and the skates in his hand?" said Portia.

"Yes, he will, though," replied William: "the sight of a church-spire calls out all his devotional feeling, which has no relation to his dress, you know. He'll walk up the middle aisle, and kneel down at the altar steps, and astonish all the respectable people in the pews, who will hold their breaths in amazement, supposing he has just escaped from some insane asylum. Meanwhile, having satisfied his religious sentiment by repeating such prayers of Socrates, Epictetus, or Taylor, as arise in his heart, he'll come out as composed, and all unconscious of the impression he has created."

And, sure enough, in about ten minutes he joined us, looking very tranquil and happy; and after talking a while about the greater simplicity of the Catholic countries, where the church-doors are always open, and no market-woman or ragged child but can step in and ask a blessing at any hour of the day or night, he put on his skates, and, bowing us a courteous farewell, pushed rapidly up the river and out of sight. The silence was now broken; and it was but natural that the conversation should fall on him who had been the cause of it.

"I will tell you," said Portia, "that I like him better, and love him less, every day. No one at the farm has been of so much service to me as he has. I feel towards him very much as you do to the Dominie." "Oh, no, indeed!" I interrupted: "I love the Dominie, and like him too, more every day. If people only <u>liked</u> me, I should want to die right away. I thought you and Erasmus were quite intimate."

"So we are, I rejoice to say. No one appears more true than he; and his mind is as pure and simple as a child's. But then, while I approach him more nearly, it is still in a less <u>personal</u> spirit."

"You are all, I see, very different from myself. I love you personally; for instance, do you suppose I love your qualities? Why, bless you, I love the braids of your hair, and the bows on your shoes. It is the peculiar <u>you</u> that makes me happy," I said.

"And I like you for saying so, although it conflicts with so much of the transcendental philosophy. But I was telling you what a great help Erasmus has been to me with my music. I never should have dared stumble through the chords and cadences in the "Men of Prometheus" and "Fidelio," if he did not sometimes hurry down stairs, and, drawing a chair beside the piano, ask me to repeat certain passages in the wonderful story. I spell out the grand sentences most awkwardly; but he, too, gets at the meaning, he says, so I dare to go on. While I execute in the execrable manner I do, I am yet drinking in life, fullest life. I tremble with emotion as I seem to be carried along in the great struggles of Humanity; and I am part and parcel of the success of the future. I hope one day to have children in whom these hesitating instincts of mine shall blossom out, freed and glorified. But look at the clouds; let them talk now."

Our German class was absorbed in Novalis's Hymns; and as discussion on the nature of Jesus was inevitable.

"Wenn ich ihn nur habe,
Wenn er mein nur ist,"

quoted Margaret. "I cannot imagine any such mystical relation between me and the great Teacher. To me Jesus was a brave, good man. I can just imagine him, with his wonderful insight, looking, without intention, into the shallow depths of those he was constantly meeting: seeing their crooked and crumpled hulls, and all their selfishness, which he knew was only blindness, and their grossness, which was blindness too; and back of all that, the inmost spirit, pure as seed-wheat. And now that we have this new chapter of magnetism opened to us, we can easily understand how he could heal the sick by sending a measure of his subtle vital forces into the exhausted nerves of the receptive and believing. If you say he was the Deity, and talk about possessing him in any other sense than that in which we possess the example and teaching of a lesser soul, then my beloved, tender hero disappears,--his example is no help to me; for the Deity, in his meanest form, would be eternally conscious that good and truth are alone valuable, and the suggestion that he could be tempted is childish."

"Then," said Sibylla, "we sweep away at a stroke all the poetry of the Christian ages, all the heroism born of a belief in a divine atoning Saviour."

"I believe it was love of love, that alone moved the world," said Portia; "and, whenever the theory of an atoning Saviour made an impression, the result was bitter feuds, brutality, Inquisitions. I do not even like to meet at every turn the cross, reminding me of the cruel (but temporary) suffering of our Elder Brother. Why should I remember my mother, as she lay slowly dying of a lingering disease? On the contrary, I love to recall her face and figure when she was in full health, and on one special occasion, when she praised our efforts at self-control, saying,--

"'Remember, my dears, you have the benefit of a whole generation of progress. You must demand great things of yourselves.'"

"Yes: I wholly agree with you," replied Margaret. "The thought of Jesus trying to inspire with some higher hopes and aims his poor oppressed countrymen in the villages and country places of Judaea, stopping to comfort this sad or sinful woman, to awaken a soul in that debased or downtrodden man, fills my heart with perpetual admiration and love. Call him 'God,' and I feel only a perplexed awe."

"If we could only be spared for a week, and could go to Concord and consult with Mr. Emerson," said Sibylla, as she gazed dreamily out of the poor little window of her room,--her room in which we had congregated,--"we should come back with clearer vision, restful and glad. His impressions would be worth more to us than the clenched reasoning of others." Her violet eyes eagerly strained forward. In spirit she was evidently tramping over the frozen Concord road.

"If we could only go to the master," she sighed, addressing herself to Portia. "We need only be absent a week, and we could walk all the way. One day to Waltham, where we could stop at my aunt's; one thence to Concord; and one for the chance of not seeing the seer the first evening. You, dear, could wear my new check-bonnet, and I should be comfortable in the old one with a veil."

"I cannot help laughing," I said, "at the great value you put on Mr. Emerson's insight and judgment; for Mrs. Enge once spoke of him in my presence as a lunatic. She went to school to him when she was a girl, and all the scholars adored him, she said; but he had allowed himself to drift into a most deplorable state of moral and intellectual obliquity. The curious part of it was, that she held him responsible for his unfortunate condition."

Sibylla, as I said, had long ago vanished. Now we heard that Camilla would shortly arrive; and she was to remain, certainly during the winter, as a boarder. Rooms of more ample dimensions than any of the others had been assigned to her; and we hoped that the jewelled grasshopper in her hair, and the soft laces that clothed her shoulders, and fell over her small firm hands, on the occasion of her first appearance among us as a visitor, did but foreshadow the paintings, the marbles, and antique furniture which we heard composed her present surroundings, and which we hoped would accompany her to her country exile. It is true, I saw people rather than their apparel or furniture; but entire abstinence from these concomitants of wealth had not in the least degree deadened our appreciation of external beauty and elegance. One chipper, industrious little woman at the Farms advanced, mildly, a "sackcloth" doctrine of her own, and refused to wear so much as a plain linen collar while slaves toiled unpaid; and one other quoted, in a colder spirit,

"And the garment in which she shines
Was woven of many sins."

The rest of us hailed with undisguised pleasure the advent among us of a small engraving, or a more delicate and brilliant piece of apparel.

Camilla had been more than a month at the Farm before she and I had exchanged a word. Then it happened that the young woman whose duty it was to mop the stairs and entries of the building to which Camilla's presence lent its principal character was taken ill, and it fell on me to make good her place. Busy with my work, I did not notice the moment when the door of the parlor opened, nor dreamed that the penetrating eyes of its occupant were bent on me, till a voice in tones of most touching entreaty, tones that recalled wailing winds and innocent childhood, at once said,--

"Could you, my dear, do you think, drop your work, and oblige me by spending a few moments in my room?"

I consented, and soon found myself charmed by her spontaneous, energetic speech; and her manner, which expressed deference, simplicity, and warmth, was quite peculiar and fascinating to me. This short, and to me brilliant, tête-à-tête ushered in a long series of interviews, as earnest, if less striking. I was only puzzled by the vehement ejaculations she indulged in during our first meeting, such as "God bless me!" and "extraordinary mistake," looking around into the corners of the ceiling meanwhile, as if seeking there a solution of her perplexity. I learned casually, when we had become well acquainted, that the kiss I had bestowed on Rückhalt's bride had caused much prejudice against me in the mind of her friend Camilla, and her surprise at the vanishing imp had expressed itself in interjections.

To my mind, no pictures or vases were necessary to the rooms Camilla lived in. A few hung on the walls, a few miniature copies of ancient marbles found place in corners; but for these I had lost my interest. She possessed the gift which made her a fine dramatic reader; and, when once she had assumed a character, she so lost herself in it, that if it happened to be Iago, or some other villain, and I the one he hated, I sat in dread lest she might forget mere personation, and, reaching over the table, should stab me with her imaginary poniard.

I did not wonder that "Father Taylor," the sailor-preacher, came out sometimes to hear her read the "Ancient Mariner" (did she ever read Mrs. Browning's "Mother and Poet," I wonder?) or, that the Water-Necken, who proved so susceptible to her magnetism, should like to bask in her generous shadow; or that she should prove such a pillar of strength in the weak hour that comes to all of us; or that Oraculum Basilius [Orestes A. Brownson], the large, angular, able advocate of Catholicism, never failed, after paying his regular visit to his brother convert Torquemada, to spend an hour in argument with Camilla.

Oraculum, who had dealt blows with a smith's hammer in the debate between capital and labor, standing foremost in demanding better conditions for labor and skill, in the second year of Brook Farm surrendered his arms, and rushed into the Church. This done, he acknowledged but one object in life; viz., to prove the Catholic Church the centre of the Cosmos; and he out-Heroded Herod, in his fierce devotion to the cause he espoused. I happened to be with Camilla on an evening when this unpolished, positive man made his usual call; and the passage-at-arms I was then permitted to witness stands out clear before my mind to-day. After a little sparring, Oraculum suddenly rose, and, planting himself with a vehement gesture in a chair that faced his opponent, said,--

"You do not place yourself on my stand-point. I say, you Protestants are a mere handful of restless, disunited vagabonds, while our Church is still a unit, and still a refuge for the greatest minds."

"My dear friend," replied Camilla, smiling, "you must not forget, that it is through the talent, through the greater individuality generated in free Protestantism, and which is transferred to the Church in the converts she makes now and then, that she keeps her tyrannical head above water today. I am as intimate with Romanism as with dissent; and I do not hesitate to say that the former is in deadly opposition to liberty. In fact, she takes freedom by the throat on every possible occasion, carefully making the sign of the cross meanwhile. What is such a unit worth?"

"Every thing. Without it chaos would come again in more appalling shape than ever. I have in my pocket a book I selected from the bishop's library, because it just suits your case. I refuse to argue with you more, since you are in so irreligious a frame of mind."

"I want to ask you just one question," urged Camilla. "Do you approve of the priests of the Inquisition roasting off the feet of the children?"

"Certainly I do," he replied. "It was much better they should have their feet roasted off in this world, than their souls should roast eternally in the next."

"What have you done with Torquemada? Three years ago he had a most ingenuous, transparent, human expression in his eyes. I don't know what you are doing with him that transforms this into a cunning, unscrupulous expression, which makes me afraid we may one day find ourselves blown up by a second Guy Fawkes."

"Prejudice, most wicked prejudice," said Oraculum, bringing his fist heavily down on the table. "That young man is destined to become a bright light in our holy Church; and I expect to see you, with many others, on your knees before him, claiming his prayers, as well as the intercession of the Mother of God. I bid you goodnight," and he left in disgust.

"Nothing ever gave me more pleasure," said Camilla to me, when we were alone together, "than the other day the sight of Torquemada's mother rising in her simple dignity from the midst of a crowd of praying priests whom her son had sent to convert her. 'I love my son John,' she said '(I know no one by the name of Torquemada); but I was at peace with God before he was born, and I am certain that giving myself up to the influences and ceremonies of his new religion would only put a thick veil between me and my Maker, and take away that peace. You are welcome to pray for my conversion, my friends, provided you do it away from my premises. I not only pray to God the Father every day, but I look around among men, my brothers, to see if I can help them; and in this last prayer I don't believe you can get ahead of me.' And the manner in which that upright old lady sailed out of the back-parlor into the kitchen gave permanent tone to my nervous system."

I remember that one morning, after an interview the night before with Oraculum, the Professor appeared at breakfast fatigued instead of refreshed by his night's sleep; and inquiry after his health elicited the following facts. Catholic converts of such marked ability as Oraculum were at once put through a course of Latin and Greek, the better to fit them for the service of the Church. But the not plastic vocal organs of the mature, self-made men were apt to make sad havoc with spondees and dactyls. The vigorous champion of the rights of labor was no exception to the rule; yet, pleased no doubt with the flexibility and expansiveness of a language with gave the verb <u>amare</u> a hundred and twenty inflections to the English five, he could not help occasionally displaying his new acquisition. The Professor, with his finely-disciplined ear, shuddered at the linguistic immorality, and the false vowels haunted his dreams of the night. It seems he had followed a crowd into the church, and Oraculum had been appointed his confessor. He made no objection to this; and, at a signal being given, proceeded to the confessional, where his old friend and newly-made Father lent attentive ear to the recital of his manifold transgressions. The affair of the calf, among others, had assumed gigantic proportions. Having finished, the Father said sternly,--

"Kneel, my son, and for penance repeat after me the 58th Psalm in the Latin Vulgate;" upon which the Professor, in mortal agony, cried out,--

"O Lord, my punishment is greater than I am able to bear!" and woke up, trembling from head to foot.

* [Georgiana Bruce Kirby], "Reminiscences of Brook Farm," Old and New, 3 (April 1871): 425-438; 4 (September 1871): 347-358; 5 (May 1872): 517-530.

BROOK FARM AND TRANSCENDENTALISM*

George William Curtis

What was known a generation ago as transcendentalism was not only a philosophy, but a life. To the world at large its most tangible phenomenon was Brook Farm, but its real power is the influence which, through those who were moulded by it, it has exerted upon American thought and society. Mr. Frothingham has written a delightful history of the transcendental epoch in its various aspects, which must become a permanent authority for a just estimate of one element in the development of our national character. A comprehensive and scholarly sketch of the rise and progress of the transcendental philosophy, which treats a subject remote from general sympathy with a certain charm which is free from superficiality, is followed by descriptions of the kind of work done by the leaders of the "newness," and of the characteristics of the leaders themselves. The germ was the study of the German philosophy of Kant and his followers, interpreted in England by Coleridge, and cultivated by a circle of Boston scholars. Perhaps the local and social spring of the movement may be found in the assemblies for intellectual intercourse at the famous Dr. Channing's. His sensitive spiritual nature, his tranquil and refined manner, and his slight person were a kind of avatar to a new impulse. Those who recall him speak of him with an affectionate reverence and tenderness which are full of suggestion of the peculiar quality of his character. His personal influence as an orator was masterful but gentle. It was the fullness of Matthew Arnold's sweetness and light. He went to lecture in Philadelphia. The hall was very full, and the great crowd listened intently. He spoke wholly without loudness, or declamation, or passion, and with entire simplicity. Presently he said, quietly, that he was fatigued, and would rest for a moment. He seated himself, while the audience remained perfectly still, and after pausing for some minutes he arose and resumed the even thread of his discourse.

Dr. Channing had already a great literary reputation, and the young scholars and seekers naturally sought him. But he was an invalid, and never an aggressive reformer, as some of his disciples became. As the questions of the time became more positive and the feeling of the scholarly circle gradually demanded some form of experimental action, the place of meeting was gradually changed to the house of Mr. George Ripley, then a settled clergyman in Boston, and his real prominence in the transcendental movement is for the first time properly stated by Mr. Frothingham. Since those days Mr. Ripley has become widely known as the chief of literary critics in the daily press, where his humane and comprehensive spirit, his ample and well-ordered scholarship, his shrewd perception and love of justice, have endeared him to writers and readers as both the truest and kindest of critics. His service in this way to American literature has been great and constant, and it is one of the debts that the country owes to the transcendental movement. In the earlier day of which the Easy Chair is speaking, Mr. Ripley was one of the few American scholars who were thoroughly familiar with German theology and philosophy, and his word had therefore a weight in the general discussion which was not surpassed. It was in his library that the project of Brook Farm took shape, and under his auspices that that Arcadian experiment was finally begun.

The name of Brook Farm has a very vague significance to those to whom it means anything whatever, and Mr. Frothingham seems to be of opinion that its story will never be adequately, even if formally, told. This is not surprising, for those of its leaders who are still living are no longer young, and the subject is not one that would readily take literary form. The most complete attempt to depict that Arcadia, but by implication and suggestion rather than by detailed description, was made in a series of papers published in early numbers of the _Old and New_ magazine. Mr. Hawthorne's references to it in his Note-Books rather dissipate any dreamy character which it may have acquired, and he always spoke of it in the tone of his notes. He expressly declared, also, that the _Blithedale Romance_ was not to be taken as a picture of Brook Farm and the life there. But that romance was the real impression which he brought away--the impression of the imagination. It could not have been written but for Brook Farm, and it is the chief purely creative product and account in literature of the spirit of that time. Mr. Emerson's essays were among the moving and inspiring forces, as they are the noble and permanent record, of the transcendental spirit.

The Easy Chair describes Brook Farm as an Arcadia, for such in effect was the intention, and such is the retrospect to those who recall the hope from which it sprang. Hawthorne's humor was always touched by the contrast between his expectation and his experience there. "I went for poetry, and I found muck," he used to say, with a smile; "I went to drive the horses of the sun, and I sat in the manure milking a kicking cow." And the curious visitors who came to see the poetry in practice, quoting George Herbert, a favorite poet of the transcendentalists,

"Who sweeps a room as for thy laws
Makes that and the action fine,"

saw with dismay hard work on every side, plain houses and simple fare, and a routine with little aesthetic aspect. Individual whims in dress and conduct, however, were exceptional in the golden age or early days at Brook Farm, and those are wholly in error who suppose it to have been a grotesque colony of ideologues. It was originally a company of highly educated and refined persons, who felt that the immense disparity of condition and opportunity in the world was a practical injustice full of peril for society, and that the vital and fundamental principle of Christianity was universally rejected by Christendom as impracticable. Every person, they held, is entitled to mental and moral culture, but it is impossible that he should enjoy his rights as long as all the hard physical work of the world is done by a part only of its inhabitants. Were that work limited to what is absolutely necessary, and shared by all, all would find an equal opportunity for higher cultivation and development, and the evil of an unnatural and cruelly artificial system of society would disappear. It was a thought and a hope as old as humanity, and as generous as old.

No common mind would have cherished such a purpose, no mean nature have attempted to make the dream real. The practical effort failed in its immediate object, but, in the high purposes it confirmed and strengthened, it had remote and happy effects which are much more personal.

It is an error, which Mr. Frothingham corrects, to suppose that many of the more famous "transcendentalists" were of the Brook Farm company. Mr. Emerson, for instance, was never there except as a visitor. Margaret Fuller was often a visitor, and passed many days together as a guest, but she was never, except in sympathy, one of the Brook Farmers. Theodore Parker was a neighbor, and had friendly relations with many of the fraternity, but he seldom came to the farm. Meanwhile the enterprise was considered an unspeakable folly, or worse, by the conservative circle of Boston. In Boston, where a very large part of the "leaders" of society in every way were Unitarians, Unitarian conservatism was most peremptory and austere. The entire circle of which Mr. Ticknor--whose lately published life and letters is a delightful book, of which the Easy Chair has before spoken--was the centre or representative, the world of Everett and Prescott and their friends, regarded transcendentalism and Brook Farm, its fruit, with good-humored wonder as with Prescott, or with severe reprobation as with Mr. Ticknor. The general feeling in regard to Mr. Emerson, who was accounted the head of the school, is well expressed by John Quincy Adams in 1840. The old gentleman, whose glory is that he was a moral and political gladiator and controversialist, deplores the doom of the Christian Church to be always racked with differences and debates, and after speaking of "other wanderings of mind" that "let the wolf into the fold," proceeds to say: "A young man named Ralph Waldo Emerson, a son of my once-loved friend William Emerson, and a classmate of my lamented son George, after failing in the every-day avocations of a Unitarian preacher and school-master, starts a new doctrine of 'transcendentalism,' declares all the old revelations superannuated and worn out, and announces the approach of new revelations." Mr. Adams was just on the eve of his antislavery career, but he continues: "Garrison and the nonresistant Abolitionists, Brownson and the Marat democrats, phrenology and animal magnetism, all come in, furnishing each some plausible rascality as an ingredient for the bubbling caldron of religion and politics." C. P. Cranch, the poet and painter, was a relative of Mr. Adams, and then a clergyman; and the astonished ex-President says, "Pearse Cranch, ex ephebis, preached here last week, and gave out quite a stream of transcendentalism most unexpectedly."

This was the general view of transcendentalism and its teachers and disciples held by the social, political, and religious establishment. The separation and speciality of the "movement" soon passed. The leaders and followers were absorbed in the great world of America; but that world has been deeply affected and moulded by this seemingly slight and transitory impulse. How much of the wise and universal liberalizing of all views and methods is due to it? How much of the moral training that revealed itself in the war was part of its influence? The transcendental or spiritual philosophy has been strenuously questioned and assailed. But the life and character it fostered are its sufficient vindication. Nothing, indeed, should teach the most positive dogmatist the value and the virtue of charity more than such a passage as that just quoted from Mr. Adam's diary. If any man in the world thought that he "knew what he was talking about," it was John Quincy Adams, and in certain directions and upon certain themes he was justified in doing so. But this allusion to Mr. Emerson, and the absolute incapacity of Mr. Adams to understand the transcendental impulse or to sympathize with it while he wrote so surely, are both amusing and pathetic. It is like stout old Admiral Montague, loyal to King George and the integrity of the British Empire, shaking his fist in rage at Sam Adam's rebel friends as they returned from the tea ships, and shouting to them that they would soon and righteously come to the gallows. How surprised would Mr. Adams have been could some good genius have whispered to him, as he denounced one of the regenerating impulses of his time, that he was doing what one of the men whom he would least like to resemble did at the beginning of the Revolution--the anonymous Boston Tory who wrote, in 1774, "That mighty-wise patriot, Mr. John

Hancock, from the Old South Meeting-house, has lately repeated a hash of abusive treasonable stuff composed for him by the joint efforts of the Rev. Divine Samuel Cooper, that rose of Sharon, and the very honest Samuel Adams, clerk."

*[George William Curtis], "Editor's Easy Chair," Harper's New Monthly Magazine, 53 (August 1876): 464-477. Octavius Brooks Frothingham's book, Transcendentalism in New England, was published in 1876.

THE BROOK FARM COTERIE*

A Peculiar Episode in the Life of Charles A. Dana

Mr. Emerson's Recollections of the Editorial Disciple of Fourier--Arbitrary, Tyrannical and Treacherous in Character

BOSTON, Oct. 29.--It was a beautiful October afternoon, just as the sun had dropped well down towards the high lands and wooded hilltops of old Middlesex, that THE STAR representative stepped out from the platform of a railway car in the quaint old town of Concord, Mass., fragrant with historic memories, and bent his steps toward the home of the philosopher, Ralph Waldo Emerson. A walk of half a mile, or such a matter, brings one to a good-sized, two-story white house, set well back from the street, with a generous L, and protected from the wind on one side by a row of tall and rather somber-looking pines. A knock at the door brings a trim servant-maid, who ushers you into a neat parlor, into which, to greet you, walks in a moment or two, Mr. Emerson. He received THE STAR representative with a characteristic courtesy that made him immediately at home.

"I have called," said the newspaper man, "to get from you, Mr. Emerson, your recollections of the Brook Farm enterprise."

"Well," said Mr. Emerson, in his peculiar deliberate manner, "I remember there were Ripley, Dana, a few others and myself. Dana was very active in the enterprise. He appeared to be an assistant of Mr. Ripley, who was at the head of the project. I was only an occasional visitor there, in the same way that many others were. I never was connected with the enterprise, though Mr. Ripley desired me and my wife to go there and enter into the plans. I thought it over, however, and decided that it was not the proper place for me or my work at that time. I never saw Dana before that time, nor have I since."

With this your correspondent withdrew, Mr. Emerson bidding him a cordial "good-bye." This morning I called upon Mr. J. S. Dwight, at his office in Pemberton square. Ben Baller has his headquarters in the two low stories of this building; and, after passing through the crowd of loafers and hangers-on which clogged the steps, and the stairs, and hallways, I found the object of my search in a room in the upper portion of the building. After stating the object of his call, your correspondent was about to dive into his pocket for his note-book when the gentleman said:

"Oh! you are an interviewer, sir, are you? Well, I do not wish to be interviewed."

"Why, sir!" replied the undaunted scribe, "I shall ask you only a brief question or two regarding some matters which transpired many years ago, and I think you will find no impropriety in furnishing me the information I wish," and THE STAR man dropped into a convenient chair and proceeded to ply the gentleman with questions. After a moment's taciturnity the latter fell very naturally into conversation, and throughout the interview treated his caller most courteously. His statements regarding the Brook Farm Coterie were, in substance, as follows:

"I myself became connected with Brook Farm at the end of the first season in '41 or '42, I think it was, and Mr. Dana had been, I think, one of the originators of the scheme, and was one of the three Directors. He was at that time apparently a very close friend and co-laborer of Mr. George Ripley, and his duties and position were all through the continuance of the society, those of direction and great influence. He also gave much of his time in teaching horticulture and arboriculture. He was of a very sanguine and confident temperament, and being in a leading position, was rather apt to take things into his own hands and go ahead according to his own ideas without consulting anybody else. His autocratic and rather domineering disposition was constantly cropping out, although I hardly recollect now any particular instance of its manifestation. He had also a very genial side, and was a man of very firm and ardent friendships.

"He had a strong will, however, and was always a little inclined to be arbitrary. He took hold of Fourierism more strongly than any of us. We all thought some of Fourier's ideas were very good, but Mr. Dana went further than any of us, and became a strict follower of those doctrines, for the time at least. Mr. Ripley, however, agreed with him substantially in this, and I think also Mr. Parke Godwin of New York. The crisis at Brook Farm I do not think was ascribable to Fourierism, but chiefly to the fact that funds were lacking, and to a conflagration, which burned a large building. Dana was the last man whom I should have thought would have taken the position he now occupies--I mean in going over to the Democratic side. He is, and I think always was, an ambitious man, and has developed, since Brook Farm days, a great love of money. The general explanation of his present attitude is his failure to get from Grant the appointment to the New York Collectorship. You remember that he quarreled with Greeley on the *Tribune*, owing to his overbearing spirit, and his next miff at Grant served, combined with a desire to keep the large subscription-list of the Sun intact by catering editorially pretty strongly to his readers' tastes, to help him on gradually, until he assumed his present attitude. He was always a scholar, and in Brook Farm days could converse fluently in German, French, and I don't know but other languages. Some of it he had picked up by contact with natives of those countries while in a store of some kind at Buffalo. His political course of late years has served to completely alienate from him almost all his old friends and associates, among them George Ripley. Somehow we never thought he could be sincere in his professed change of sentiment, and his new front has been something of a puzzle and mystery to us all. What opinions he now holds upon Socialism I do not know. The change in him in other respects, at least, has been very great."

*"The Brook Farm Coterie," New York *Star*, 3 November 1878; reprinted from Kenneth Walter Cameron, *Transcendental Log* (Hartford: Transcendental Books, 1973), pp. 318-319.

BROOK FARM RECOLLECTIONS*

Belle C. Barrows

. . . .
Mr. John S. Dwight, so well and widely known as the founder of Dwight's Journal of Music, being present, was called upon by Dr. Ellis to follow Mr. Frothingham. His plea of inability was not accepted by the chairman, who carried his point, much to the satisfaction of the audience.

Remarks of John S. Dwight

As an old Brook Farmer, I may be allowed to protest against the dream aspect which has been so strongly presented. I think it was very practical; and most of us thought it was, and we had very practical and common-sense men and women amongst us. They were of various classes. Some were idealists and ideal thinkers of the Transcendental School, so called, though they never called themselves so. That was rather a nickname. There were men from farms there. There was a printer's office, there were carpenters' shops; for they needed all those industries combined with the school, making a very varied society. It was my privilege to know Mr. Ripley very intimately for a number of years before he conceived that experiment. When I first came out of Divinity School at Cambridge, he was my first warm, helpful, encouraging friend. I was at his house almost daily during that famous controversy with Andrews Norton. I knew the whole of it as it went on. I talked with Mr. Ripley, and heard him read his manuscript.

After I lived in Northampton, I was very much attracted to his idea which resulted in Brook Farm. His aspiration was to bring about a truer state of society, one in which human beings should stand in frank relations of true equality and fraternity, mutually helpful, respecting each others's occupation, and making one the helper of the other. The prime idea was an organization of industry in such a way that the most refined and educated should show themselves practically on a level with those whose whole education had been hard labor. Therefore, the scholars and the cultivated would take their part also in the manual labor, working on the farm or cultivating nurseries of young trees, or they would even engage in the housework.

I remember the night of my first arrival at Brook Farm. It had been going on all the summer. I arrived in November. At that time, it was a sort of pastoral life, rather romantic, although so much hard labor was involved in it. Hawthorne was there then, but he left about that time. He knew very little about it, certainly nothing of it as an organized industrial experiment. But he was pleased to live on a farm, and he liked to drive oxen, and he would drive till he got himself tired through the day, and shut himself up in his room in the evening. [Laughter.] So it is wholly a mistake that the "Blithedale Romance" describes Brook Farm. There is nothing of Brook Farm in it except the scenery. None of the characters represent people at Brook Farm. It has been supposed that the heroine was Margaret Fuller, but she was never a member. She was only an occasional visitor, a friend of Mr. and Mrs. Ripley. She made us very delightful visits.

The great point aimed at was to realize practical equality and mutual culture and a common education for the children in a larger sense than prevails in ordinary society. This phase of the life lasted two or three years, until it began to grow a hard toil for pecuniary reasons, when Albert Brisbane came along, full of the doctrine of Fourier, a great <u>doctrinaire</u> himself. He made us frequent and long visits, and Mr. Ripley and Mr. Dana and others became greatly indoctrinated. Some of us received it only tentatively and partially. We were inclined to feel our way along. We could see something fine in the views, and much that seemed practical. To some, they seemed somewhat visionary, but we were glad to have it tried, so far as we could; but the Fourier idea implied a community of several thousand people in the phalanstery and a very large domain and a great common building, an enormous palace, which would cost millions of money. We were never more than a hundred, often not that; and we had found it hard to get people enough of the right kind to do what work was required. Everybody went into the work heartily, and everybody tried to help every other. There was a great sweetness and charm in the sincerity of the life.

The educational part consisted partly in our education of one another, and partly in the school, which was also one of the means of support of the community. Pupils were taken from outside, who lived there, and were taught by Mr. and Mrs. Ripley and others. There were some young people who came and lived there simply as boarders, from a certain romantic interest in the ideas, but not committing themselves to them by membership. Such were the two Curtises, George William and Burrill, two most attractive young men.

I remember the night I arrived there. They were all at tea in the old building, which called the Hive. In a long room, at a long table, they were taking tea; and I sat down with them. When tea was over, they were all very merry, full of life, and all turned to and washed the dishes, cups and saucers; all joined in, the Curtis brothers, Charles Dana, and all. [Laughter.] It was very charming. It was quite a lark, as we say. Much of the industry went on in that way, because it combined the freest sociability with useful acts.

When it was attempted to try the ideas of Fourier in one department, that of the organization of industry, and to some extent the matter of education, we of course felt our great limitations. We could only construct more rudimentary "groups and series." It was a mere pretense, hoping that it would grow to something. The idea of most of us was that, beginning with what we felt to be a true system, with true relations to one another, it would probably grow into something larger, and that by bringing in others we should finally succeed in reforming and elevating society, and put it on a basis of universal cooperation. Communism it was not, because property was respected. Some were allowed to hold and earn more than others; only justice was sought for in the matter of labor and in the distribution of any surplus, if there were any, which seldom occurred. [Laughter.] Capital, labor, and skill each had their fair proportion in the division, and the same person might share under each of those heads. It gave labor the larger share,--five-twelfths, and skill three-twelfths. By skill is meant the organizing head in industry. That was the whole of our equality. The social education was extremely pleasant. It hardly went so far as our friend intimated. For instance, in the matter of music, we had extremely limited means or talent; and very little could be done except in a singing class, and we had some who sing a song gracefully and accompany themselves at the piano. We had some piano music; and, so far as it was possible, care was taken that it should be good,-- sonatas of Beethoven and Mozart, and music of that order. We sang masses of Haydn and others, and no doubt music of a better quality than prevailed in most society at that date; but that would be counted nothing now. Occasionally, we had artists come to visit us. We had delightful readings; and once in a while, when William Henry Channing was in the neighborhood, he would preach us a sermon.

I do not think Brook Farm was wholly a dream. I do not think it was wholly nothing, in looking back upon it. I think it was a good deal. It was a good deal to me. I think every-one who was there will say so, though it is extremely hard to tell of it. The truth is every resident there had his own view of it. Every one saw the life through his own eyes and in his own way. Naturally, they formed groups, and one group was not like another. Certain ones were just as individual as in any common society. I felt and still think that it was a wholesome life, that it was a good practical education. I have no doubt I should not have been living at this day if it had not been for that life there, for what I did on the farm and among the trees, in handling the hay and even in swinging the scythe. But those who survived and been active in their experiences have certainly, most of them, shown themselves persons of power and faculty, with as much common-sense on the average as ordinary men. I do not think it was a dream.

The audience was a little surprised when Mr. James Sturgis, a prominent Boston merchant, arose and confessed that he, too, had been a "Brook Farmer." Mr. Sturgis was promptly ordered to the front, and compelled to tell his experience.

Remarks of Mr. James Sturgis

I was one of the Brook Farmers for eight months. It happened in this wise. Mr. Robert G. Shaw sent me out to the West Indies in the winter of 1841, and in the spring I came home from Puerto Rico bringing four Spanish boys, none of whom could speak English. I talked Spanish, and they were in my care to be educated; I sought counsel of my friend and brother-in-law, at West Roxbury, Mr. Frank Shaw, who said, "Why don't you take them to the Community?" "Because that involves the necessity of my going," I replied. He said, "You can't do better." So I went. It was the most delightful and the most improving eight months that I ever remember to have spent in my life. It was a time that set me seriously to thinking about Unitarianism. I sought counsel of Dr. Putnam. I used to walk over on Saturdays seven miles to my father's house in Roxbury, as I had charge of the Sunday-school in Dr. Putnam's church.

But what I rose for was to mention why we didn't succeed. There were two material reasons. One was, that instead of a farm, we had a great gravel heap. I know it because Quincy Shaw, Burrill and George Curtis and I used to plough and hoe it. [Laughter.] In the forenoon, from half-past eight or nine, I taught. In the afternoon, I "drove team." I had two yoke of oxen and a horse. We used to take turns in driving and in holding plough. We all worked that summer together. I was as vigorous as any man could possibly be. I used to walk that seven miles, sometimes getting wet quite through, but I survived it. The land we broke up was gravelly, and it did not return in kind for the work that was done.

That was one reason. There was another. Naturally, in our mixed association, we got in the wrong characters. We got in lazy folks, regular drones. I foresaw then that we were getting an element that was afflicted with this lazy streak. The associations, the charming life that was led with such people as Mr. and Mrs. Ripley, George Curtis, and Charles Dana (who taught German as well as Greek) was delightful, and I thought we had very good music there. I used to play the flute, and thought it very fine. [Laughter.] We went to the "Eyrie" in the evening, and had conversations, reading, and music.

The thing went to the bad because it was a hard soil, and because a great many of the people did not want to work a great deal. Still, I can testify to the effect on myself for the eight

months that I was there,--that they were of more
service to me than any eight months I have ever
lived. I felt better and was better than I have
ever been since; I look back with the greatest
pleasure, and shall carry a red-letter feeling
about it, to the last of my days.

*Belle C. Barrows, "Brook Farm. What it was and
What it Aimed to Be," Christian Register, 61 (9
March 1882): 1. The beginning of the piece, an
address on Brook Farm by Octavius Brooks
Frothingham, has been omitted.

THE BROOK FARM PERIOD IN NEW ENGLAND*

Thomas Wentworth Higginson

The death of Ralph Waldo Emerson recalls to public attention that extraordinary period of seething radicalism which prevailed in New England, and to some extent beyond it, when he was in his prime. It was an era so unlike the present that it seems centuries away. The eighty-two pestilent heresies that were already reckoned up in Massachusetts before 1638, or the "generation of odd names and natures" which the Earl of Stratford found among the English Roundheads, could hardly surpass those of which Boston was the center and Horace Greeley's Tribune, to some extent, the organ, between the year 1840 and the absorbing political excitement of 1848. The best single picture of the time is to be found in Emerson's lecture on "New England Reformers," delivered in March, 1844; but it tells only a small part of the story. Carlyle's works had stimulated youthful minds in England; Fourier's writings had made a certain impression in France; and German literature played an important part in the whole movement; but America was, after all, the chosen scene.

The mental agitation ranged from the most cultivated to the most ignorant persons; German theology, as interpreted by Brownson and Parker, reached one class, while the Second Advent movement fired another. The Anti-Slavery agitation was a feeder to the whole excitement, supplying a class of persons who were ready to forsake all and follow conscience. The Hutchinson family were its minstrels--a band of Puritan Bohemians--five or six long-haired and black-eyed striplings, grouped round one rose-bud of a sister. Edward Palmer fulminated against the use of money; phrenology and physiology, then ranked together, contributed to the speculative enthusiasm; Alcott preached what Carlyle called "a potato gospel"; Graham denounced bolted flour; the water-cure was coming into favor; the body must be fed and clothed and bathed upon new and saintly principles. The wildest speculations and practices not only prevailed, but must be linked together; reform was not a series of convictions, but a general attitude; you were expected to accept the whole "sisterhood of reforms," as now to vote the whole party ticket. When, in 1847, I went to reside for some years in a manufacturing town in Massachusetts, where the operatives were still chiefly American farmers' daughters, one of my radical acquaintances was quite amazed that I, who passed for a reformer, was yet unacquainted with "the Riggs girls," who worked in one of the mills. "Not know the Riggs girls!" he said. "You ought to know <u>them</u>! Interested in all the reforms--temperance, anti-slavery--bathe in cold water every morning, and one 'em's a Grahamite." I afterward became acquainted with these young ladies, and found them exceedingly sensible and well-informed women.

Mr. Emerson, in a paper in the "<u>Dial</u>" for July, 1842, on the "Convention of Friends of Universal Reform" in Boston, says truly of that gathering: "If the assembly was disorderly, it was picturesque. Madmen, madwomen, men with beards, Dunkers, Muggletonians, Come-outers, Groaners, Agrarians, Seventh-Day Baptists, Quakers, Abolitionists, Calvinists, Unitarians and Philosophers--all came successively to the top." The phrase "men with beards" is of itself characteristic of the period; for then almost every reputable man went shaven, and beards were regarded as indicating the worst forms of social heresy. Charles Burleigh was even reproached with blasphemy in the newspapers, I remember, for a length of beard and hair which gave him an undoubted resemblance to the early pictures of Christ. Lowell, then in the first flush of his youthful radicalism, wore his beard also, and it was considered an artist's whim in both poet and painter when Page depicted him under that guise, in the portrait which now looks down the stairway at Elmwood. Thus, between the things that were not really eccentric but only seemed to be, and the things that were half crazy but seemed to their projectors to be sane, it is plain that good sense had a hard time of it. Yet what a period it was in which to be born and reared; what infinite hope, what boundless hospitality to what was called "the newness," what mutual help and kindliness among the "like-minded!" I always thought that its chief benefit came to those who, like myself, appeared on the scene just too late to be active participants in any excesses, but in time to share the impulse and the glow.

It shows that good sense on the whole prevailed under all vagaries, when we consider that in all these circles Mr. Emerson was revered; and that his calm nature, shrinking from extremes, held its own way undisturbed through everything. Through what adulation, what deference, did that man live! I remember that after one of the courses of lectures in Boston he used to hold receptions at the rooms of a cultivated young bachelor of that city who was like the Riggs girls "interested in all the reforms." This youth was especially interested. Zealous in behalf of Fourierism--the outside of his door displayed a blazing sun with spreading yellow rays and this motto in the center: "Universal Unity." Beneath it was another inscription in neat black and white letters: "Please wipe your feet!" Into this domain, thus emblazoned and thus guarded, the philosopher and his proselytes would enter and commune after a lecture, and the group of admiring youths and maidens around the seer was as well worth studying as anything which their teacher could give. I remember, for instance, that Mr. Emerson had been telling me, one evening in the winter of 1848-9, of Clough's new poem in hexameters then just published, which at first bore the name of "The Bothie of Toper-na-Vuolich." Being baffled by the Gaelic name, I offered Mr. Emerson a pencil and card to write it down for me; as I withdrew, a maiden stepped modestly forward with duplicate card and pencil, saying, "You promised it to me too, Mr. Emerson." To her succeeded a second maiden, "And to me, Mr. Emerson"; and when yet a third appeared, the sage said, his wonted smile broadening a little, "Do you also wish the name of the book?" "Oh, anything, anything," responded the confused girl, eager only for the autograph, and careless whether it came in the shape of a Gaelic name or one in Choctaw.

I was never a resident of Brook Farm even for a day, but used to make brief calls there with a cousin of mine who, as niece of Mrs. Ripley, had access to the charmed circle. To us young people it seemed a perpetual "lark," one round of Gypsy parties and picnics, with only so much of hard work as might make any other picnic amusing. The first person pointed out to me on my first visit, I remember, was George William Curtis, who in shirt sleeves and high boots, as became a picturesque young amateur agriculturalist, was escorting some ladies about the grounds. In general, the "Community" youths, as they were called in the neighborhood, were inclined to a style of blouse then recently imported from England (not France), and a cross between a hunting shirt and an English farmer's smock frock. These were also worn by Harvard students in those days; but the young men at Brook Farm superadded little picturesque vizorless caps; a costume in which Burrill Curtis, brother of George William, was as beautiful as a young Raphael. I remember it as very characteristic that Charles Dana, now editor of the New York Sun, who was the most influential among the younger leaders of the "Community," kept himself strikingly free from all these innocent fopperies, and always looked like a well-educated and manly young farmer. On the other hand, he had the reputation, I think, of throwing rather less of generous idealism into the affair than was contributed by the others, and people missed in him--as Mrs. Ellen Hooper wrote that they missed in Emerson--"the heat that ofttimes breeds excess."

Brook Farm, which had always a certain flavor of foreignness, retains it up to the present day. When I last visited it, the chief buildings were occupied as an almshouse for German paupers; and they had laid out a quaint little burial ground, full of old-world names and pious Lutheran phrases, which seemed as remote from our modern American life as were the studies and the talk of those who first made the place famous. Elsewhere the change has been more complete. All that period of seething excitement has passed away; the leaders are gone, the followers are rapidly going; and nothing brings it so vividly back to my mind's eye as the occasional sight of some surviving brother of the Hutchinson Family in a concert-room, still exhibiting the long hair now whitened, and the broad collar that needs no whitening, and the vague benign smile that yet speaks unfalteringly of "a good time coming" with no date fixed.

*Tho[ma]s. Wentworth Higginson, "The Brook Farm Period in New England," Demorest's Monthly Magazine, 18 (July 1882): 534-535.

REMINISCENCES OF BROOK FARM*

George P. Bradford

I joined the Brook Farm, of which George Ripley may be held the founder, on the last day of May, 1841. Part of the company had already begun work there about the first of April. Some engagements prevented my joining them until the last of May, although I had enrolled myself among them some time before. Among those I found there were Mr. and Mrs. Ripley; Miss Marianne Ripley, a sister of Mr. Ripley; Nathaniel Hawthorne; and Warren Burton, who had been a Unitarian clergyman, and was the author of several little books, among them "The District School as it was."

Mr. Ripley, who had been for some time the minister of a Unitarian congregation in Boston, was a scholar of much metaphysical and theological acuteness and learning, of a sanguine temperament, and with a remarkable power of rapid acquisition and perception--perhaps a little hasty in his conclusions, and with other characteristics of a sanguine temperament. His mind was filled and possessed with the idea of some form of communism or co-operation, and some mode of life that seemed to produce better conditions for humanity; and was informed to some extent of what had been said and written on these subjects. Whether he was at this time acquainted with the ideas and works of Fourier, I cannot say; my own impression is that he was, but others, who are perhaps better informed than myself, tell me that he did not become acquainted with them till later, after he had been some time at Brook Farm. I think he must, at least, have known something of them through the writing of Albert Brisbane. When he became acquainted with them he was at first certainly not disposed to adopt them fully; but later he and other members tried to arrange the institution on principles of Fourier's theories. Finding many disposed to sympathize practically or theoretically with his views and plans, he went forward with an ardor and a zeal that were inspiring to those who came in contact with him, with a genuine and warm interest in the idea of association, and faith in the benefits it promised to humanity. Full of enthusiasm for his hopes and schemes, he threw himself into them with disinterested zeal, and worked long and earnestly and with much self-denial for their accomplishment. Mrs. Ripley, too, who was of an energetic and enthusiastic temperament, entered into his views very heartily, and was always a prominent and important person in the conduct of the enterprise, and entered with zeal and efficiency into all the departments in which she could take part. There appeared a just and favorable notice of her in some pleasing papers on Brook Farm, in the "Atlantic Monthly," written by one of our zealous and very useful co-workers.[1]

With them came Miss Marianne Ripley, who had had a school for young children in Boston, several of whom she brought with her. She lived in a small house close by the farm,--which we called the Nest,--and had a warm interest in the enterprise.

Charles A. Dana, now editor of the "New York Sun," was an important member; and for a long time,--I think till the close of the institution. He came to us from Harvard College, which he had been obliged to leave, I think, from some trouble with his eyes. He was sanguine in temperament, with all the ardor of youth, and of great natural energy and rather arbitrary will, of fine personal appearance and attractive qualities in some other respects. Being, as I think, somewhat of a doctrinaire, he embraced the ideas and modes of operation with ardor and systematic energy; and, as he brought with him from Harvard the latest improvements in scholarly law, filled an important place as teacher, worker, and counselor. Dana did not come at the beginning, but later than myself, in the course of the first summer.

Minot Pratt, who with his family came in the course of the first summer, was a very valuable accession to our society. He had been a printer, but was drawn to the Brook Farm enterprise by sympathy with its object and the mode of life, as well as by his taste for agriculture, which last he retained during his life. He was a man of singular purity and uprightness of character and simplicity of taste, and was in many ways a very valuable member. In the later years of his life he was much devoted to the study of botany, and had a very peculiar, personal, and most extensive practical knowledge of the plants of Concord, where he passed the remaining years of his life after leaving Brook Farm.

A man who proved to be a valuable and generally liked member of our company was John Cheever. He was said to be son of an English baronet, and once held some position, I think, in the government of Canada. What the previous life of Cheever had been I cannot say. We found him intelligent, kindly, obliging, and very capable and useful in some directions. His case was a pathetic one: from his former experience in life and a natural insight into character he seemed especially drawn to persons of superior culture and refinement, who in their turn became much attached to him; yet he always seemed to feel a sort of gulf between them and himself.

Then a very important person to us in our inexperience in farming was Tom Allen, a young farmer from Vermont who had become "interested in the idea"--this was one of our pet phrases. He was valued and rather looked up to for his knowledge of farm work, and had pleasing traits of natural refinement. Besides those I have mentioned, there were otheres of marked and interesting character-- among them several young women, who, if not much known to fame, made a strong and lasting impression on the friends who had the good fortune to know them and enjoy their friendship.

I joined the company, as I said, the last of May. I arrived at evening, and the first impression was not very cheerful, the whole aspect of things being a little forlorn. Perhaps the company were tired out with the hard farm work, which I think the novices found more exacting than they had expected. Taken from books and comparative luxury and elegance of living, and obliged to work, day in and day out, in shoveling in the barn-yard, which Mr. Ripley called his goldmine, they were quite wearied and naturally a little depressed. But the next day, June 1, made ample amends. It was to be a sort of holiday. Various groups of ladies who had been pupils and friends of Mrs. Ripley--many of them with their young children--came out from the city to pass a festive day. The excitement of the arrival of the successive parties; the exuberant spirits of the children on their holiday, on this loveliest of

June days, and amid the very charming fields, woods, and knolls that made up or surrounded the farm, and gave name to the place; the enthusiasm of the new devotees to a life that looked so beautiful and fascinating on such a day; the interest of those from the outside world who came to see old friends in so novel an environment, gave a sort of glamour to the whole scene, and to the enjoyment of the day. It seemed <u>Arcadia</u> <u>redux</u> at least, if we had not got <u>Astraea</u> <u>redux</u>. To the new inmates and cultivators it appeared the promise of a new, beautiful, and poetical life. We were floated away by the tide of young life around us. I dwell a little on this day, which may seem to my readers very like an ordinary picnic, because it was the type and precursor of many such golden days that at intervals came to throw a bright light over our life, mingled, as it was, with heavy and burdensome toil and care for some of us. There was always a large number of young people in our company, as scholars, boarders, etc., and this led to a considerable mingling of amusement in our life; and, moreover, some of our company had a special taste and skill in arranging and directing this element. So we had very varied amusements suited to the different seasons--tableaux, charades, dancing, masquerades, and rural fêtes out of doors, and in the winter, skating, coasting, etc. I have some vivid and pleasant recollections of exciting scenes by moonlight on the knolls, meadows, and river, with the weird aspect of its wooded banks under the wintry moon.

One great charm of the life at first, and indeed long after, was in the free and natural intercourse for which it gave opportunity, and in the working of the elective affinities which here had a fuller play; so that although there was a kindly feeling running through the family generally, little groups of friends drawn together into closer relations by taste and sympathy soon declared themselves. For the first summer certainly, and indeed long after, the mode of life was felt to be very charming by most of those who were there. The relief from the fetters and burdensome forms of society,

> The greetings where no kindness is,
> And all the dreary intercourse of daily life,

was a constant delight to those who had suffered from them in the artificial arrangements of society; the inmates were brought together in more natural relations, and thus realized the charm of true and hearty intercourse; and at the same time the relief and pleasures of solitude were not wanting: one could withdraw to the solitude of the woods, or of his own room, without offense to any.

There was for a long time a large element of romantic feeling and much enthusiasm, especially among the young and more inexperienced, and those who knew nothing of the embarrassment of providing ways and means. For there was much in the existing conditions of our life to excite and promote this enthusiasm: the picturesque situation, with something of wild beauty, with the rocks, woods, meadows, river, and the novelty of our position, where each step was often a new experiment, and with new aspects ever developing themselves. Nor was this enthusiasm confined to the young and more ignorant; there was something of the tête montée pervading the family which led sometimes to those vagaries or hallucinations which afforded many a derisive laugh to the world without. But if in some instances there was a slight falsetto tone, there were a great deal of genuine faith and hope in the idea, and a conviction that this was, in many respects at least, a truer and better, as well as happier, life than that of the unfortunates who, according to our phraseology, were still in civilization (for this was a term of somewhat sinister import with us,) and--perhaps among the sensitive and thoughtful carried to a foolish excess--a feeling of pity for the civilized, as we denoted those not yet emancipated and still struggling with the evils of civilized life. At the same time, let me say that it seems to me, as I recollect, that the feeling with which the more serious and thoughtful went into this enterprise was very simple, and with no special pretension or assumption of superiority.

.Their motive and object was to work out for themselves a life better suited to their tastes and feelings than was possible in the common social arrangements, and which was thus deemed more consonant to the real demands of humanity.

The condition was somewhat like that of travelers in a new and unknown country. New vistas were constantly opening, and new aspects developed. The effect was a sort of exhilarating surprise and excitement, such as comes in traveling among new scenes.

Much of the work the first summer was making and getting in the hay from our very extensive meadows and fields. This was pleasant work, and I have very agreeable recollections of raking and otherwise working over many an acre in close company with Hawthorne, with whom I first became acquainted here. He, as I understood him, was attracted to the enterprise by the hope of finding some more satisfactory and congenial opportunity of living according to his tastes and views than in the common arrangements of society, and also of uniting successfully manual with intellectual work. But he was, I think, disappointed in this, and found it not easy to combine writing with severe bodily toil; and as the former was so manifestly his vocation, he gave up farm work at the end of the first summer, and although he remained there some time longer, part of the following winter it was as a boarder, not as a worker. The younger people, as usual, had their admiration and their worships, and Hawthorne was eminently fitted to be one of these, partly from the prestige of his reputation, partly from real appreciation of his genius as a writer, as well as from the impression made by his remarkable and fine personal appearance, in which manly vigor and beauty were combined. He was shy and silent, and, though he mingled with the rest of the company in the evening gatherings in the hall and parlor of the Hive, he was apparently self-absorbed, but doubtless carefully observing and finding material for his writing. The incident introduced into "The Blithedale Romance" which is commonly considered as giving the result of his life and observation at Brook Farm,--the drowning of one of his characters--with its ghastly features, did not really occur here, but in another place at some distance, and really had no connection. We had a good deal of enjoyment in becoming acquainted with and practising some of the industries of life unknown to us before, and in this, besides the excitement and novelty, was an accession of power in the exercise of some branches of this knowledge, humble as they may seem. Besides the agricultural knowledge and experience so interesting to many of us, there was a feeling of healthy reality in knowing and coming into close contact with some of the coarser forms of labor and drudgery which go to make up that "demi grind" of life so distasteful to Mr. Mantalini.

For instance, we spent some pleasant days working on a peat meadow. Interesting, indeed, was the charming situation, surrounded as it was by woods, and lying along the pretty Charles River near Dedham, Massachusetts; the learning something of a very old, but to us new, kind of industry in the various operations of paring, cutting, and stacking the peat.

I think Hawthorne was with us on some of these occasions. Then there was the great work of the wash-room, into which a large number of our company were drawn or thrown out, according to experience of fitness or the needs of the household. I may perhaps be allowed to dwell rather fully on some personal experiences, and indulge in some egotistic narration, on the ground of the "magna pars fui"; for besides serving a while in the wash-room, and pounding the clothes in a barrel or hogshead with a sort of heavy wooden pestle,--in which process I learned something of the mystery of that remarkable disappearance of buttons from garments in passing through the laundry, so inconvenient and vexatious to bachelors,--and wringing them out, not so simple a process as it might seem, I had for a considerable time the chief care of the clothes-line and of hanging out; for it was a part of our chivalry, in order to save labor and expense to the women, for the men to take on themselves, or have assigned to them, some of the harder and more exposing portions of the work. I have labored in the above-mentioned process of pounding the clothes by the side of some since well known and distinguished in the literary and political world. Mrs. Ripley, too, whose most important function, besides a sort of general superintendence, was teaching, but whose zeal and energy led her to take part in various industries, sometimes shared in the labors of the wash-room.

Then there was the experience of milking the cows, which could not be omitted by those bent on agricultural education; so some of us learned and practised the mystery of this accomplishment, somewhat to our own satisfaction, but apparently not so much so to that of the animals. But in time matters arranged themselves, and we came to the conclusion, reluctantly perhaps, that the old Philistine way might, after all, be the better, more sensible, and more economical; viz., that work requiring skill and experience should be executed by those who had the proper training, rather than by amateurs, however our culture might suffer by the loss. But let it not be supposed that we had none but unskilled workers. There were some men of skill and experience in various departments, and incapable amateurs could be easily reformed out of office, as our system was flexible and readily yielded to the demands of our household work.

I may mention, as an instance of the way in which we accommodated ourselves to our needs, our arrangements of the waiting department. When our table had grown so large that it was found inconvenient to pass the dishes backward and forward, and as the getting up from the table to help ourselves to anything we might want seemed not quite orderly, a special corps of waiters was detailed for this work, and to this were assigned some of the younger and more ornamental members of the company.

A difficulty we found in the attempt to unite work of the head and the hands was the loss of time in passing from one to the other, especially for those engaged both in out-of-door work or other manual labor and in teaching. Thus, something of this kind might be likely to occur: we might leave our hoeing, weeding, haying, etc., and go from the fields to the house for a lesson with some pupil who, himself zealously engaged in hunting or trapping woodchucks, muskrats, or squirrels, or like absorbing occupation, might not be mindful of the less important lesson.

The question is naturally asked, What were the financial resources, and when the funds for the daily support of the family? The purchase of the estate, and the carrying on of the farm and household were, at first, and for a few months (through the first summer perhaps), the private enterprise of Mr. Ripley; and those of us who went there did so by some arrangement with him, most of us working for and with him, and receiving in return our daily support without any very definite or exact bargain. There were also boarders and scholars from whom, as well as from the sale and use of some of the various products of the farm--milk, hay, vegetables, etc.--the necessary funds and means of support were derived.

After a while the company resolved themselves into a community, with a systematic organization and with certain conditions, and soon, I think, were regularly incorporated as a sort of joint-stock company. In course of time several trades were introduced, and with the farm products contributed something to the necessary fund; but the income at first, and for some time, was mainly derived from boarders and scholars, some of the latter paying a part or the whole of their board by their work in various ways. This brief sketch of the ways and means is very imperfect, as it is aside from my general design, which is to give mainly my personal reminiscences and impressions.

The situation of our farm was very pleasant. It lay between the towns of Dedham, Newton, and West Roxbury, of which it formed a corner. About the house were wooded knolls, fields, and hills sinking down into a wide meadow that extended to Charles River and bordered on it. The place was well adapted to some of our winter pastimes,--sledding, coasting, skating,--of some of which scenes on moonlight nights many of us have a vivid and agreeable recollection.

Through the meadows ran the lively brook from which we had our name; at a little distance from the houses was a fine upland pasture which also sloped down to the river, and was a favorite resort for sunset views and twilight walks.

But the farm, though having many picturesque charms, was not adapted to be a very profitable one, as much of the land was not well suited for culture, consisting largely of a meadow that bore little but coarse grass, and pastures with rocky ledges--picturesque, indeed, but clothed with a thin, hard soil. There were beautiful and interesting localities in our neighborhood, where we found pleasant walks, or which we utilized for our rural fêtes.

The Hive, the original farm-house and first residence of our company, was soon found insufficient for our growing numbers, and considerable additions were made from time to time;

but our numbers still increasing, the Hive could not well hold us all, and we were obliged to swarm. So the Eyrie, after much planning and discussion, was decided on and begun. It was planned with much care and deliberation, but one might perhaps think that more regard was had to esthetic considerations than to those of ordinary comfort and convenience. It was pitched high on a rock, whence its name, and with fine picturesque rocks all around; but to climb the shelf on which it stood in wet, snowy, or scorching weather was not easy or comfortable; neither was the journey in the deep snow and mud through which our path lay to and from the Hive, where the operations of cooking and eating were carried on. Besides, there was no well, only a rain-water cistern, which want involved the trouble of fetching water for some purposes.

But the situation was charming, and very near was a beautiful grove of pines--so well known to the inmates, habitués, and loving visitors of Brook Farm--where so many delightful days were passed, and so many charming fêtes and entertainments of various kinds enjoyed by those who had the luxury of being idle. Many of our company had a fancy for climbing these trees, and some, a still more odd one of perching or roosting like birds on the highest branches. Besides the Eyrie, there were added to our building, in course of time, the Cottage, a pleasant and pretty building where were held many of the gatherings for amusements, and later the Pilgrim House; still later, shops and buildings for the various kinds of industries were introduced.

The Eyre itself was a sort of romance of houses; it had no kitchen or fireplace, and so was dishonored or degraded by no culinary uses. One striking thing about it was its acoustic character; it seemed constructed on some, I know not what, acoustic principles by which the sounds of each and all the rooms were, as it seemed, audible in every other; as it was the place for musical instruction, and the scene of the musical exercitations of troops of young beginners, one can, or perhaps cannot, imagine the discomfort of this remarkable property in this singularly constructed building; and though I had at one time a charming room there, I have not very charming recollections of the dreary monotony of scales and exercises through the long, sleepy summer days.

I have some pleasant recollections of the large parlor in the Eyrie, which was designed with special reference to our evening gatherings of various kinds for amusement or improvement. We had many visitors from the outside world of civilization, among them some persons of interest and distinction.

Miss Margaret Fuller (afterwards Countess Ossoli) was one of these, and was often there as a friend of the Ripleys and of others in the company, as well as from interest in the enterprise and sympathy with its objects. She was to us an interesting and instructive visitor, and would sometimes hold conversations, a favorite mode of teaching with her. Then, too, among our visitors was Orestes A. Brownson, whose active brain led him to the various new movements of which the air was full at that time, and finally to a very old institution. He was also a friend of George Ripley--whether then a Romanist I cannot say. One of the visitors best known to the world was Robert Owen of Scotland. He was naturally interested in our experiment, as he had been engaged in something of a co-operative or communistic character at New Lanark, Scotland. I recollect that I received an agreeable impression of his great simplicity and transparency of character, as well as his earnestness and warm humanity. Then Miss Frances Ostinelli, afterward well known in opera as Madame Biscacciarti, spent some time with us. Her fine voice in its youthful purity and freshness was a great delight to us, as her youthful beauty and charm were very fascinating to some of the younger members of our company. Then there were the Hutchinsons, a family well known at that time, and a marvel for their sweet singing, and this especially in the interests of antislavery and temperance. The accord of their voices was very pleasing. A great charm of their singing was a sort of wild freshness, as if brought from their native woods and mountains, and their earnest interest in the objects that formed so much the theme of their songs.

We had in our vicinity some agreeable neighbors: among these Theodore Parker, who was a personal friend of Mr. Ripley and others of us, whose church some of us attended, and who often came to see us; for though he did not enter fully into the idea and plans of the "Association," he of course looked with generous interest on all that promised benefit to humanity. There were also near us other families to whose broad and liberal sympathy, generous assistance, and genial society we were much indebted.

Besides, there came from time to time to see us reformers of a humbler or milder stamp, with various schemes and dogmas for reforming society: vegetarians, come-outers from Church and State, to some of whom no doubt the former was, in the rather strong language current at the time, the "Mother of Abominations." Then there were long-bearded reformers dressed all in white, which was in itself a protest against something, I hardly know what; for a very liberal hospitality was exercised from the beginning, for which I think great credit is due to Mr. Ripley.

There were also those who came to observe and make trial of our mode of life, or as candidates for admission on a sort of probation; for, in the narrowness of our means and accommodations, we could not take all that offered themselves. Mr. Ripley, who, as I have said, was somewhat sanguine in his way of looking at persons and things, would bring us from time to time accounts of applicants that looked to him very desirable, but who on further consideration were not accepted; for a very important question in regard to those who wished to join us was the Shylock one, "Is he a good man?"-- and this in the Shylock, and not in the ethical sense,--and "Is he sufficient?" and perhaps our applicants were not so apt to have the former sort of goodness as the other, that of a more transcendent kind.

Our enterprise attracted a good deal of attention and interest, and we certainly had the satisfaction of being much talked about, for good or for evil--chiefly the latter. Indeed, it seems strange that it should have been looked upon so unfavorably, and have excited, I may almost say, such bitter hostility.

If the world chose to think us very silly and childish and ridiculous in our mistakes, hallucinations, and vagaries, and that we had a foolish pretension and self-complacency, it was fair and reasonable enough in them to have their laugh at us; but these follies of ours, if they were so, were very harmless, good-natured, and well-intentioned, and with these there were a real earnestness of philanthropy and worthiness of purpose, which certainly deserved some respect, and were not properly marks for ridicule or malice. This prejudice was no doubt due in some measure to false or exaggerated accounts of our doings which were circulated and, naturally enough, in many cases innocently believed. There were criticisms on our fare, which was sometimes not very sumptuous, and on our style of living, which was not very elegant. But we did not go there for luxury, and if there was no elegance, there was certainly a good degree of refinement--as far as consistent with our conditions. As an instance of this I may mention that the attempt was made to give, as far as possible, separate rooms to those who desired it. One very current and common misapprehension was that the members of our company were agreed, for the most part in views of extreme radicalism and hostility to the common beliefs and institutions of society. But in fact no such uniformity existed; on the contrary, there was a great variety of shades of opinion and feeling.

Indeed, there were some who might be considered quite conservative, and often children from families of conservative parents, who were well enough acquainted with the leading persons to have confidence that they would get no harm. Some of the stories to which I have alluded related to the way in which Sunday was regarded and treated-- stories of disrespect and desecration of the day, as it was considered, which shocked some persons, but I think without much ground. Quite a number inclined to go to church, some to Boston, some to Theodore Parker's church, which was at that time in West Roxbury. Others chose to spend the day walking in the woods or other beautiful localities about us. But if not observed with much rigor, it was generally, as far as I recollect, a quiet and peaceful day, and this was in accordance with the wishes and tastes of the principals of the company. At one time, I recollect, Mr. Ripley gave on Sunday afternoons some account or explanations of Kant's philosophy to those who wished to hear him. It should be considered that great freedom existed and pervaded our mode of living, and the company in general did not feel responsible for the eccentricities of some individuals, or authorized to interfere with them, except perhaps in extreme cases.

One of the interesting features of our life was the pleasant and favorable influence with which the young were surrounded. With great freedom in the modes of instruction and discipline, there was no lack of thoroughness, for the most part; and, what was important, there was an inspiring influence either in the circumstances surrounding, or in the modes of imparting knowledge of a very varied character in an informal and genial way, by a variety of teachers with whom the pupils were thrown into near and friendly relations. In our easy way the teachers and pupils interchanged functions, the pupils becoming teachers and <u>vice versa</u>. Some of the pupils have become well known in various ways. General Frank Barlow, so honorably distinguished in our civil war, and politically since, was then but a young boy. George Weeks [Wells], who went from us to the Williamstown college, where he graduated with honor, became a lawyer, and also had some judicial position. At the first sound of the call to arms to suppress the Rebellion, he joined the volunteers, I think as captain in the First Massachusetts Regiment, distinguished himself as an officer, and after a gallant career died or was mortally wounded on the field, in some battle of western Virginia, having risen to the rank of general.

Then there was George William Curtis, of late so prominent in the literary and political world, and a number of others since esteemed and honored in the community.

Isaac Hecker was there for some time, attracted by the object and character of the enterprise. He afterward went over to the Romish Church, where he has been a good deal distinguished, and active in the formation of a new order called the Paulist Fathers.

John S. Dwight, so well known to the musical world for his zeal and services in the cause of the higher music in our neighborhood, came early with the others of his family, and remained a long time, till the final abandonment of the enterprise. Of course his taste and zeal in the interest of the best music could not fail to be of very great value in our community, among whose objects artistic cultivation held a high place. There were many others whose memory and friendship are sacredly and lovingly cherished by many of us, but this seems hardly a place to give publicity to their names.

I have spoken of the gatherings at the Eyrie, where were passed many pleasant and profitable evenings; when some lion of special note came along, it often was an occasion for discourse or conversation on his speciality. The scene was pretty and interesting.

In the evening of our washing-day the folding of the clothes gave occasion for pleasant and social meetings.

An amusing and rather odd practice was the frequent writing of notes among those who were constantly meeting each other for work, etc. Perhaps it was that the various sentiments could not be so well expressed *viva voce*, and pen and paper gave better opportunity for more full and considered explanatory statements and epilogues, as needed, than the winged words of speech. One of our number, quite a singular character, had the habit of administering advice and reproof, of which he was rather lavish, on little scraps of paper, which he left on the floor or ground where the objects of his censure might find them. The notes I mentioned above were generally put on the table at the plate of the persons for whom they were designed. These may seem poor and trifling details, but some of those who were at Brook Farm may be pleased to recall the amusing, the trifling details and incidents of our life. But I must not omit among our social pleasures the gatherings in the barn in summer for preparing vegetables for the market, and other social work. Those who have not had the experience cannot know what a stately room for company a large barn is, with its lofty roof, the sweet scent of hay for perfume, the twittering of the swallows overhead for music, and the cool breezes passing so freely through. Our meetings here were at times enlivened by what we pleased ourselves with thinking was wit. Various classes were from time to time formed for reading and studying together. One I recollect was a very agreeable opportunity of reading Dante in the original (we read in turn, the whole or nearly the whole) with a number of cultivated, intelligent, and appreciative persons, those of better knowledge of the language helping the others. Mrs. Ripley was one of this class. in the summer we often had our readings out of doors, sometimes on one of those pleasant wooded knolls I have mentioned.

But I find that the limits to which I must confine myself will not allow me to speak of many of the varied aspects and features of the life at Brook Farm, or to give any detailed account of its course, progress, or final abandonment, which, besides, would be beyond the scope of this paper, professing as it does to give my personal reminiscences--in a somewhat discursive manner.

And now I wish to express for myself the very agreeable and, more than this, very affectionate remembrance of this rich and interesting episode of our lives, which feeling, I believe, is shared by many others. There were, no doubt, some dissatisfied or discontented on one ground or another, and, of course many shortcomings and imperfections in carrying out the idea and professed object of the institution. But I fully believe that many, very many, who were there look back upon it as one of the most profitable as well as delightful parts of their lives, and with warm feelings of affection and respect for its objects, and on the whole for the way in which the attempt was made to realize them. To many young people especially it was an opportunity of great and lasting benefit as well as of enjoyment. To such persons of high aims and aspirations, but whose life had been straitened and hampered by unfavorable conditions this opportunity of a life freed from many of the embarrassing conventions of society, and where feelings of humanity, sympathy, and respect for all conditions of life and society were cherished and professed as the basis of the association,--in habitual intercourse, too, with persons of cultivation and refinement, of varied acquaintance with society and the world, surrounded by those of friendly and kindly character and of aims at least theoretically humane and unselfish, to many of whom, too, were drawn by the elective affinities into close and confidential intimacy,-- was a very valuable and precious one, and was felt and appreciated as such by them at the time, and remembered with a tender and grateful interest. And some there are who still revere all the dreams of their youth, not only those that led them there, but those also that hovered around them while there and gave a color of romance to their life, and some of whom perhaps still cherish the hope that in some form or mode of association, or of co-operative industry, may be found a more equal distribution of the advantages, privileges, and culture of society--some mitigation of its great and painful inequalities, a remedy, or at least an abatement, of its evils and sufferings. But it may be thought that I have dwelt too much on the pleasantness of the life at Brook Farm, and the advantages in the way of education, etc., to the young people, which is all very well, but not quite peculiar to this institution, and some may ask what it really accomplished of permanent value in the direction of the ideas with which it was started. This I do not feel that I can estimate or speak of adequately; neither is it within the scope of this paper. But I would indicate in a few words some of the influences and results that I conceive to belong to it. The opportunity of very varied culture, intellectual, moral, and practical; the broad and humane feelings professed and cherished toward all classes of men; the mutual respect for the character, mind, and feelings of persons brought up in the most dissimilar conditions of living and culture, which grew up from the free commingling of the very various elements of our company; the understanding and appreciation of the toils, self-denial, privations which are the lot to which so many are doomed, and a sympathy with them, left on many a deep and abiding effect. This intercourse or commingling of which I have spoken was very simple and easy; when the artificial and conventional barriers were thrown down it was felt how petty and poor they are; they were easily forgotten, and the natural attractions asserted themselves. So I cannot but think that this brief and imperfect experiment, with the thought and discussion that grew out of it, had no small influence in teaching more impressively the relation of universal brotherhood, and the ties that bind all to all, a deeper feeling of the rights and claims of others, and so in diffusing, enlarging--deepening and giving emphasis to--the growing spirit of true democracy.

*"A Member of the Community" [George P. Bradford], "Reminiscences of Brook Farm," Century Magazine, 45 (November 1892): 141-148. Keyed to the title is this note: "The association continued in existence and operation until some time in 1847, after the loss by fire of a very extensive building (called phalanstery) before it was finished. The whole enterprise was abandoned mainly, I think, from financial troubles and embarrassments." Keyed to the designation of authorship is this note: "The author of this paper died recently, at an advanced age. He was a man somewhat of the Emersonian type, of singular purity and loveliness of character. He was a teacher by nature as well as by profession, and one whose influence was as elevating as it has been abiding in many lives."
 1. Miss Amelia Russell, formerly of Milton, not now living. [Bradford's note]

A BOY'S RECOLLECTIONS OF BROOK FARM*

Arthur Sumner

Let it be understood, at the outset, that I know very little about the origin or general scope of the famous Brook Farm enterprise. I only present my own life there, so far as I can recall it. I was about sixteen years old at the time. The impressions of my year at Brook Farm remain perfectly distinct in my mind, after a lapse of fifty years. But a great deal passed before me which I took little interest in, at the time; and so it would be unsafe for me to say much about the purpose which drew the people together. I know that when I first went there they repudiated the name of Fourierites; nor was it, at any time of my sojourn, a genuine socialist community. The elders formed an association, to which they contributed their labor, and their money, if they had any. But the principal income of the society or, as it was called, the Community, was derived from the boarders, who were not regular members of the association. There were many boarders; and most of them were young people, who received instruction from the members, though there was no regular school. I was one of the scholars; and very little did I learn. That was my own fault. I have never regretted my idleness. I was too busy in the fields and by the river to study. Plenty of time for that afterwards.

We Brook-Farmers were exceedingly happy people, and perfectly satisfied with our little isolated circle. We always spoke of the outer world of "civilization" (a term of contempt) as "outside barbarians." But by and by the "barbarians" began to encroach. Towards the close of my year, Fourierism came to be discussed by the members. Meetings were held in the long dining-room of The Hive. We boys took very little interest in these proceedings; but we understood that the theories of Fourier were to be adopted. To what extent they were I did not know at the time, nor do I know now. Soon after this agitation began, some very unpleasant people appeared upon the scene. They seemed to us boys to be discontented mechanics. They soon fell into a group by themselves. After dinner they would collect together in the great barn, and grumble; and when the others passed through, the malcontents eyed them with suspicion, and muttered, "Aristocrats!" all because they knew themselves to be less cultivated and well-bred. Yet there was the kindest feeling of brotherhood among the members; and it did not need that a man should be a scholar or a gentleman to be received and absorbed.

I remember one sour-looking apostle, with scowling brows, whose whole talk was hate. He kept a glass shop in Boston, and but for this circumstance would have thrown stones at all the world; but he made a good living out of that established order which made him swear so.

About this time a famous Socialist, Albert Brisbane, used to visit the Community, and harangue the people, yet not in a way to secure the constant attendance of the youngsters. A story was told of him. He and others were lying out in the grass in the moonlight. "What a beautiful world! What a heavenly moon!" said one. "Miserable world! Damned bad moon!" was poor Brisbane's reply.

The outcome of this fermentation was the building of a huge frame-house, called the Phalanstery, which, being burned down before it was quite put up, the Community fell flat and soon dispersed. There was not much capital, and very little business sense; and the soil was poor, though the landscape was beautiful.

This famous experiment, since known almost the world over, had a life of seven years. There were a hundred people present during my time; but I cannot remember more than three married couples, though there were several betrothals which afterwards led to marriage.

I don't believe anybody was ever hurt by being at Brook Farm. The life was pure, the company choice. There was a great deal of hard work, and plenty of fun,--music, dancing, reading, skating, moonlight walks, and some flirting in pairs. After the dispersal, the people went back to the world, and most of them prospered.

Mr. George Ripley was the head man. His sunny, beaming face, cheerful kindness, and elastic step are not to be forgotten. Yet he could look stern. I remember we had some <u>tableaux vivants</u>.

He stood for a Suliote chief at bay, with his daughters clinging around him. The thing was taken from an annual. Mr. Ripley came in hastily from work, and made no change in his clothes, though he did take off his spectacles. He took a fine, heroic pose, and with a leopard-skin thrown over his breast, he and his Greek daughters looked fully equal to the occasion. It is perfectly certain that he would have faced a real danger with equal composure.

Mr. Ripley favored our going to church; so they used to rig up a two-horse hay wagon, of a Sunday morning, and ride over to Theodore Parker's meeting-house in West Roxbury, a pretty village two miles away. I think I went once. This was in the earlier part of Parker's ministry, before he had become obnoxious to "true believers." Many years after this ancient history, I used to visit a young lady in West Roxbury--a farmer's daughter--who told me that Mr. Parker had always been greatly interested in the young people of the village, and had thrown open his library and his study and himself to all the girls and boys who would come to see him. There were also several families of cultivated people. The effect was marked. As in Concord, there grew up a circle of studious, thoughtful, refined young people, reading books not commonly read in small towns by farmers and others of the working people.

The Rev. William Henry Channing, nephew of the famous Dr. Channing, came out several Sundays to preach to us at the Pilgrim House; so our religious wants were not neglected. Yet the grown people were freethinkers. All that I remember of Mr. Channing is that his sermons were beautiful, and that he stood in the end of the parlor, with a high, white forehead in striking contrast with a sun-browned face.

Not all the people of the present day, who read the New York <u>Sun</u>, are aware that Mr. Charles A. Dana was a member of the Brook Farm Community, and the companion of those unworldly philosophers. He was Mr. Ripley's right-hand man, and between them there was a most affectionate and jovial friendship. I call to mind Dana's vigorous stride, hearty laugh, and belted blouse. Like the rest, he taught and worked and sang, and then worked again. He was the bass in a choir which sang <u>Kyrie</u>

Eleison, night and day. It seemed to me they sang it rather too often; but I might have been mistaken.

I cannot forbear to speak of a young man who was at Brook Farm during the early part of my time. He would not recognize the description of himself, could he see it; but all the old Brook-Farmers would. His name and work are known wherever Americans are found. He was a comely youth of eighteen, and when I first saw him he was chopping fagots with a billhook behind the Erie all alone. His face and manners, his singing, and his general tone made him very attractive to women, and I think equally so to men. I know one boy who was almost as well pleased with him as any girl would be. I am what is left of that boy; and the young man was George William Curtis. I speak of his early years, because of the contrast between the guitar-playing, serenading, moonlight young fellow and the earnest reformer he soon grew to be.

Mr. John Dwight used to come in from his toil in the hot sun at noon, to give me a lesson on the piano; and after faithfully doing that job, he would lie down on the lounge and go to sleep, while I played to him. What a piece of nonsense it was, to have a man like that hoeing corn and stiffening his fingers! But the idea was (I think) that all kinds of labor must be made equally honorable, and that the poet, painter and philosopher must take their turn at the plough or in the ditch. Mr. Dwight had a quite feminine sweetness and delicacy of nature. I suppose only the non-musical public need to be told that he was afterwards the editor of Dwight's Journal of Music. Boston has only lately mourned his death.

To me this year of my youthful life stands out single and conspicuous. Simply as a happy memory, it is inestimable. I learned little or nothing from books, and only worked occasionally in the fields, just to amuse myself. But the regular members worked in the house, or out of doors, at general farm work, domestic duties, and in giving lessons to the pupils. The ladies used to go round from house to house, to do the chamber work in the morning; and in rainy weather they were sometimes escorted by us boys, who held our umbrellas over them. The washing and ironing were done at the Pilgrim House, by another "group." There it was that I first learned to iron towels. I think there were only two paid women servants, and they worked in the kitchen. The waiters at the table were selected from the regular members, under the direction of Mr. Dana as head waiter. They were skilful, assiduous and very gay.

The Farm had about one hundred acres. Lying in the gently hilly country that stretches southwest of Boston, bordered by primeval forests of pine and dotted with elms and (am I right?) ash-trees, with the beautiful river Charles not far away, you can conceive how delightful was the landscape wherever we went; in summer or winter, in the woods or by the river, boating, skating, or walking, there was nothing that was not beautiful. And we were all alone. Except for an occasional farm wagon that rumbled along the quiet country road skirting one side, I never saw any but our own people, though I wandered for miles through the forest and down the river.

I remember a fancy-dress picnic in the woods, which might have furnished Mr. Hawthorne his scene in the "Blithedale Romance." The big dog and the Indian chief were there, and Silas Foster, but no Zenobia. I am glad to say that there was never at Brook Farm anybody remotely resembling Zenobia; because if there had been, Hawthorne would never have presented this superb creature. I am often asked this question, so I make the answer. The Indian chief of our picnic was a young fellow,--George Wells,--a hero among us boys, tall, straight and handsome, with long, fair curls hanging down his shoulders (the fashion at the Farm). He was bright, kind and strong, and could do everything that a boy ought to do, and better than any of us. He afterwards became distinguished in the Massachusetts Legislature, in the ante-bellum days, where he contended successfully with the veteran Caleb Cushing about the stirring issues of that day. Wells was killed in Virginia, while colonel of the Thirty-fourth Massachusetts and commander of a brigade. I do not remember Silas Foster's name; but I recall his beautiful smile and white teeth. Across half a century, this plain, sun-browned farmer, who spoke little, but had a kind voice and pleasant ways, stands before me so clearly that I could paint his portrait. I do not say that Hawthorne had him in mind; but he was our head farmer, just as Silas Foster was in the "Romance."

Hawthorne lived at Brook Farm in the early days, but I never saw him there. Afterwards I saw him for just one second. It was at the door of Miss Peabody's book room in West Street. Oh, ye old Bostonians, most blessed of mankind, what happy memories are associated with that famous room, the resort of poets, philosophers, painters, thinkers! Mr. Hawthorne appeared for an instant at the door, and then vanished; but not before I had taken an impression of him, which may be wrong, but is ineffaceable. What I saw, with near-sighted eyes, was a rather tall, youngish, well-made, poetical-looking man, who came to the door and fled away before the crowd.

Margaret Fuller spent three days with us at Brook Farm in my year, and I had the honor of sitting alone with her in the library of the Eyrie for one hour. She was quite unconscious of my presence, though I sat near her, and could not take my eyes off her face. I have no idea why I did so look at her, but I did. Associated with Miss Fuller in my memory, because he shared her tragic fate, was Horace, youngest brother of Charles Sumner. Horace was living at the Farm when I first came there.

We had a great deal of company,--curious tourists from abroad, artistic people, and socialists. It became necessary to charge a moderate price for their accommodation. The houses were, first, The Hive, largest and oldest. It was an old farmhouse, standing near the quiet country road, the land sloping down in front to a pretty brook which ran through the farm to join the river. Close by was a magnificent elm. The Hive contained the kitchen and dining-room, and thither flocked the whole Community, summoned three times a day by a bugle horn, which set the black dog a-howling. The other houses were about a quarter of a mile away, and a few hundred yards from each other. One of them was built by Mr. Morton of Plymouth, and was called the Pilgrim House. Mr. Morton was the father of Mrs. Abby Morton Diaz, who was at one time a member. She was a pretty girl. Near by was a brown house called The Cottage. The first time I slept at the farm I was put into a room in this house, and, the night being cool, I got up and laid a table upside down on the bedspread as a blanket. I do not recommend the expedient, but I slept well that night. Next to The Cottage was The Erie, a square, frail house, standing on some high terraces, and looking over a wide prospect of meadow and hill. Back of it, within a few rods, a pine forest stretched away, I don't know how far.

Many years afterwards I went to view the old scenes, and found the Second Massachusetts Regiment encamped on the grounds, and ready to go to the front. The Erie had gone,--nothing left but the cellar, in the middle of which stood a tall pine-tree. But this was not my first return. Once I rode out of Boston on horseback, and found, attached to the Pilgrim House, the scene of so many merry dances, a great yard, surrounded by a high, open fence, which corralled a pack of screaming urchins belonging to the Roxbury poorhouse. As I rode by they ran along the fence after me, with such remarks as naturally suggest themselves to persons of their condition. I went on, and came to a high knoll in sight of the river, crowned with a clump of ash-trees. I was looking for the grave of the old cook, whom I shall call Hannah. She was lame and suffered much pain, and was therefore cross; but I remember she sometimes spoke pleasantly to me, and I have pleasant memories of her. Indeed, she had a perfect right to be cross; she was quite alone in the world. Hannah died while I was there, and was buried on this lonely, breezy knoll. Her grave had been protected by a fence of two rails, and shaded by the beautiful summer trees; but I could not now find her grave, nor any vestige of it.

I must tell who "we boys" were. During my year there were not many. There were two Spanish boys from Manila, who had been consigned by their father to a Boston merchant, to be sent to school; so they were kept at Brook Farm for several years. They learned very little; but that was just as well, for one was dull, and the other was a leper, and died at sea on his voyage homeward. There might have been a dozen more boys. For a little while there was a crowd of Cuban boys,--most unpleasant fellows, haughty, jealous, quarrelsome and suspicious. There was one, however, Ramon Lacuna, who had none of these traits. A tall, fair-haired stripling from Virginia was my crony. If young Booth is yet alive, and should see this, it may interest him to know that I remember him perfectly and can see his blue eyes to-day.

Lucas, the Spanish leper, had a broad, good-humored face, and was an exquisite waltzer. Poor fellow, he grew worse before the Community broke up; and his father, a Manila lawyer, abandoned him, stopped the supplies, and cast him off! But the Boston merchant took care of him, and finally put him on board a ship bound to Manila. He died and was buried at sea.

A queer character was a man named John Cheever. He came over to this country as valet to an English baronet, who spent a day at Brook Farm and died suddenly the day after. What John's means of subsistence were I do not know; but long after I left, I was told that he wandered away and was never heard of again. He had droll, quaint ways of talking; and though treated on terms of perfect equality, being a general favorite, he never abandoned the deferential, formal manner of a well-trained English servant. He wrote to me after I left; and you would have thought he was addressing a duke. I wish I had that letter. I kept it until five years ago; and the old yellow leaves, with the queer style and formal speech, were the only relic I had of Brook Farm.

It is often asked, "Why has no one written a complete history of this queer little Community, giving its bearings and results upon the social problems, and describing the extent to which Fourierism was adopted?" Perhaps the reason is that it never had any result, except upon the individual lives of those who dwelt there. And perhaps the best way to give an idea of Brook Farm is simply to sketch what one saw and did there. It was a beautiful idyllic life which we led, with plenty of work and play and transcendentalism; and it gave place to the Roxbury poorhouse.

*Arthur Sumner, "A Boy's Recollections of Brook Farm," New England Magazine, 10 (May 1894): 309-313.

REMINISCENCES OF THE BROOK FARM ASSOCIATION*

J. Homer Doucet

I

I am to give some of my reminiscences of the Brook Farm Association. It is now more than half a century since the events I am to recall have passed into history, or, I might say, oblivion. Forgetting the lapse of time, you might imagine that the writer was then a man of mature age, capable of appreciating the full meaning and value of the experiment in which he was taking part. Not so. I was not then qualified, either by age or education, to fully appreciate and understand the great principles of social regeneration promulgated by the teachers of the new dispensation. The opinions which I now entertain of the significance and value of the experiment, and of the men and women engaged in it, have been formed by subsequent study and reflection.

The social experiment at Brook Farm has always excited a lively interest among those who are inclined to the study of social phenomena, and great desire has been expressed, at various times, to learn the facts relating to the origin of the movement, and the home life of those who took part in it. I have often been asked why it is that the real inner history of Brook Farm Association has never been written. Some years ago I met Mr. W. H. Channing in this city. He told me that contemplated writing such a history--but he never did.

Robert Carter, in an article entitled "The Newness," in the Century for November, 1889, said that the movement which culminated in the establishment of Brook Farm Association and other similar communities had its origin in the introduction of German literature and philosophy among the scholars of New England. What influence the study of Goethe, Schiller, Lessing, Jean Paul Richter, Hegel and Kant may have had in the inauguration of a movement diametrically opposed to the spirit of the philosophy which they taught is not apparent on the surface, and will remain an unsolved enigma, unless we inquire into the intellectual phenomena which characterized the decade from 1830 to 1840.

This period was marked by intense mental activity. The work, however, was aggressive and disintegrating. German literature and philosophy, as well as the works of Carlyle and Emerson, exerted a powerful influence in accelerating the disintegrating movement, but could not initiate the reconstructive movement. The new philosophy, or transcendentalism, spread like a mist, through which the rays of the new light were refracted, vitiating the perception and the judgment, leading to exaggeration in the estimate of opinions, and to extravagance in thought, speech, and conduct.

During this period Boston had reason to be proud of the brilliant galaxy of illustrious names which justly entitled her to be called the Athens of America.

Emerson, Thoreau, Bronson Alcott, Theodore Parker, James Russell Lowell, John S. Dwight, W. H. Channing, and many others more or less gifted as writers and speakers, were among the disciples and teachers of the new philosophy.

Among the most notable women who graced the literary circle of this period were Mrs. George Bancroft, Mrs. Lydia Maria Child, Mrs. Emerson, Mrs. Horace Mann, Mrs. Theodore Parker, Mrs. Hawthorne, Mrs. Wendell Phillips, Mrs. George Ripley, Mrs. Anna Shaw, Mrs. Putnam, and Miss Caroline Sturgis.

Margaret Fuller had suddenly reached the zenith of her short but brilliant career. She was a prodigy of learning and a most brilliant conversationalist. She aspired to be the Corinne of America. Weekly, she would discourse to the élite of Boston society on the genealogy of heaven and earth; the will and the understanding; the celestial inspiration of genius; the perception and transmission of divine law, and so forth.

A writer in the Dial said: "The movement is, in every form, a protest against usage, and a search for principles." The protest against usage became a revolt against all constituted authority. The sovereignty of the individual and the finality of private judgment was considered to be the supreme law from which there could be no appeal. Government, institutions, laws, the church, and established usages of society, were scouted and ignored. With some this movement to realize perfect freedom from all social restraints degenerated into license and anarchy. "The search for principles" did not produce very satisfactory results, and did not advance the cause of exact knowledge to any great degree. The method of research was either mythological or metaphysical,-- and in no wise scientific. Miss Margaret Fuller, for instance, used to illustrate her lectures by reference to Greek mythology. Man, in his complex nature, was studied and analyzed metaphysically; human nature was unduly exalted, and human rights empirically defined as absolute and inalienable.

But this disintegrating movement had reached its limits, the mass had been reduced to its ultimate atoms, and the work of reconstruction was about to commence. Emerson had given up preaching because he did not believe in oral prayer, and because he would not officiate at the Lord's Supper, which symbolizes the brotherhood of man, to a people whose daily practices, in the marts of trade, gave the lie to the doctrine. Ripley, Dwight, Allen and Ballou had ceased to speak to those who would not understand the true democracy of religion. Channing continued to speak, here and there, but had no abiding place. Theodore Parker made his own platform, and fought a noble fight for truth and humanity to the end. Thus it will be seen that these men, in the midst of their brilliant surroundings, had become isolated. They were no longer in accord with the spirit that dominated the church and ruled in every business transaction of the day. The world seemed to have nothing for them to do. There was no career but literature open to them, but they realized that the existing evils were inherent in the constitution of society itself and could not be eradicated by philosophy or preaching. So they set themselves to the task of reconstructing society upon new lines wholly outside the great stream of human activities which had flown down the ages from the first. I do not know how it is now, but at that time everybody who had an "ism" to coddle came to Boston to have a convention. Convention week was usually in the last part of May. The several halls in Tremont Temple were always engaged on such occasions, and, oftentimes, Faneuil Hall and other large halls in various parts of the city were occupied by a coterie of enthusiastic and excited men and women bent upon nursing some pet scheme to advance the temporal or spiritual welfare of suffering humanity. At one of these conventions Adin Ballou, who had established a community at Hopedale, Mass., read his annual report, in which this characteristic passage occurred: "We are not distillers of intoxicating liquors, to cover the world with drunkenness. We are not fabricators of swords, guns and other deadly weapons. We are not manufacturers of slave manacles and scourges. We are pursuing no anti-Christian industry. We have eschewed these abominations, and testified against all such perversion of human industry, skill and capital. We have no government craft, no priest craft, no education craft, no bossing craft, no exclusive privilege class or order among us to be salaried, fattened and effeminated at the expense of our little commonwealth. All things necessary to be done are done for the common good on equal terms." Bronson Alcott founded a community in the town of Harvard, about forty miles from Boston. He seemed to have gathered about him the most eccentric disciples of the "Newness." Robert Carter describes some of the ludicrous notions and extravagances in which some of the associates indulged. Bronson Alcott and Thoreau seemed to have no other object in view than to teach the world how little human beings could subsist upon.

II

About the year 1841 the disciples of the new dispensation gathered at Brook Farm. Mr. Robert Carter gives the number of the first members at about one hundred. This is incorrect. The number of men did not exceed ten. For a long time the membership did not exceed forty. But the number of scholars increased rapidly, and at the time of Mr. Carter's visit the whole population may have come up to one hundred. Among the very first members of the Association were George Ripley, the founder of the institution; Charles A. Dana, William Henry Channing, John S. Dwight, Warren Burton, Nathaniel Hawthorne, George William Curtis, and his brother Burrill Curtis. "The avowed object of the Association was to realize the Christian ideal of life, by making such industrial, social and educational arrangements as would promote economy, combine leisure for study with healthful and honest toil, avert collision of caste, equalize refinement, diffuse courtesy, and sanctify life more completely than is possible in the isolated household."

Brook Farm derived its name from a brook which ran in front of the main building and which separated us completely from the outer world. Between the brook and the old farm house, which stood upon a ridge, there was a flower garden and strawberry bed, and adjoining this was the nursery. We boys hoed and prepared the soil, and the young ladies planted the flowers and attended to the strawberry bed. The crop of strawberries never was very large, and I never knew what became of it. The farm contained about two hundred acres "of good land," so says Mr. Carter. This, also, is an error, so far as the quality of the land is concerned. The soil was the most barren and unproductive that could be found anywhere this side of the bad lands. The surface was studded with large rocks, sand hills and clumps of stunted pine trees. There was very little produce on the place, and this not by any fault of the farmers. The head farmer, or chief of the farmers' group, was efficient and practical. He understood the business thoroughly. The fault was in the land. No one but a transcendentalist philosopher could have imagined that such land could ever be made to pay for its tilling. Yet we planted potatoes and raised very good crops. Often have I seen Mr. Ripley marching toward the potato field, with his schoolboys in military array, hoes at "carry," and a fine Newfoundland dog bringing up the rear. Nature had lavished her choicest gifts upon George Ripley, and the schools had developed and ripened them in full fruition. He was a thoroughly classical scholar; a profound thinker, conversant with ancient and modern literature and philosophy; an accomplished and logical speaker, and a ready writer. He was of polished manners, and his presence was commanding. He possessed great self-control. Under a load of cares that would have crushed any man less happily constituted no shadow of doubt or discouragement ever darkened that bright, open and cheerful countenance. He always met every one with a smile and an encouraging word. He was very ready in joke and repartee. One time, at a convention in Boston, he commenced his speech thus: "The first requisite--" at which juncture he made a misstep and came near falling from a narrow platform on which he was standing. Without the least hesitation, as though it was part of his speech, he continued: "--that we shall not fall in this cause."

Before I joined the Association quite a number of the old members had gone back to the world to engage in the strife for fame and wealth in the seething cauldron of civilized life. Nathaniel Hawthorne, whose chief occupation had been the feeding of the pigs and the care of the stock, said that he "declined to be made a chambermaid to a cow." He had invested all his savings in the Association, and, I believe, he lost all. George William Curtis and his brother were not actual members. Mr. Curtis returned to New York, where his noble words and gifted pen were always on the side of right and progress.

For the first two or three years there was no other source of revenue but that derived from the farm and the school. The school was very good, not simply because of the great learning of the teachers, but because the free intercourse of the pupils with men and women of such exquisite culture and refinement could not but exert a powerful influence in the development of the best elements of human nature and the formation of correct habits of life. During the two and a half yars of my residence there I never heard loud or boisterous language used, I never heard an oath, I never saw or heard of any one quarreling; I never knew that any one was ever accused or suspected of having acted in an ungentlemanly or unladylike manner anywhere on the place.

The proximity of the Farm to Boston and other large towns, its natural beauty and great salubrity, offered unequal advantages as a location for the establishment of a large and prosperous school. But the bitter attacks of the press, and the vile vituperations and slanderous lies that were continually circulated all over the country against us, prevented many from sending their children to our school. The income from this source, therefore, never was large enough to meet the necessary expenses of carrying on the Association. Some other means had to be devised to meet the exigencies of the case. It was finally decided to enlarge the industrial field by establishing various mechanical trades. In order to accomplish this object new buildings had to be erected and great additions made to the old ones to accommodate the people who were expected to come.

When the Association first took possession of the farm there was but one farm-house, used in common, which stood near the road. This was originally a double house, containing four rooms on each floor, with kitchen and shed. As the Association increased in numbers new buildings were added, so that when I joined in the spring of 1844, there were several good houses on the place.

First, there was the old farm-house, greatly enlarged and improved. It was called the "Hive." It contained two rooms on one side, rather dingy and bare of furniture. These were for general use. The men usually gathered in these rooms to read or chat while waiting for dinner. On the other side there was a large dining-room. The whole family, now numbering over two hundred, could be seated at two long tables extending the whole length of the room. Back of the dining-room was the kitchen, then the bakery, and a room used for laundry purposes, after which came the shed for the storage of wood and farm implements. The story above this long array of miscellaneous rooms was divided into many small rooms used as dormitories, in which lived most of the mechanics and farmers, especially those with families.

The next house erected was the "Aerie," thus called because it was built upon a rock, quite a distance back of the ridge. It contained two large rooms on the first floor. One was occupied by Mr. Ripley as an office, library and recitation-room. The other was used as a reception and meeting-room. Above these were several other apartments. The front room was occupied by Mr. and Mrs. Ripley, and the others by the younger pupils.

Now I should mention the cottage, which was by far the prettiest building on the place. It was built by a lady who occupied a part of it during the first period of the Association's existence, but who left when the character of the movement was entirely changed by the introduction of mechanical trades and the organization of the industries according to the system of Charles Fourier. The cottage was used for school purposes. It was fitted up with regular school furniture and two or three pianos. John S. Dwight and Charles A. Dana continued to occupy rooms in the cottage after it was converted into a school-house. Near by, at the extreme edge of the ridge, there was a queer-looking building. It was intended for two families--houses placed "dos à dos" instead of side by side. It was called the "Pilgrim House," not because it was devoted to the reception of strangers, which might naturally have suggested the name, but because the builders of it were two brothers from Plymouth who intended to live in it. They did not sympathize with the new state of things and did not come. The Association, I believe, acquired possession of it on very favorable terms. The basement of this house was used by the laundry group as an ironing-room. Although I lived in it for over two years I never was in any of its apartments except the ironing-room and that which I occupied. On my side of the house there were two large rooms connected by folding doors. I occupied the back room. This room was also used during the day by the sewing-group, my bed being placed in an alcove or small apartment under the stairway.

The front room of this structure was occupied by the editorial staff--Ripley, Channing, Dwight, Dana, Orvis, Allen and others--who were often busy here correcting proofs and discussing the merits of certain productions and the propriety of admitting them to the pages of the Harbinger. These discussions were at times very animated, and always interesting and instructive to me. On one occasion there was a heated debate between Messrs. Ripley, Channing and Dwight on the one side, and Dana on the other. Dana had written a scathing review of some of Edgar Poe's poetic effusions. There were three men against who Mr. Dana seemed to cherish the most intense dislike. The first was Edgar Poe, the second was Anthon, author, or, rather, compiler of a Classical Dictionary, and the last, but not least, was Fenimore Cooper. Greeley, I believe, shared Dana's dislike for Cooper. In this case it was urged that the review was unnecessarily harsh, if not cruel--that whatever Mr. Poe's failings were, he, unquestionably, possessed in a high degree the true spirit of poetry--that it was the duty of the reviewer simply to point out the defects or the beauties of a literary production.

Mr. Dana's contention was that Poe had published a poem for which he had received a certain compensation. The poem no longer belonged to him; it belonged to the public. He had said nothing against Poe personally, but he claimed the right to say what he pleased about the poem. Mr. Dana had his way in this case, and, I think, he used to have his way in almost every case.

Mr. Dana's personal appearance at this time was quite striking. He was quite thin, and on that account appeared taller than he really was. His features were expressive of great firmness and executive ability. His step was firm and elastic, indicating that his nerves as well as his muscles were of iron. He was a fine classical, German, and French scholar. He was by all odds the best teacher we had, and the only one who had any idea of discipline. He had the best method of imparting knowledge of any teacher I ever saw. While always kind and considerate, no one cared to incur his displeasure by coming to the recitation-room unprepared for the lessons. Mr. Dana was very watchful, and he used to make the rounds of the several buildings, at night, to see that everything was right and safe. There was a rule that all should be in their own dwellings by ten o'clock.[1] "One evening there was a party at the Cottage playing whist. All belonged at the Cottage except one who was a pupil and lived at the Hive. Being absorbed in the game and not noticing the hour, they were startled by the appearance of Mr. Dana, on whose countenance they observed a menacing expression. The young man was austerely questioned as to his being at that hour--a quarter past ten-- absent from his dwelling-place: 'And how do you expect, sir, to enter the house, when you know the doors are locked at ten?' The young man did not seem at all disconcerted, and answered quietly: 'Oh, that is of no consequence, sir: I always get in at the pantry-window.' A burst of laughter greeted this answer, in which none joined more heartily than the questioner himself." One evening, about eleven o'clock, I was studying in my room, when Mr. Dana unexpectedly entered. I saw by his looks that there was something to displease him, but I could not imagine what it could be. I was not left long in suspense. I was suffering with a sty or something of the kind on one of my eyes. I had it bandaged with a handkerchief and was reading with the other--a very foolish thing for me, or any one else, to do. He asked me what was the matter with my eye. I told him. He looked at it and simply said, "Young man, this must stop," and marched out again.

III

During this period Brook Farm was the ideal of philosophical anarchists, though this name was not then known. In its origin, as we have said, the Association was a protest against the conventionalities of social life, the church, and the existing political and economic conditions. There was no law to limit the freedom of the individual, and no systematic organization of labor. Every one worked hard and enthusiastically for the success of the Association, without much, if any, direction from any quarter. But the Association was now in a transitional state. The period of involution was at an end, and the period of its organic life was about to commence.

The industrial plant consisted mainly of a large two-story wooden building, recently erected, in which all industrial operations were to be carried on. In the basement there was a good steam-engine. The first floor was wholly occupied by a sash and blind factory. On the second floor there were the printing office and presses, shoemaker shop and block-tinware manufactory. The tailoring department was at the Pilgrim House.

With the accession of so many new members and the establishment of these new industries a more systematic organization of labor became a pressing necessity. One of the new members was strongly imbued with the ideas of Charles Fourier, and urged the propriety of organizing the industries according to the system of the great French socialist. A correspondence was finally commenced with some gentlemen of New York, who were disciples of Fourier. Among them may be mentioned Parke Godwin and Albert Brisbane. For once New York had got the start of Boston on a new "ism." The works of Fourier were procured and zealously and understandingly studied. Soon Albert Brisbane came to us to explain the social philosophy of the master whose pupil he had been, and to assist in organizing labor upon the new system. Brook Farm always was an association--a joint stock company, not a community. Applicants were not called upon to surrender their worldly possessions to the common fund. All investments were credited to the investors, who were to receive four per cent interest. Those who had nothing to invest gave their labor and skill as equivalents. All met on the same footing. The period of probation was three months. When the applicant knew that his name was to come up before the august tribunal of the chiefs for approval or rejection, I am sure, judging by my own feelings, that he waited with fear and trembling for the final decision. A two-thirds vote was necessary for affirmation. No one, to my knowledge, ever was rejected after having served the full three months' probation. Efficiency and skill in labor, a genial and friendly disposition, were sure to win from all a hearty welcome.

Outwardly there was no sign indicating that a radical change had taken place in the internal economy of the Association. Yet every industry had been systematically organized into groups and series of groups. In order to secure the greatest freedom to the individual, every one was left free to elect, according to aptitudes or affinity, in which group or groups he would work. Each group elected its own chief; the duties of each were clearly defined and the chief was held responsible for the performance of the work assigned to it. Labor was made attractive by the facility which the division of labor afforded alternations from one group to another. These changes tended to bring new faculties into play and developed the social feelings. It is a fact, that after a fair day's work, either in field or shop, no one complained of weariness, and all were ready to engage in the amusements of the evening. The system may seem arbitrary or fanciful, but it is quite natural and in the line of the evolution of our industrial system. It is nothing more than the division of labor and the differentiation of organs which constitute the basis of modern economics and social science. Every large industry to-day is really organized into groups and series of groups--only the groups are called "gangs" and the chiefs "bosses." Division of labor is a necessary condition of the final integration of the individual into the collective body on the industrial plane. There can be no organism without organs, and the union of a certain number of individuals to perform a function constitutes the ultimate unit of the social organism.

The functions of production and distribution were carried on by the associates themselves, who paid no tribute to any class for superintendence. The products were to be distributed in certain proportions to capital, talent or skill, and labor. There is one peculiarity about the principle governing interest that should be noticed. It was estimated that the deterioration of industrial plants would necessitate their renewal every twelve years. The original capital, becoming thus periodically exhausted of its productive power, ought, in justice, it was claimed, to cease to share in the products of present labor. In order to eliminate it from the category of productive forces, interest was computed on a sliding scale which would extinguish it every twelve years. The power of capital to draw interest was not therefore perpetual, and did not, as in the present system, remain forever a fixed charge upon the industries of the people.

Our experiment was now in full blast. The hum of industry had become a fact in our midst. The puffing of the steam-engine, the buzzing of the saws and the screeching of the planing machine as it tore madly through the wood, were melodious sounds to our ears. Many hoped that the experiment would prove a success and add much to our scanty resources. But I suspect that others, and those best qualified to judge, were not so sanguine. Indeed, every one ought to have seen that the difficulties in the way of success were inherent and insurmountable. The sash and blind factory was the most extensive plant on the place. The cost of its steam engine and machinery was considerable, and it was expected that the income from this outlay would be correspondingly large. But the location was as unsuitable for the establishment of remunerative industries as it was favorable for the establishment of a prosperous school. The Farm was situated nine miles from Boston, our nearest market. There was no railroad. The lumber had to be hauled from the yards of Boston with horses.

Then the bulky finished products had to be transported to market by the same means. Although Mr. George Hatch, the chief, understood the business thoroughly and was very active, he could not compete on equal terms with the manufacturers of Boston. Still, the work was going on in every department; the shoemaking, tailoring, and printing groups were busy most of the time, but the work was not profitable. I have never learned whether the <u>Harbinger</u> paid expenses. The circulation was quite large for such a paper, but many of the subscribers, I know, were delinquents.

To outsiders, and, in fact, to many of the members, it did seem as though the experiment was a success. But the committee of ways and means knew that the income of the various trades did not more than cover the additional expenses. Under these trying conditions the question of retrenchment was always in order. Miss Ripley, our chief cook, puzzled her brains to devise means to lessen the expenses of the table. The allowance of butter never was very large; it now became microscopically small; and coffee was reserved for particular occasions. The food, however, was always good and of sufficient quantity. The bread was of superior quality. Baldwin, the chief of the baking department, was a skilled baker from Boston. As he did not wish to be confined to the bakery every day, he taught the art of baking bread to three or four young men, who would take turns in relieving him. I was one of these. Baldwin was always watchful, in order that nothing should go wrong with the bread. One day I made a batch of ginger bread and forgot to put any ginger in the batter. The chief was a great stutterer. He came in just as I had the batch out of the oven. My ginger bread looked fair to the eye and tempting to the palate. I was proud of it. Baldwin took a piece, which he tasted. He looked puzzled. "Well," I asked, "don't it taste good?" "Yes," replied he; "gin-ger bread without any gin-ger in it." I got out of this scrape very well, and my reputation did not suffer much. But I soon made another and more serious mistake. It was the day for Boston brown bread. The ingredients were properly mixed, but I should have added a lump of common bread dough to leaven it. I forgot to put in the leavening lump and my Boston brown bread was a total failure. It looked very much like Bronson Alcott's unleavened black bread, only it was not molded into the shape of various animals as his was. Alcott resorted to this device to make his bread more palatable. As it was, the bread was not eatable, but as we could not afford to lose it, Miss Ripley sliced the bread and fried it in fat. It made good toast, and, I believe, was all consumed. It was a long time, however, before the chief allowed me again to relieve him.

I was also a member of the nursery group. We voted to do the nursery work from four o'clock A. M. to seven o'clock A. M. Dana was the chief. At four o'clock precisely he would go round to call his men up. We would crawl out half asleep, but work, nevertheless, like beavers, weeding and hoeing until the horn for breakfast sounded. This was a welcome signal. In the laundry group, my work was to take the clothes from the boiler and carry them to the tubs. In the ironing room my principal work was to turn the crank of the mangler. This mangler, the only labor-saving machine we had that I remember, was a very clumsy affair. It consisted of a huge box, weighted with stones, running on four wooden rollers. The sheets were placed between the rollers, and by turning the crank the huge box was made to travel up and down until the sheets were pressed smooth.

Mrs. Ripley was chief of the washing and ironing departments. She was a remarkable woman--a blonde, tall, erect, graceful in all her movements, a finished scholar and a brilliant conversationalist. Margaret Fuller, as you know, did all the talking herself; but Mrs. Ripley had the rare tact of bringing out the very best there was in others. Yet this woman, so refined and cultured, was working like a slave, often for ten hours a day, in the sloppy wash room or in the hot ironing-room, not only willingly, but even cheerfully, speaking a pleasant word to this one and that one as she directed them in their work. Associated with Mrs. Ripley in the same group I remember a short, plump, busy little lady who was a great favorite with us all. One little girl used to call her "lady love." She was very clever in clear starching. Her work was to clear-starch the garments of the women. Each woman was allowed to put in two pieces weekly. Seeing our friend always engaged in starching muslin, a witty little girl gave her the name of "Miss Muslin"--a name which, if not as poetical, was at least quite as appropriate as the first.

There was a middle-aged man who was placed with us by an English nobleman. John [Cheever] was very observing, and few personal peculiarities ever escaped his notice. He was witty, and some of his aphorisms were replete with wisdom. If anything went wrong anywhere he referred to the matter by saying "there is something rotten in the State of Denmark," or, "all things will find their level." There were only three books in his opinion worth having--the Bible, Shakespeare and Burns. One woman who was very tall and erect, he always addressed as "your perpendicular majesty," and she very good naturedly responded to the name.

Although our life seemed monotonous, we managed to get a great deal of enjoyment out of it. Wednesday evenings we usually had dancing. Everybody danced--most of us for the pleasure derived from it, others from a sense of duty. Ripley, Channing, Dwight and Allen added much to our enjoyment by their participation in the dancing. We had charades, tableaux vivants, mock trials, readings and recitations very often. One of the most ludicrous performances was a speech by Baldwin, assisted by Mr. Ripley. Baldwin was a very tall man. Mr. Ripley stood very close to Baldwin's back, with his arms passed over the latter's shoulders. Both were enveloped in a sheet, which concealed Mr. Ripley's head and body. Baldwin did the speaking and Mr. Ripley performed the gestures. This combination produced very comical effects, especially when the stutterings came in. One evening we established a camp of gipsies in the pine woods back of the Aerie. The tents, the flickering fires, the kettles hanging from crossed sticks, the dusky figures moving silently among the trees, the gaudy costumes of the women telling fortunes, made it one of the most unique and realistic scenes I ever witnessed. Our gipsy camp was voted a great success. Music, however, was the principal source of enjoyment. Mr. Dwight was a thorough musician, though his selections were usually too classical for those of us who were not musically educated. We had several members who had good voices, and a lady from Boston who possessed a very beautiful and well-trained voice. These adjuncts added much to our musical entertainments.

During my sojourn at the Farm I remember that there were a number of illustrious visitors, among whom was Robert Owen, the great philanthropist and communist. The evening discussions of social problems were always exceedingly interesting, but were doubly so during Owen's visit. He insisted, of course, that a community of property was the only system that would effectually prevent the concentration of wealth in the hands of the few, eradicate poverty, abolish slavery and war, and usher in an era of plenty, peace and harmony over the whole earth. Mr. Owen was a grand old man, whose heart, at eighty-four, was still young and responded generously to every humanitarian effort.

On the 3d of March, 1845, a large edifice which had been in process of erection since the spring of 1844, was destroyed by fire. The total expenditure upon the building, including the labor performed by the associates, amounted to about seven thousand dollars, and three thousand dollars, it had been estimated, would be required for its completion. As it was not yet in use by the Association, and until the day of its destruction, not exposed to fire, no insurance had been effected. It was built by investments in our loan stock, and the loss fell upon the holders of partnership stock and the members of the Association. Many suppose that the destruction of this building was the cause of the final dissolution of the Association. Such was not the case. Although the disaster was a great blow to our hopes, it occasioned no immediate discomfort, and the routine business was in no way interrupted. The very next day, had it not been for the smoldering ruins, a stranger would not have supposed that a great calamity had befallen us. The school and the industries were going on as though nothing unusual had happened. Undoubtably unfavorable economic conditions hastened the dissolution, but they were not the primary cause of it. Many similar associations and communities had sprung up at about the same time all over the Eastern and Western States, and, while some of them were financially prosperous, all, excepting the Oneida Community, gave up their experiments, about the same time, ostensibly for various reasons, but,

I believe, from the same ultimate cause. The fact is, that the exceptional intellectual and moral movement in which all had their origin had become exhausted; the wave of enthusiasm and lofty aspiration, which swept the land from East to West, had spent itself, and ceased to be an inspiring and vivifying principle, not only in the particular individuals thus effected, but in the community at large. It was, even then, indistinctly perceived that these societies were outside the lines of the natural evolution of society, and broke the historical continuity of the movement.

These unsuccessful attempts to reform society upon arbitrary lines prove, merely, that evolution cannot be forced out of its natural course, however noble the ideal for which we labor may be. But they do not prove, as some assert, that the _laissez faire_ philosophy is the only true course, nor that the object sought to be attained--the establishment upon earth of a true human brotherhood--is not the goal toward which all evolution tends. I cannot accept the brutal philosophy which the biological branch of political economists teaches, that man, together with all animate nature, shall eternally struggle for existence--that this is according to an inexorable law from which there is no escape; that the millions must toil, suffer and die miserably, that the select few, the "fittest to survive," may revel in luxury and live sumptuously. This philosophy, although promulgated in the name of science, is not true. It is a calumny against human nature. If the law of evolution is inherent in the nature of things, it is within the possibilities of the future that man shall evolve from the animal plane, where brute force is the only reason of things--the only law--to the human plane, where reason, enlightened by science, shall rule, and where love shall sanctify every relation and still every discord of life. I believe that the goal of human progress is the establishment of a social state in which justice, freedom and universal order shall prevail, and in which the sublime thought of the fatherhood of God and the brotherhood of man shall rest, like a benediction, equally upon all.

*J. Homer Doucet, "Reminiscences of the Brook Farm Association," Conservator, 5 (January, February 1895): 164-165, 180-182; 6 (March 1895): 4-6. Keyed to the title is this note: "This narrative will be published in three or four parts. Dr. Doucet, its author, is now a practicing physician in Philadelphia. He was born in Three Rivers, Canada, in 1822. His stay at Brook Farm was from the spring of 1844 to the summer of 1846. He has written and spoken multifariously upon the labor and other social questions."

    1. Atlantic Monthly, October and November, 1875 [1878]. [Doucet's note]

BROOK FARM*

Annie M. Salisbury

"The full history of Brook Farm can only be written by one who belonged to it, and shared its secret; and it doubtless would have been written before this had the materials been more solid. Aspirations have no history." Brook Farm Community, as it has erroneously been called, was not in the usual sense of the word a community-- George Ripley, the leading spirit, disclaims the appellation. The association was formed by the most highly intellectual and morally noblest men and women of New England, to enable them to live a life freer from the "trammels of civilization," as they would express it; or, as we should say, more free from the tyranny of social life with its senseless despotism. Fifty years ago a Boston Unitarian pastor was looked upon as a beacon light intellectually, as also the highest type in purity of life and motive; but feeling that there was much sham in the pulpit, George Ripley was said to have made the remark that he "could pray by the job no longer." I do not vouch for the truth of it. German transcendentalism (if anyone happens to know what that may mean) was rife in Boston at that time, too. I quote from O. B. Frothingham's works: "It must be remembered that projects of radical social reform were in the air at this time. Carlyle was thundering against shams in religion and politics; Dickens was showing up the abuses, cruelties and iniquities of the established order, Kingsley was stirring in the caldron of social discontent. * * * Seeds were ripening in France as well as in England, in fact all over Europe, for the great revolt of 1848. The influence of the new ideas was felt in the United States. We have the testimony of James Martineau to the fact that Dr. Channing, for a time, fell under the fascination of some of the speculative writers * * * who held forth the promise of a golden age for society. Rousseau and others entertained the idea of going to South America to plant an ideal society. Similar plans were eagerly discussed among the friends of progress in Boston."

Mr. and Mrs. Ripley were prominent as talkers and eager as listeners. Mrs. Ripley was a woman of burning enthusiasm, warm feeling and passionate will. Theodore Parker made the following entry in his journal: "Mrs. Ripley gave me a tacit rebuke for not shrieking at wrongs, and spoke of the danger of losing our humanity in abstractions." Dr. Channing had said in a letter to Rev. Adin Ballou, dated Feb. 27, 1841, two months before the beginning of Brook Farm, "I have for a very long time dreamed of an association to which the members, instead of preying on one another, and seeking to put each other down, after the fashion of this world, should live together as brothers, seeking one another's elevation and spiritual growth." That this spirit was carried out at Brook Farm was evident to all who entered into the life there. "Though the institution was far from being religious in spiritual purpose," their strong faith in the "divinity of impulse," as Frothingham has expressed it, could not but be misleading when carried to the extent to which it was there. Even the German transcendentalist was not perfect--except, perhaps, in his own eyes. Their confidence in individual freedom might have been dangerous, but it was only considered "freedom to become wise and good, simple and self-sacrificing, gentle and kind."

There was no theological creed, no ecclesiastical form, no inquisition into opinions, no avowed reliance on superhuman aid. The thoughts of all were heartily respected; and while some listened with sympathy to Theodore Parker, others went to church nowhere or sought the privileges of their own communion. By far the greater part of the people went to church nowhere. It was very decidedly not popular there to go to church! It savored too strongly of bondage to <u>civilization</u>! "It has been well said that the aim of the association was practical, not theoretical, not transcendental, not intellectual; in the same breath it must be added that it was in a high sense spiritual; that it was practical because it was spiritual; that while it aimed at the physical and mental elevation of the poorer classes, it did so because it believed in their natural capacity for elevation to children of God. * * * More than this, they felt themselves to be Christians. The name of

Jesus was always spoken with earnest reverence." In 1841 the earliest articles of association were subscribed to by George Ripley, Nathaniel Hawthorne, Minot Pratt, Chas. A. Dana, William B. Allen, Sophia W. Ripley, Maria T. Pratt, Sarah F. Stearns, Marianne Ripley, Charles O. Whitmore. Following are a few of the leading articles:

Articles of association made and executed this twenty ninth day of September, one thousand eight hundred and forty-one, by and between the several persons and their assigns, who have given their signature to this instrument, and by it associated themselves together for the purpose and objects hereinafter set forth:

Article I. The name and style of this association shall be The Subscribers to the Brook Farm Institute of Agriculture and Education; and all persons who shall hold one or more shares of the stock of the association shall be members; and every member shall be entitled to one vote on all matters relating to the funds of the association.

Art. II. The object of the association is to purchase such estates as may be required for the establishment and continuance of an agricultural, literary and scientific school or college, to provide such lands and houses, animals, libraries and apparatus as may be found expedient or advantageous to the main purpose of the association.

Art. III. The whole property of the association, real and personal, shall be vested in and held by four trustees, to be elected annually by the association.

The site of Brook Farm was a pleasant one, not far from Theodore Parker's meeting-house in Centre street, and in close vicinity to some of the most wealthy, capable and zealous friends of the enterprise. It was charmingly diversified with hill and hollow, meadow and upland. It possessed, moreover, historical associations which were interesting to its new occupants. Here the "apostle" Eliot preached to the Indians; his grave was hard by. The birthplace was not far distant of General Warren of Revolutionary fame. The spot seemed particularly appropriate to the use it was now set apart for. Later experiences showed its unfitness for lucrative tillage; but for an institution of education, a semi-aesthetic, humane undertaking, nothing could be better. In a letter to Emerson, Mr. Ripley says, "I recollect you said if you were sure of compeers of the right stamp you might embark yourself in the adventure; as to this, let me suggest the inquiry whether our association should not be composed of various classes of men. If we have friends whom we love and who love us, I think we should be content to join with others, with whom our personal sympathy is not strong, but whose general ideas coincide with ours and whose gifts and abilities would make their services important. For instance, I should like to have a good washerwoman in my parish, admitted into the plot! She is certainly not a Minerva or Venus; but we might educate her two children to wisdom and varied accomplishments, who otherwise will be doomed to drudge through life. The same is true of some farmers and mechanics whom we should like with us." This letter shows the truly philanthropic spirit which characterized the founders of Brook Farm Association; the wholly unselfish idea they were trying to carry out. In another letter to Emerson, after giving an account of the plans of the association, he says, "I can imagine no plan which is suited to carry into effect so many divine ideas as this. If wisely executed, it will be a light over this country and this age. If not the sunrise, it shall be the morning star. * * * I shall be anxious to hear from you. Your decision will do much towards settling the question with me--whether the time has come for the fulfillment of a high hope, or whether the work belongs to a future generation." It is interesting to know the light in which the practical mind of Emerson viewed the experiment. He says in a letter to Mr. Ripley, "It is quite time I made an answer to your proposition that I should venture into your new community. The design appears to me noble and generous, proceeding, as I plainly see, from nothing covert or selfish or ambitious, but from a manly and expanding heart and mind. So it makes all men its friends and debtors. * * * I have decided not to join it, and yet very slowly, and I may almost say with penitence. I am greatly relieved by learning that your coadjutors are now so many that you will no longer attach that importance to the defect of individuals, which you hinted in your letter to me, I or others might possess--the painful power, I mean, of preventing the execution of the plan. My feeling is that the community is not good for me, that it has little to offer me which with resolution I cannot procure for myself; that it would not be worth my while to make the difficult exchange of my property in Concord for a share in the new household. * * * It seems to me a circuitous and operose way of relieving myself to put upon your community the emancipation which I ought to take on myself. I must assume my own vows. I do not think I should gain anything, I, who have little skill to converse with people, by a plan of so many parts, and which I comprehend so slowly and bluntly. I do not look upon myself as a valuable member of any community which is not either very large or very small and select; I fear that yours would not find me as profitable and pleasant an associate as I should wish to be, and as so important a project seems imperatively to require in all its constituents." In regard to the pecuniary success of the farm, he says he read Mr. Ripley's letter to Mr. Edmund Hosmer, a very intelligent and upright man in the neighborhood, who admired the spirit of the plan, but "distrusted all I told him of the details as far as they concerned the farm. * * * He thought Mr. Ripley should put no dependence on the results of 'gentleman farmers' such as some he had named. If his [Mr. Hosmer's farm] had been managed in the way Brook Farm was managed, it would have put himself and his family in the poorhouse long ago." An article in the Dial (Margaret Fuller, Jan. 18, 1842)[1] gives a very clear idea of the aims of the association: "The attempt is made on a very small scale. A few individuals who, unknown to each other under different disciplines of life, reacting from different social evils, but aiming at the same object--of being wholly true to their natures as men and women--have been made acquainted with one another and have determined to become the faculty of the embryo university. In order to live a religious and moral life worthy the name they feel it necessary to come out in some degree from the world and to form themselves into a community of property so far as to exclude competition and the ordinary rules of trade; while they reserve sufficient private property, or the means of obtaining it, for all purposes of independence and isolation at will. They have bought a farm in order to make agriculture the basis of their life; it being the most direct and simple in relation to nature. A true life, while it aims beyond the highest star is still redolent of the healthy earth. The perfume of clover lingers about it. The lowing of cattle is the natural bass to the melody of human voices. * * * All labor, whether bodily or intellectual, is to be paid at the same rate of wages, on the principle that, as the labor becomes merely bodily, it is a great sacrifice to the individual laborer to give his time to it. * * * Another reason for setting the same pecuniary value on every kind of labor is to give outward expression to the great truth that all labor is sacred when done for a common interest. Saints and philosophers already know this, but the childish world does not. * * * Nor will this elevation of bodily labor be liable to lower the tone of manners and refinement. The 'children of light' are not altogether unwise in their generation. They have an invisible but all powerful guard of principles. Minds incapable of refinement will not be attracted into this association. It is an ideal community and only to the ideally minded will it be attractive; but these are to be found in every rank of life, under every shadow of circumstance. Even among the diggers of the ditch are to be found some who through religious cultivation can look down in meek superiority upon the outwardly refined and book learned." Emerson says, "The founders of Brook Farm should have this praise; that they made what all people try to make, an agreeable place to live in." All comers, even the most fastidious, found it the pleasantest of residences. It is certain that freedom from household routine, variety of character and talent, variety of work, variety of means of thought and instruction, art, music, poetry, reading, masquerade, did not permit sluggishness or despondency; broke up routine. There is an agreement in testimony that it was to most of the associates education; to many the most important period of their lives, the birth of valued friendships, their first acquaintance with the riches of conversation, their training in behavior. The art of letter writing was immensely cultivated, it is said. Letters were not only flying from house to house, but from room to room.

It was a perpetual picnic, a French Revolution in small, and age of reason in a patty pan. "No doubt there was in many a certain strength drawn from the fury of dissent." Thus Mr. Ripley told Theodore Parker, "There is your accomplished friend; he would hoe corn all Sunday, if I would let him, but all Massachusetts could not make him do it on Monday."

Hawthorne was with them a year at the first, and was quite enthusiastic for a time. He as there at the beginning of 1841, and his notebooks contain much that is interesting. But Hawthorne's temperament was not congenial with such an atmosphere, nor was his faith clear or steadfast enough to rest contented on its idea. His, however, were observant eyes; and his notes being soliloquies, confessions made to himself, carry honest impressions.

"BROOK FARM, April 13, 1841. I have not yet taken my first lessons in agriculture, except that I went to see our cows foddered yesterday afternoon. We have eight cows of our own. There is a most vicious animal in the yard, a transcendental heifer belonging to Margaret Fuller. She tries to rule every other animal and a guard has to be placed over her while the others animals pass in and out. [Whether the fact that the creature belonged to Miss Fuller, or that it was a Transcendental animal, caused it to be so undesirable a companion is not announced.] I intend to convert myself into a milkmaid this evening; but I pray heaven that Mr. Ripley may assign me the kindliest cows in the herd, otherwise I shall perform the duties with fear and trembling.

"April 14. I did not milk the cows last night, either because Mr. Ripley was afraid to trust them to my hands or me to their horns, I know not which. * * *

"April 16. I have milked a cow.

"April 22. I read no newspapers and hardly remember who is President, and I feel as if I had no more concern with what other people trouble themselves about than if I lived on another planet.

"May 1. All the morning I have been at work under a blue sky on a hillside. Sometimes I have felt as if I were at work in the sky itself, though the material in which I wrought was the ore from our gold mine * * * There is nothing so disagreeable or unseemly as this sort of toil as you think. It defiles the hands, indeed, but not the soul. * * * I do not believe that I should be so patient here if I were not engaged in a righteous and heaven-blessed way of life.

"May 11. We have been employed partly in an augean labor of cleaning out a woodshed. * * * These jobs are not at all suited to my taste.

"June 1. I think this present life of mine gives me an antipathy to pen and ink even more than my custom-house experience did. In the midst of toil, or after a hard day's work, my soul obstinately refuses to be burned out on paper. It is my opinion that a man's soul may be buried and perish under a dung heap, just as well as under a pile of money.

"Aug. 15. Even my custom-house experience was not such a thraldom and weariness as this. Oh, labor is the curse of the world, and nobody can meddle with it without becoming proportionately brutified.

"SALEM, Sept. 3. Really, I should judge it to be twenty years since I left Brook Farm; and I take this to be one proof that my life there was an unnatural and unsuitable, and therefore an unreal one. The real _me_ was never an associate of the community. There has been a spectral appearance there sounding the horn at daybreak and milking the cows and hoeing the potatoes and raising the hay, toiling in the sun and doing me the honor to assume my name. But the spectre was not myself."

"Hawthorne was elected to high offices, to those of trustee of the Brook Farm estate and chairman of committee of finance, but he told Mr. Ripley that he could not spend another winter there. * * * His rather sombre view must be accepted as the impression of one peculiar mind. In his 'Blithedale Romance,' Hawthorne disclaimed any purpose to describe persons or events at Brook Farm and expressed a hope that some one might yet do justice to a movement so full of earnest aspirations." Miss Fuller was never a member, though going there frequently, and sometimes remaining for a longer or shorter time, and always in strong sympathy with the movement. She delighted the people with her "conversations," which she had just established in Boston. One who was there at the time says, "She made plenty of money with her talents, which money she religiously devoted, as she had promised herself, to the education of her brothers." A lady who has written some very interesting articles on life at Brook Farm says, "Seldom is an aspiration, or even an ambition, fulfilled according to its original form and dimensions, because of the every varying changes constantly taking place on the surface of character, if not at its depths. Having earned our money we apply for our loaf, and are surprised, it is not unlikely, at the shape, at the color, or at the larger or smaller proportion of it. How few of us understand that in any case we have fully our money's worth. I had prayed for arithmetic and history and the companionship of my equals, and I had found opportunity for unlimited culture and a company of advanced thinkers, large-hearted, pure-minded, religious and cosmpolitan. * * * Work had its own zest; study adorned all that lay below it; intimate friendships filled all the spaces between. If the loaf were too large, of necessity I could not appropriate the whole. I did indeed seem to be receiving my own with compound interest. * * * Democracy and the highest mutual and spiritual culture were evidently the animating ideas at Brook Farm. Had the world denied you opportunities for culture, here your souls should be attended to at once. Did you desire chirography or Sanscrit--it was all one. Hence in the course of time there were classes in German, French and European history, in Italian, Greek and mathematics. Two Hibernian sisters were learning to write."

Though not many were blessed with the talent of the above writer (Mrs. Georgiana Bruce Kirby, who has written a very interesting book, "Years of Experience") the place was an El Dorado to many who had only their own hands to help them to an education.

My brother was an enthusiastic member of the association from 1842 to the end, and an indefatigable worker in season and out of season, feeling amply repaid by the cause for which he was laboring and the people among whom he labored. I remember seeing in a letter written to him a year or two after he left Brook Farm by one who was a co-laborer with him there, "I hear from you no longer; have you gone over entirely to those miserable civilizees, and forgotten the glorious freedom of Brook Farm?"

I was a pupil there in the summer of 1843. At first all who were members or pupils were expected to work a certain number of hours in the day; but as funds were very much needed and there seemed no other way to raise them, pupils were taken as at other schools, for pecuniary compensation. George Ripley was teacher for intellectual and moral philosophy and mathematics; and his accomplished wife--who, I think, was said at that time to be the most learned woman in Boston, than which no greater praise could be given in America--was teacher in history and modern languages; George P. Bradford took the department of belles lettres, Charles A. Dana had classes in Greek and German; John S. Dwight in Latin and music, and lesser lights in other branches. Many were glad to avail themselves of opportunities thus afforded on any terms. Probably purer people as to moral status or as many highly intellectual people were never assembled in one company. But, though all worked, it was the workers who did the work, there as elsewhere; while the theorizers theorized beautifully and gave a charm to the common life. I would not imply that any one of the members shirked unpleasant labor. The elegant Mrs. Ripley is said to have worked ten hours a day in the laundry at times; but what I would imply is that a skilled laundress might have done the same work in six hours, perhaps better. "She worked in the laundry until the necessity of economizing strength compelled her to resort to lighter labor in which her natural elegance and refinement of judgment were required." Mr. Ripley never shrank from the most menial work about the barn. "He liked to milk cows, saying such an occupation was eminently favorable to contemplation, particularly when the cow's tail was looped up behind." I recall the figure of John S. Dwight as I used to see him in his tunic (the regulation garment of the masculine members of the association), moving among us in the most quiet and unostentatious manner, not at all as if he knew himself the bright musical light of the time, as he was. Some one says, "This winter brought us a cordial sympathizer and earnest laborer, John S. Dwight, and with him all sorts of talk about the meaning and use of music and much delicate improvisation. Soon there was a class of little ones crowding around the gentle, genial master, singing from the first Boston School Singing Book (has there been so sweet a collection since?) and later a larger class who attacked the glees in 'Kingsley's Choir,' and presented Mozart's seventh and twelfth masses. How modestly he speaks of the mass clubs which sprang up about that time, not only at Brook Farm but in Boston and of the writing and lecturing on the great masters, as if he himself had not been the sole instigator and unwearied worker, assisted, no doubt, measurably, by the articles of Miss Fuller. First it was necessary to create a larger want for something better than the Swiss Bell Ringers and mangled psalmody; then he set himself to work to cause to be assembled the talent that would supply, while it increased the demand. It will never be known by what studied and persistent manipulation a sufficiently large public was brought to believe that Beethoven's symphonies and Mozart's masses were divine creations, and as such their performance should be called for by all lovers of fine music." George William Curtis and his 'English Oxford brother,' Burrill, were notable residents at that time. Mr. George Curtis showed then the material that was in him, and gave promise of the power he was to wield in later years and the stand he was to take for humanity. But the elder brother Burrill had a look as if he were above earth. In one of the magazines of a few years ago I saw an article in which it was stated that an artist in Europe had requested him to sit for a head of Christ. His name was not given, but I felt sure from personal recollection of the circumstances that the person spoken of was the 'Oxford' brother of G. W. Curtis. Charles Dana of the New York Sun was one of the active and enthusiastic members. There were several houses; the Hive, where we took our meals, and where all work pertaining to the culinary department was carried on; Pilgrim Hall was another building, sometimes called the Morton House, built by the father of Mrs. Diaz, who was Abby Morton when at Brook Farm. But the most beautiful for situation was the Eyrie, built on high land and overlooking the Charles River. I was so fortunate as to have a room there, and in the same house were Mr. and Mrs. Ripley, also George W. and Burrill Curtis. But the idyllic phase of Brook Farm was nearly ended. Thus far there had been no organization. The name was an afterthought. The constitution was not written till the experiment was several months old. The principle of freedom from all restraints but those of reason and conscience made the managers jealous even of apparent control. The policy of non-intervention was carried as far as it could be without incurring the risk of Anarchy. This was not unfitly called the "Transcendental period." As early as 1843 the wisdom of making changes in the direction of scientific arrangement was agitated; in the first months of 1844 the reformation was seriously begun. There was an enthusiastic meeting held at Boston in behalf of Fourierism. Brook Farm was represented, and Mr. Ripley made an earnest speech. Albert Brisbane was the most prominent person associated with Fourier in this country. He was a powerful instrument in the conversion of Brook Farm. He came there often; at first for a few days only, but afterward residing several months. "He was a man of ability and enthusiasm, an intellectual visionary. In the mere name 'phalanx' he seemed to hear trumpets of the angels. * * * In April, 1844, a convention of associationists was held at New York. * * * Burning words fell as if from inspired lips; Channing, Dana, Greely, Godwin, each in characteristic style and all with deep sincerity, poured out their souls." In March, 1845, the Brook Farm "phalanx" was incorporated by the Legislature of Massachusetts. "The change to Fourierism made essential changes; a different people, more practical and prosaic, came hither. It frightened away idealists whose presence had given to the spot its chief attraction and injured the pastoral bloom which beautified it." The building of the Phalanstery, that all might be under one roof, which required all their available funds or more, was the next thing in order. This was much disapproved of at the time by people who sympathized in their aims but thought the method impracticable. When nearly finished the building took fire. This was on the night of March 3, 1846. In the unfinished state of the building, and with the water facilities at hand, it was impossible to save it, and with its downfall burst the beautiful bubble for which they had labored so earnestly, and from which they hoped such high fruition.

"The sternness of the waking does not destroy the beauty of the dream. Brook Farm was an idyl, and in the days of epics the idyl is easily forgotten."

*Annie M. Salisbury, <u>Brook</u> <u>Farm</u> ([Marlboro, Mass.: F. B. Estabrook, 1898]); reprinted, with slight changes, from "The Real Brook Farm," <u>Boston</u> <u>Evening</u> <u>Transcript</u>, 27 October, 3 November 1894, pp. 13, 13.

1. The reference is to Peabody's "Plan of the West Roxbury Community" in the January 1842 <u>Dial</u>, which is printed above.

A SURVIVOR OF "BROOK FARM"*

M. Betham-Edwards

That fact should be more romantic than fiction in the case of a work like Hawthorne's famous story may sound paradoxical. Yet anyone who has heard the narrative of Brook Farm from the lips of a survivor, that survivor an Anna Blackwell, must so put the case. In the new suburban district of Hastings, lying to the east, and called Clive Vale, lives a remarkable woman, one of several remarkable sisters; the name of Dr. Elizabeth Blackwell, the first Englishwoman to receive the degree of M.D., is now of European reputation; a second sister, Dr. Emily, is one of the leading physicians of New York; Miss Blackwell, their elder, the subject of the present paper, has worked in quite other fields. With her long and most successful career as Parisian Correspondent of leading colonial papers, with her works as poet, writer of fairy-tales, and essays on occult subjects, we are not concerned. For the moment it is the story, the true story, of Brook Farm with which we are privileged. Everyone presumably has read Hawthorne's entrancing story--everyone, by the way, but Miss Blackwell! Why, indeed, should she turn to pages which but faintly echo vivid memories of the past? Presumably, also, everyone knows that Brook Farm was an experiment based on Fourier's celebrated work; in other words, a Phalanstery, or associated home, no labour being paid for, all conventional distinctions being done away with, the Golden Age being brought about by rich and poor, ignorant and instructed sharing the "brown bread" of life.

Miss Blackwell, it is not necessary to say, is a lady of advanced age; but age is relative, and the bright eyes, the clear voice, the alert memory make it difficult to believe that she is telling us of 1842.

"Yes, it was in 1842 that I spent some weeks at Brook Farm, a period I look back to as the happiest of my life," she began, her handsome face brightening as she went on. "We were about a hundred, and all had brought to the scheme the most desperate devotion. Some of our number were rich, some poor, the former keeping up the place, the latter earning their livelihood; none paid for board and lodging and all performed a certain amount of manual labour. We were, too, of all ages and conditions--the young, the old, the married, the single. Hawthorne often visited the place, but never resided there. Foremost of our Phalansterian family were Mr. Charles Dana and Mr. Ripley, scholar and preacher, both eminent men and both accompanied by their wives. Mr. Dana used to get up at five o'clock and milk the cows; Mrs. Ripley superintended the laundry, all domestic and industrial work being, of course, accomplished on the premises. We had among us an amateur shoemaker, also a carpenter, baker, &c., every branch of labour being shared by both sexes. It was a principle of Fourier that, in so far as was practicable, men and women should work together. The daily programme was arranged according to Fourier's group system, each member choosing the groups that best suited him. I worked in no less than eleven, but could not get into the favourite one, that of the washing-up. So popular was the washing-up of plates and dishes that newcomers had to wait long for a chance of admittance to the office. All the prettiest girls were in this group, and, of course, there was a great struggle among the men to enter the ranks. The work was all got through in the highest spirits; talk, laughter, story-telling accompanied every task. A good deal of flirtation went on, and during its brief existence many marriages were made at Brook Farm. Nothing more delighted the rest than any sign of love-making! I must now tell you of my own 'groups.' One of these was the lamp-cleaning and dressing department. We had seventy-two lamps, and each process had its group. Thus one set of workers collected the lamps, another cleaned them, a third--myself among the number--trimmed the wicks, a fourth filled the receptacles with oil, and so on. I also belonged to the 'baby group,' being fond of babies. One hour daily I attended to the infant Phalansterians. Then I belonged to the 'waiter group.' We had no paid servants, and, after being waited on at table ourselves, we waited on others. This was an amusing and lively service.

"All arrangements were on a scale of primitive simplicity, our food consisting chiefly of breadstuffs, dairy produce, fruit, and vegetables. The evenings were given up to recreation, lectures, dancing, music, and so on. One of our number, Mr. Dwight, was an accomplished musician. We all put on our best clothes when work was done; and now I must tell the history of the Brook Farm bonnet. The ladies had only one bonnet between them, and when any of us wanted to catch the Boston stagecoach, each by turns utilised the bonnet. Ah, it was a happy, happy time!" And then the narrator paused and sighed.

"And why did Brook Farm come to such a speedy end?" I asked.

"My own connection with it ended in this way. At the time of my stay I had under my care a younger sister, and, as there was no room for her, I felt compelled to leave on my charge's account. But the failure of the experiment was a sheer matter of money. Want of funds brought about the ultimate fiasco. Brook Farm, as I knew it in 1842, consisted of half-a-dozen old houses in the country lying near together. This arrangement was naturally very inconvenient, especially in winter. After some time, money was collected for building, and new, commodious premises were begun. When near completion, the place caught fire; some of us suspected the work of an incendiary and the promptings of theological intolerance. It had not been insured, and, no further money forthcoming, the scheme fell through. But it was a sad pity!"

A sad pity, indeed! Brook Farm the dream, however, will keep alive memory of Brook Farm the reality. What, perhaps, the combined millionaires of the New World could not effect has been achieved by a quill and a ream of paper. Zenobia of the crimson flower and meek little Priscilla are among the immortals of fiction.

---

*M. Betham-Edwards, "A Survivor of 'Brook Farm,'" The Sketch [England], 23 (24 August 1898): 210.

THE BROOK FARM ASSOCIATION*

John T. Codman

Very few persons can tell why the ideas and doings of a small gathering of friendly persons, who joined themselves together under the name of the Brook Farm Association for Education and Industry, should have such a tenacity of interest as to be preserved and read with unwavering interest after the long distance of time that has intervened since that event took place in West Roxbury, near Boston, the spring of the year 1841. But as time goes by the marked individuality of the character of many of its members, the truth and purity of their motives, their wide departure from the established ways of living, together with their intellectual ability and social standing, continue to attract the attention of thoughtful and religious persons, while their relation to the great cause of universal social reform and the fine suggestiveness of their way of life interest also the lovers of justice and progress; and the curious are not wanting who speculate on what might be the result of the universal application of the princples they there advocated and the life they there tried to lead.

Rev. George Ripley, a Unitarian preacher, settled over a parish in Boston, Mass., a graduate of Harvard College, a deep student of literature and religious philosophy, well acquainted with the newest and best thoughts of the European writers, German, French, and English, and with many of those brilliant souls who were and are still influencing and molding the minds and ideas of the inhabitants of the young American Republic, is solely responsible for the Brook Farm movement, and no one has ever disputed the oneness and purity of his motives in its formation,--the good of humanity. No cheap ambition, no desire for notoriety, no scheme of profit was ever charged to him, for he had earned and secured intellectual and social position, and he had financial means enough, with New England economy, to live an easy life, and he and his wife were surrounded by hosts of admiring friends.

Over the households, particularly of New England, had reigned the Calvinistic ideas of religion. Never, perhaps, had they been so firmly anchored elsewhere, never so persistently practiced. The God of vengeance sat on his mighty throne. In the fall of Adam every soul fell from God's grace. All men, women, and little children were depraved. All must repent, even of what they never intended to do, and what they never had done, else their soul-bodies would be plunged into a lake of fire and burning brimstone, there to be in torment never ceasing. But a strong reaction began to take place from these ideas. It seemed the very horror of them was not consistent with the goodness of the Creator and with the idea of an all-wise and loving Father. The old school of theology neither presented logic or wisdom in man's creation, nor love in man's soul torment.

The typical preacher of the new theology was William Ellery Channing. The logic of his doctrine was that the human soul was inherently good, but the atmosphere in which it lived was bad, and that we should reform it,--that we should abolish the national sin of African slavery, be temperate and honest and practice the Christian virtues, and that the highest virtue of all time was to lead every day a just life. But Mr. Ripley had preached and taught these things for a dozen years with all the sincerity of his heart, yet his congregation to the great reality of such a life seemed to be indifferent. Outside of his church was gathered together a coterie of friends, scholars, writers, philosophers, philanthropists, and men of ideas. They had either thrown overboard the crude theology of the past or they doubted its logic. They called their gathering "The Symposium," but they were nicknamed "The Transcendental Club" and called "Transcendentalists." What this name meant was a mystery to many and is so now. Mr. Ripley defined it thus:

> There is a class of persons who desire a reform in the prevailing philosophy of the day. These are called Transcendentalists, because they believe in an order of truth that transcends the sphere of the external senses. Their leading idea is the supremacy of mind over matter. Hence they maintain that the truth of religion does not depend

on tradition or historical facts, but has an unswerving witness in the soul. There is a light, they believe, which enlighteneth every man who cometh into the world. There is a faculty in all-- the most degraded, the most ignorant, the most obscure--to perceive spiritual truth when distinctly presented; and the ultimate appeal on all moral questions is not to a jury of scholars, a hierarchy of divines, or the prescriptions of a creed, but to the common sense of the human race.

There is another class of persons who are devoted to the removal of the abuses that prevail in modern society. They witness the oppressions done under the sun and they cannot keep silence. They have faith that God governs man; they believe in a better future than the past; their daily prayer is for the coming of the kingdom of righteousness, truth, and love; they look forward to a more pure, more lovely, more divine state of society than was ever realized on earth. With these views I rejoice to say I strongly sympathize.

One is almost amazed at the amount of brilliant talent existing and developed in this Symposium. It had the cream of New England's ability, and although its membership did not contain either Holmes, Longfellow, or Whittier, it had, besides Mr. Ripley, the Channings, William Ellery, William Henry, and Walter, Emerson, Lowell, Cranch, Story, John S. Dwight, Hawthorne, Theodore Parker, Bancroft, Bronson Alcott, O. A. Brownson, and others, and for ladies Margaret Fuller, the Peabody sisters--Elizabeth and Sophia,--Miss and Mrs. Ripley. Theological and social questions were uppermost in discussion. Mr. Ripley believed that the condition of the surroundings of our people thus described by Channing should be changed: "Of modern civilization the natural fruits are contempt for others' rights, fraud, oppression, a gambling spirit in trade, reckless adventure and commercial convulsions, all tending to impoverish the laborer and to render every condition insecure. Relief is to come and can come only from the new application of Christian principles, of universal justice and universal love, to social institutions, to commerce, to business, to active life." Some one should set the example of a radical departure from present modes of daily life! If no one else would do it, Mr. Ripley would. He would begin it in a humble way, if he could find a few friends to follow him. Who would go? His friend Rev. John S. Dwight, of Northampton, son of Dr. John Dwight, physician, of Boston, was one, and Samuel D. Robbins thought he would go, but no one else in all that brilliant assembly of souls, howsoever much they wisely theorized, did actually promise to do so. Yes, there was that quiet, modest young writer, just coming into note, friend of the Peabody sister, especially of Sophia, Nathaniel Hawthorne, but the end proved that his connection with the party was more of a poetic fancy on his part than a conviction of the moral grandeur of Mr. Ripley's movement. Brave Minot Pratt, who represented the hard-working side of the scheme, being foreman printer in the office of the Christian Register, a liberal newspaper of Boston, deserved the credit of being the first "workingman" to volunteer to come into the circle of the adventurers.

Contrary to what is often supposed, Mr. Ripley had no great scheme in his mind, no thought that he was going to reform the whole world, neither did he expect to build up a great human institution or a large socialist colony. The now popular word "socialism" was then hardly in use. After preliminary preparations had been made, he left his pastorate and Boston with his wife and sister, and a small party of friends, about fourteen in all, on the 29th of March, 1841, to occupy Brook Farm in West Roxbury, nine miles from the city hall in Boston. He had always insisted on a Christian life as the only test of a Christian faith, now he meant to put in practice the lessons of his own pulpit, says his biographer. There were two hundred acres in the property, one hundred and seventy in the homestead lot, on which there was a solitary farm-house of two stories in height, pleasantly overlooking the domain with its meadow and the small brook that gave the name to the place. A school for the instruction of the young was immediately started. The combination of manual and intellectual labors was a permanent theory, and here was a chance to exemplify it. The capacity and standing of the teachers secured to it pupils from first to last, a number of whom have since then occupied prominent places in life, the most noted example being the late George William Curtis. There was no farmer among the first settlers, and a Mr. Allen was hired as leader in that department until after the first season, when Mr. Pratt succeeded him. The policy of the Association was not fixed as to its enlargement, and in their condition they allowed parties to build two new houses on the domain for their private use, the Cottage and the Pilgrim House. The old farm-house they called the Hive, and enlarged its capacity. On a prominent point of the farm the Association built a little square house, the Eyrie, with suitable parlor to entertain the numerous guests and inquirers who began to shower down upon it in large numbers.

The regulations of the Brook Farm Association were fixed by a constitution and by-laws, and were of a simple character.

No one should interfere with his associates' religious convictions. The principles of right and justice, believed to be known to all, should be the motives to govern its life. Domestic servitude should be done away with. The day's work should be not more than ten hours long. The meeting for business or pleasure should terminate at 10 p.m. One dollar for a day's work should be paid to each worker. If there were more than that amount earned, it should be divided among them at the end of each year. Individual rights should be respected. Every one's goods and little belongings were their own and not to be interfered with. The farm and collective property was represented by stock paying ordinary interest. There was no common property but what was earned.

All the members of the Association, and the pupils of the school as well, were expected to employ themselves some time each day with manual labor. All dined together in a common dining-room at the Hive. Everything there was very plain, but neat and clean. No one wanted to disobey the common rules of personal neatness expected of them. The farmer left frock and soiled apparel in a dressing-room, and put on a belted tunic, adopted as a convenient, easy, and comfortable dress, before going in to meals. The bugle call notified him half an hour before dinner to leave his work, which might be in distant fields.

The result which is found to be similar in all such experiments took place. Conditions for a dozen persons had to be expanded to those suitable for a hundred or more who were new to the life and its duties. The social life began to be charming, but the cash receipts, with a generous treatment of open table to visitors, and the unaccustomed handling of farming implements, were not fully up to the income needed.

Mr. Ripley wrote of it a few months after its commencement: "We are now in full operation as a family of workers, teachers, and students. We feel the deepest convictions that, for us, our mode of life is the true one, and no attraction would tempt any one of us to exchange it for that we have quitted lately."

What turn affairs would have taken in the long run cannot be told, but future labors might have overcome the loss of a couple of thousand dollars or so that took place during the first two years, but a new problem came up that produced a change in basic ideas of the little community. A furor for socialistic life had been aroused in the country by the preaching and teaching of Albert Brisbane, Horace Greeley, Parke Godwin, William Henry Channing, and others, in the New York Tribune and elsewhere, who took for their ideal the system suggested by Charles Fourier, of Besancon, France, and nicknamed "Fourierism." A dozen and more unwise attempts soon sprang up in the northern States, and were weak, futile, poverty-stricken from the start, each differing from the others in some vagaries. One was founded on non-resistance, some on community of property, which idea was utterly at variance with Fourier's theories, and Bronson Alcott brought up the rear with an attempt to realize an ideal life by reading Plato and living on a fruit and vegetable diet. On one point Mr. Ripley agreed with them all, for the idea they all held in common was the brotherhood of humanity and the good of the human race. "It was but an idle dream to attempt to form a Phalanx with the men and means at hand," said Mr. John S. Dwight in speaking of its afterward. "It was a mere pretense, hoping that it would grow to something. The idea of most of us was that, beginning with what we felt to be a true system, with true relations to one another, it would probably grow into something larger, and by bringing in others we should finally succeed in reforming and elevating society and put it on a basis of universal co-operation." Mr. Ripley had become convinced that Fourier's ideas of industrial co-operation were in the main correct. They were his own religious ideas translated into daily life--a working plan for great moral and physical forces, the map and guide of the divine way to study and organize the social trend of human lives. With infinite courage and hope Mr. Ripley and his little band of workers pushed on. Revising its constitution and procuring a charter, it added new industries to the farm-work, such as shoe-making, sash and door-making, rule-making, the manufacture of Brittania ware, lamps, teapots, etc., and on the farm added the tree-nursery, greenhouse plants, and flower cultivation. But the most important work undertaken was the starting of the Harbinger, a weekly journal devoted to social and political progress. Mr. Ripley, Mr. Dwight, and Mr. Dana were its editors, Mr. Treadwell and Mr. Butterfield its printers. The ability of the editors attracted a large number of brilliant writers to it. Soon after this the Association, which numbered a hundred persons, found a positive need for more accommodations and better ones, and planned and commenced to build a large wooden building near the center of the farm for a unitary home, large enough to accommodate all the families then residing on the place. It was one hundred and seventy-five feet long, three stories high, with spacious attics, divided into pleasant and convenient rooms for single persons. The second and third stories were divided into fourteen houses, independent of each other, with a parlor and three sleeping-rooms in each, connected by piazzas which ran the whole length of the building on both stories. The basement contained a large and commodious kitchen, a dining-hall capable of seating from three to four hundred persons, two public saloons, and a spacious hall and lecture-room. Seven thousand dollars had been expended on this building, and three thousand more would have made it available for use. The insurance on it had run out only a few days before, and it was by the oversight of one of the directors that it had not been renewed. On the evening of March 3, 1846, it caught fire from some defect in stove or chimney and burned to the ground, it being a total loss to the Association.

Life, charm, sociability, novelty, enthusiasm, and work all reigned at Brook Farm. Hundreds and hundreds of outsiders and friends came to visit the place, among them many distinguished intellectual men and women, many artists and musicians, clergymen, theorists, cranks and oracles of various sorts, and their theories ran "from grave to gay, from sober to severe." Surely there is something in associated life that attracts curiosity, to say the least about it. Many of the visitors added a charm to it by giving specimens of their talents. Sometimes it was William Henry Channing who held a choice religious service in a noble grove of pine-trees not far from Hawthorne's "Eliot's Pulpit." Sometimes it was a full evening of song, flute, and piano, and sometimes classes or informal talks among the books in Mr. Ripley's library or in one of the parlors. It might be Curtis or Cranch, Channing or Margaret Fuller, or Emerson even, but he fought shy of the Association after the advent of "Fourierism" so called; but it will in my opinion take many Emersons to make one man who can approach the intellectual grandeur, the great outreach of mind, the intense love and reverence, the veneration and childlike trust in the Creator of the heavens and the earth that Fourier had.

True to their ideas, no Brook Farmer interfered with another's religious creed. The larger portion of them were radical to the prevailing orthodoxy, but there were Catholics, Swedenborgians, and Jews among the number, and those who wished went to hear Theodore Parker, not then become famous, at his church two miles away in the old village of West Roxbury, where he resided.

The industries started on the Farm were all fairly at a good average for profit, but they were demanding continual outlay to bring them upon a paying basis. The school paid, but it was not large enough, and the peculiar surroundings about it had kept down its numbers. Two or three years would seemingly have developed each of the industries into a fine business. They had no rich friend to stand by them at this time with a small amount of capital to tide them over the shoals. The plan of life seemed then to the public much more unreasonable than it does now. If the balances had been even, and there had been no increasing debt, they might have stood the loss of the "Phalanstery" by fire; they would have stood the poor fare and the uncomfortably crowded rooms, but hope of expansion was lost with the burnt building, and the break-away commenced, and although there was no "sauve qui peut," no haste in leaving, one after another found labor and homes elsewhere. The Association dissolved, and the world called it a failure.

But how shall I, who was only a young and humble participant in the work and ideas of this unique company's scheme of life, describe its results? If there was any one who suffered more than a temporary deprivation from his or her Brook Farm labors in the great moral attempt at the alleviation of the condition of the masses of our people and the cause of universal justice, I do not know who it was. If there has been any such case, there is set against it an almost universal remembrance of love and gratitude for the days spent there and to the kindly fate that led their lives into its social circle, and their feet over the green fields and sods trodden by the worthy souls led by the whole-hearted, God-trusting, truthful, high-minded George Ripley.

Years after the decline of the Association, amid the hates engendered by political strife and the pressing cares of business and devotion to pecuniary gain, Mr. Charles A. Dana wrote of his old home as follows:

It is not too much to say that every person who was at Brook Farm for any length of time has ever since looked back to it with a feeling of satisfaction. The healthy mixture of manual and intellectual labor, the kindly and unaffected social relations, the absence of everything like assumptions or servility, the amusements, the discussions, the friendships, the ideal and poetical atmosphere which gave a charm to life,-- all which the mind turns back with pleasure as to something distant and beautiful not elsewhere met with amid the routine of this world.

Many of the little band did not think the dissolution was an end to associative life. They believed that long before this time the world would have found out the beauty and use of the cooperative life and that the country would be dotted with little "Phalanxes," as we were pleased to call them. Some left the Farm with great gladness in their hearts, for they found there among the co-operators companions who made good husbands and wives, for there, in a few weeks or months, a better knowledge could be formed, a truer and more absolute and certain estimate of character, than by years of fashionable flirtation. The women were always well dressed; there were no party dresses, all shine, lace and glitter, and household wrappers all slouched, torn, and drabbled. The situation of all was to stimulate them to neatness in personal appearance, even if the material was of the cheapest kind.

Did the experiment shipwreck the members? No; I say, decidedly, no! Mr. Ripley had sacrificed all his means even to his personal library of choice books, but the world was large and his faith in the goodness of God and his greatest creation, man, was still triumphant. He and his wife went to Long Island and there taught school awhile, but gradually Mr. Ripley commenced writing for the press, and finally earned with his pen a competency. Mrs. Ripley, less hopeful than her husband, wavered in her liberal doctrines, and under the depression of failure joined herself to the forms of the Catholic Church. During a temporary illness of Mr. Ripley the Harbinger, which had been removed to New York, suspended publication. Mr. C. A. Dana continued the editorial work first commenced at Brook Farm, and became finally the editor of the New York Sun, reaping a large financial reward. Mr. John S. Dwight also went into editorial work, founding the Journal of Music, which lasted many years, and was finally absorbed into one of the trade journals. I single out these three men, because to them should be credited the fact of their remaining all through the experiment and of occupying the most prominent positions before the public in regard to it. But I should be especially derelict in my duty did I not remember Miss Marianne Ripley, Mr. Minot Pratt and wife, and many others, who by their fidelity to what are called "humbler duties" were towers of strength to the little association.

To the young persons on the farm it was all that Mr. Dana had said of it, and more. The atmosphere was of self-reliant freedom. The courteousness of the older to the younger was much appreciated; the mingling together of old and young in their amusements, dances, tableaux, etc., knitted them together with a grand family feeling, and as the pupils of the school were expected to join the residents in manual labor, it very largely prevented anything like a school clique on the place, and the lads and lassies were always ready to assist with their persons and purses any proposed social entertainment.

Sometimes the men assisted in doing what is called "women's work," in the hard labor of the domestic series. Mr. Ripley went into the cattle group every morning, and Mrs. Ripley at first did some heavy washing, for which the outside public expended on them a great deal of unnecessary sympathy. They were showing that they honored honest toil, that they were willing to do anything necessary,--all that they would ask any one else to do. Be assured that there were always those present who had so high an esteem for them they would not have allowed them to do hard labor unless it was their own personal wish. It was not imposed on them.

The work was done in this manner: Three or more persons made a group. Three or more groups of a kind made a series, as the farming series or the mechanical series. All the series were united under a general direction made of the heads of the series.

There was no community of property. All the ownership was represented by stock. Had the Association made progress in wealth, it would doubtless in time have absorbed the stock and reduced the private ownership of the general goods into general ownership. The greatest center of attraction of its social life was the meeting daily of all hands at a common table in the Hive.

Elsewhere, in my "Memoirs," I have given many interesting details of the daily life of the place which it would be out of place for me to repeat here.

Did the Brook Farmers find any satisfaction and truth in the life at their farm? Yes, say I. If not, I would not have known it. In the half-century that has passed since then, out of the many connected with it, I have never heard of any one of the number who has publicly or privately said the cause and the life were failures. They unanimously decided that it contained elements of truth that belonged to a higher development of life than the present state of civilization. "Civilization," says a profound writer, "develops the elements which enable man to obtain his destiny and happiness, but it is neither his destiny nor does it secure him happiness."

Referring to Brook Farm in "The Blithedale Romance," Hawthorne said it forty-seven years ago: "More and more I feel that we had struck upon what ought to be a truth. Posterity may dig it up, and profit by it." That is my opinion, and it is also my opinion that posterity is here now and ready to revive the work of the early co-operators.

Mr. Ripley at the time of its operation wrote: "The work we are engaged in is not destruction, but true conservatism. It is not a mere revolution, but as we are assured, a necessary step in the course of social progress, which no one can be blind enough to think has yet reached its limit."

---

*John T. Codman, "The Brook Farm Association," Coming Age, 2 (July 1899): 33-38. The reference to Codman's book is to his Brook Farm: Historic and Personal Memoirs (Boston: Arena, 1894).

A GIRL OF SIXTEEN AT BROOK FARM*

Ora Gannett Sedgwick

Of all the memorable company whom I found seated at the tea table when I arrived at Brook Farm, a few weeks after its opening, not one is now alive. I myself, sole survivor of the men and women who occupied that first table in the Parlor of the Hive, have already passed nearly a lustrum beyond the allotted term of life.

I realize, therefore, that if I am to comply with the repeated requests of many friends, and record my recollections of the earliest days of what, with Hawthorne, I may call "my old and affectionately remembered home," I must not longer defer the task. I esteem it both a duty and a privilege not only to correct some inaccuracies and supply some omissions in the accounts of those less familiar than myself with the inner life of those early days, but also to express my gratitude to my friends and teachers at Brook Farm for the noble, sweet simplicity of the life there, which has been to me one of the most precious influences of the past threescore years.

The idea of Brook Farm originated with Rev. George Ripley, settled over Purchase Street Church in Boston, and his wife, Sophia Dana Ripley, a niece of Richard H. Dana, the poet and scholar. Mr. and Mrs. Ripley had boarded for several summers at the Ellis Farm in West Roxbury, and were convinced that it was the ideal spot for their enterprise. They invited all interested in their scheme to meet at their pleasant home in Boston one evening a week, through the winter of 1840-41, to discuss the matter and form definite plans. These meetings called together such "cultivated and philosophic minds" as Margaret Fuller, Theodore Parker, William Henry Channing, John S. Dwight, David Mack, and others of similar character and culture. The proposed association became the current topic of conversation in Boston and the neighboring towns. Some laughed at it, of course, but some were as much frightened as men and women have been since by the talk of the anarchists.

I was then a girl of nearly sixteen, living in a college town. My mother, a woman of rare discernment, wishing to send me away to a good school, and knowing that teaching as well as farming was included in the scheme, attended the meetings at the Ripleys' house, not without some opposition and ridicule from her Philistine friends.

Before her marriage, Mrs. Ripley, then Miss Dana, had been a most successful teacher in Cambridge. She was a woman of elegant manner and perfect self-control, qualities which insured her a remarkable degree of influence over her pupils. My mother felt that she could intrust my intellectual and moral training to her with the greatest confidence; but my father was a clergyman, with a large family and the usual small income of his profession, and there was some hesitation. On learning, however, that I could work four hours a day for my board, leaving only my tuition to be paid for in money, my parents decided to send me.

One pleasant afternoon in June, 1841, my father drove over to West Roxbury with me in the family chaise, with my trunk securely strapped beneath, and left me at the Nest. This was a small house occupied by Miss Ripley, a sister of George Ripley, and a few young boys brought with her from her school in Boston, among them two sons of George Bancroft. In the care of these children and of the house I was to assist her. We all took our meals at the Hive, and in the autumn went there to live.

The Hive was the Ellis farmhouse, one of the lovely old New England houses with a broad hall running through the whole length, and having a door at each end. From the left side of his hall, as you entered, a staircase went straight up to the second floor. The walls of the hall were lined with open bookshelves filled with rare English, French, and German books, belonging to Mr. Ripley, who had, I imagine, one of the finest libraries in Boston at that time, especially in foreign works. After the Eyrie was built the Hive became merely the working headquarters, and this library was removed to the new building; but the books were always free to all, a fact which showed the real generosity of Mr. Ripley.

There was a comfortable sofa in the hall, under the stairs, on which Nathaniel Hawthorne, who then occupied the front room at the right, used to sit for hours at a time, with a book in his hand, not turning a leaf, but listening with sharp ears to the young people's talk, which he seemed to enjoy immensely, perhaps with the satisfaction of Burns's "Chiel amang ye takin' notes." It is, however, but just to Mr. Hawthorne to say that, whatever use he made in The Blithedale Romance of the scenery and "romantic atmosphere" of Brook Farm, he cannot be accused of violating the sanctities of the home and holding up to public observation exaggerated likenesses of his associates there. I spent some delightful hours with him the winter he died, and he assured me that Zenobia represented no one person there.

The company on which my eyes fell, when I arrived at the farm, included Mr. and Mrs. Ripley; George P. Bradford, kinsman and friend of Emerson; John S. Dwight, musician and scholar, founder and editor of the Journal of Music; Nathaniel Hawthorne, then a young man, not yet married, but engaged; Rev. Mr. Burton, a Unitarian clergyman; Miss Sarah Stearns, niece of Mr. Ripley, a young woman of much culture and charm; the family from the Nest; and a pupil of about my own age, tall, fair-haired, and beautiful to look upon, Ellen Slade, mentioned by name in Hawthorne's American Note-books, and the original Diana of that book and The Blithedale Romance, with whom I was proud to be associated.

There soon came others to our little company: Miss Georgiana Bruce, one of the most interesting persons at the farm, the writer of Years of Experience; Minot Pratt, who brought with him his wife and two little sons, one of whom afterwards married Annie Alcott, the Meg of Little Women. The Pratts were admirable people, and became very useful members of the association. Mr. Pratt, a printer, wanted, I imagine, more liberty to labor as he chose, and to find time for reading and study, and took an important part in the farmwork. Mrs. Pratt I remember as a most kind and motherly woman.

Charles A. Dana, the late editor of the New York Sun, then a handsome collegian, came over from Cambridge and passed a day or two in the course of the summer, and later took up his abode with us.

Theodore Parker's farmer, William Allen, had been deeply interested in the idea of the association, and soon came to take charge of the farm. This new farmer, William, was a sturdy young fellow from Westmoreland, Vermont. He married just before coming to us, and brought his pretty wife, Sylvia. These four were, I think, among our most efficient workers. The education of their hands had not been neglected, and these were well trained by good heads. It was such as they, perhaps, who kept the daily machinery running smoothly.

William, as I remember him, must have been a man of power in his way, as he was the head farmer, and the four or five men who fitted boys for college (I fancy this was the surest source of income to the association) must have been directed by him and his brother in all the work of the farm. I remember well that George P. Bradford and Mr. Hawthorne had the care and milking of the cows, but not to the exclusion of other less Arcadian labors, as is evident from the American Note-Books. Mr. Hawthorne seems to have had a rather tender feeling for his charges, expressing forcibly in The Blithedale Romance, chapter xxiv., his indignation at their "cold reception" of him on his return from an absence of several weeks. I recall distinctly the names of two cows, Daisy and Dolly, from the fact that Messrs. Hawthorne and Bradford were particular always to assign to these cows adjoining stalls in the barn at night, because they were always together in the pasture. I recollect also Mr. Bradford's often begging me to stop at the gate through which the long line of cows came at evening, and watch the varying and interesting expressions on their faces.

The pigs too came in for their share of Mr. Hawthorne's care. When, in the following winter, the Brook Farmers, as a delicate attention, sent a sparerib to Mrs. George S. Hillard, with whom he was then staying in Boston, he raised his hands in horror, and exclaimed, "I should as soon think of a sculptor's eating a piece of one of his own statues!"

Besides those whom I have mentioned others joined us, with well-trained hands, but not of such good New England blood. I recall among them two Irishwomen, one of whom, a fine cook, had lived with the Danas and others of the best families of Boston. This woman came to Brook Farm for the sake of her beautiful young daughter, an only child, who looked like a Madonna and possessed much native delicacy. Her mother was desirous that she should be well educated. These women were perfectly welcome to sit at the table with us all, but they preferred not to sit down until the two courses had been put upon the table, if at all.

As I remember our meals, they were most delightful times for talk, humor, wit, and the interchange of pleasant nonsense. When our one table had grown into three, Charles A. Dana, who must have been a very orderly young man, organized a corps of waiters from among our nicest young people, whose meals were kept hot for them, and they in their turn were waited on by those whom they had served. I have seen Mr. Dana reading a small Greek book between the courses, though he was a faithful waiter. The table talk was most delightful and profitable to me. Looking back over a long and varied life, I think that I have rarely sat down with so many men and women of culture, so thoroughly unselfish, polite, and kind to one another, as I found at those plain but attractive tables. All seemed at rest and at their best. There was no man, tired with the stock market and his efforts to make or to increase a big fortune, coming home harassed or depressed, too cross or disappointed to talk. There was no woman vying with others in French gowns, lace, and diamonds. The fact that all felt they were honored for themselves alone brought out more individuality in each, so that I have often said that I have never elsewhere seen a set of people of whom each seemed to possess some peculiar charm.

I do not recollect Hawthorne's talking much at the table. Indeed, he was a very taciturn man. One day, tired of seeing him sitting immovable on the sofa in the hall, as I was learning some verses to recite at the evening class for recitation formed by Charles A. Dana, I daringly took my book, pushed it into his hands, and said, "Will you hear my poetry, Mr. Hawthorne?" He gave me a sidelong glance from his very shy eyes, took the book, and most kindly heard me. After that he was on the sofa every week to hear me recite.

One evening he was alone in the hall, sitting on a chair at the farther end, when my roommate, Ellen Slade, and myself were going upstairs. She whispered to me, "Let's throw the sofa pillows at Mr. Hawthorne." Reaching over the banisters, we each took a cushion and threw it. Quick as a flash he put out his hand, seized a broom that was hanging near him, warded off our cushions, and threw them back with sure aim. As fast as we could throw them at him he returned them with effect, hitting us every time, while we could hit only the broom. He must have been very quick in his movements. Through it all not a word was spoken. We laughed, and his eyes shone and twinkled like stars. Wonderful eyes they were, and when anything witty was said I always looked quickly at Mr. Hawthorne; for his dark eyes lighted up as if flames were suddenly kindled behind them, and then the smile came down to his lips and over his grave face.

My memories of Mr. Hawthorne are among the pleasantest of my Brook Farm recollections. His manners to children were charming and kind. I saw him one day walking, as was his custom, with his hands behind his back; head bent forward, the two little Bancrofts and other children following him with pleased faces, and stooping every now and then with broad smiles, after which they would rise and run on again behind him. Puzzled at these manoeuvres, I watched closely, and found that although he hardly moved a muscle except to walk, from time to time he dropped a penny, for which the children scrambled.

Among our regular visitors in that first year were: Emerson, who came occasionally to spend a day; Margaret Fuller, who passed weeks at a time with us; and Theodore Parker, who was a frequent caller. The last, a warm personal friend of Mr. Ripley, lived within walking distance, and we were often amused at the ceremonies of his leave-taking. When he took his departure, after spending two or three hours in close conversation with Mr. Ripley, the latter always started to accompany him part of the way; at the end of a mile or so, when Mr. Ripley turned back, Mr. Parker, in his turn, became escort, Mr. Ripley resuming the role when Brook Farm was reached. In this way, the two men, always absorbed in conversation, walked back and forth, until sometimes another couple of hours were added to the solid talk.

Wendell Phillips came once, but I was away and did not see him. On my return I was flattered to hear that he had asked for me; but my pride had a fall when I learned that he had supposed the "Ora" of whom he had heard so much to be a favorite cat.

All sorts and conditions of men were kindly received at Brook Farm, and of course many peculiar persons came to claim our hospitality. I remember well the man mentioned by Mr. Codman, in his book on Brook Farm, who, when Mr. Ripley offered to show him to his room for the night, declined, averring that he never slept, and would sit up all night in the parlor, which he was allowed to do.

As our family soon grew too large for the Hive, two other houses were built while I was there. One, perched on a hill not far from the Hive, and built upon the rock, was named the Eyrie. In this was a good-sized room for our musical evenings and dancing; also a library, to which, on its completion, the books were removed from the hall in the Hive. At the Eyrie Mr. and Mrs. Ripley had their rooms; also my sister, who came a year after me, and myself, with several other young people; but we continued to go to the Hive for our meals and recitations. That the Eyrie was built on a Scriptural foundation I know, from having once seen the elegant Burrill Curtis, brother of George William Curtis, filling the oil lamps of the house on the cellar floor of solid rock.

Mr. and Mrs. Minot Pratt took charge of the Hive, and there all the cooking and washing were done. Mr. Bradford continued to keep his room there until he left, I believe.

One of the houses was a cottage built in the form of a cross, by a cousin of Mrs. Wendell Phillips, a wealthy lady, who lived in it herself [Mrs. A. G. Alvord]. Charles A. Dana and other young people also had rooms there.

Later, Ichabod and Edwin Morton, of Plymouth, Mass., who came to Brook Farm after I left, built a large home after Fourier's plan, with a common kitchen, dining room, and laundry on the lower floor, and separate rooms above. This was called the Phalanstery. I think it was the outcome of a pet plan of Mr. Ripley's. The inmates might either eat at the common table, or, by paying a certain sum, might have their meals sent to their apartments. This would clearly indicate that Brook Farm was not a community, as so often miscalled, but an association, where the members could more easily live out the aims for which it was founded.

Possibly the whole settlement might in time have grown to be a sort of co-operative village, but unfortunately the Phalanstery was burned to the ground, in March, 1846, before it was quite finished. The financial loss was heavy, and I know that the destruction of the Phalanstery was a great blow to the association in many ways.

Perhaps my recollections of Brook Farm are tinted by the rose-colored optimism of sixteen, but as I have grown old, and, looking back to the general standard of half a century ago, have compared the lives led at Brook Farm with the most useful ones of these days, I am more and more convinced that my estimates were true, that there was very much "sweetness and light" there,--a light too bright for most people at that time to bear.

With the progress of time, as higher moral and scientific developments have improved the internal as well as the external vision, the world is coming to see that living for others is true living. Certainly, most of the persons whom I knew at Brook Farm lived on a higher plane than their contemporaries, recognizing, as they did, others' needs as of equal moment with their own. I can recall so many unselfish, loving, gentle-mannered people that I am sure that if others of a different stamp did come, they could not have lived contentedly there, but must have slid out. Thank God, there were always enough of the old stock left to keep the spirit of the place as it had been at first. Among the boarders, too, were some who entered into that spirit, and though not sharing the labors, yet added greatly to the pleasures of the association. Among these I remember particularly Mr. Charles Newcomb, of Providence.

One may easily imagine the influence such a man as George P. Bradford had on the people assembled at Brook Farm. He knew the woods and fields well,--indeed, all outdoor things: the flora, especially, which as my memory recalls it, was very rich; astronomy, too. Many, many nights he showed us the constellations, quietly talking of all this beauty in a way that inspired love and reverence in us.

He loved the beautiful pine wood that we called the Cathedral, using is as a magnificent hall, for our amusements. Hawthorne tells in one of his Note-Books of the masquerade we had there, where more beautiful people met, I think, than usually falls to one's lot to see in a lifetime.

The brook he loved, I fancy, as much as I did, as it ran in front of the Hive, through the large green meadow; talking sometimes in a serious undertone, sadly, as if finding fault with me, and sometimes so gay and frolicking that even now, after more than half a century, it comes to me as a voice either blaming or making me joyous.

The dearest friend I have ever had since I left Brook Farm often used to stop beside some singing brook, as we were driving through the country, and ask me: "How about this brook? Isn't its voice as sweet as the one at Brook Farm?" But only once did I ever hear one that even approached to the sweetness of Brook Farm's brook, and I believe firmly that the memory of its voice has helped many of those who were happy enough to have heard it to bear their successes and failures with gratitude, sweetness, and strength. I have often wondered if such a place, so pure, refined, and entirely democratic, could have been started nearly "sixty years since" in any other place than the United States, and in Boston or its vicinity.

The boys studying there did not fight, as at other schools, for they were treated courteously, and had fewer rules. My tender conscience, however, has kept alive the memory of my connivance in one violation of a rule. One of my morning duties was to dust and adorn the parlor in the Hive, after it had been swept. Mrs. Ripley had made a strict rule that none of the boys who used that room for morning study should enter it before I had finished my task. Early one morning, on entering the room, dust-cloth in hand, I was surprised to see there three boys on three different sides of the room, each in a chair drawn forward from the wall, with heads bent over their books, apparently deeply absorbed in study. Not a head was raised nor a movement made, when I went in. "Boys," I said, "you know you mustn't be here." "Oh, please let us stay, Ora, and we won't disturb you a bit. We've dusted our chairs,--see," and, suiting the action to the word, they polished their chairs with their coat sleeves.

Finding them bent upon staying, I crossed the hall to the dining-room and told Mrs. Ripley. She went immediately back to the parlor with me; but the room was empty, the boys having jumped out of the window. I continued my dusting. Soon one of the delinquents thrust his head in at the window and said: "Now, Ora, if you'll dust that sofa, you may take as much time for it as you please; and then I'll come in and put my feet up on it, so as to be out of your way, and I'll read hymns to you just the way some of the Unitarian ministers around Boston do." As some of the Unitarian pulpits in Boston and vicinity were filled, at that time, by men with very peculiar voices and styles of delivery, the temptation was too great to be resisted. The entertainment was certainly unique and mirth-provoking. My entertainer, George Wells, became one of the youngest judges ever on the bench in Massachusetts. Later, the dear fellow gave his life to his country in the civil war. Some years after leaving, he said that he felt all the good there was in him he owed to Brook Farm.

In keeping with this testimony of Judge Wells was a remark once made to me by George William Curtis, when staying at our house in the course of one of his lecturing tours: "In many places where I lecture I meet old Brook Farmers whom I have not seen for years, and they are always, I find, among the very best people of the place."

The teaching at Brook Farm was fine, and, to one who really wished to learn, of the very best kind. It was not confined to daytime study hours, for some, not only the teachers, but of the scholars, used to work a portion of each day on the farm. In order to get our work done early enough for the evening pleasures, among which we reckoned Mr. Ripley's classes, Georgiana Bruce, Sarah Stearns, and myself, whose duty it was to wash the tea dishes, used to hurry through the task with great rapidity, the young men helping by wiping them. I recollect particularly one evening in the moral philosophy class,--which must have been very interesting to rouse and keep the enthusiasm of a girl of sixteen,--when the question of free will came up. Mr. Ripley read aloud Jonathan Edward's famous chapter on Golden, Silver, Wooden, and Pottery Vessels, and this was followed by a most exciting discussion between Mr. Ripley and Miss Bruce.

The arrival of George William Curtis, then a youth of eighteen, with his brother Burrill, two years his senior, was a noteworthy event in the annals of Brook Farm, at least in the estimation of the younger members. I shall never forget the flutter of excitement caused by Mr. Ripley's announcing their expected coming in these words: "Now we're going to have two young Greek gods among us." Nor have I forgotten their first appearance at the gate at the bottom of the hill leading to the Eyrie. This was the gate by which I had stood, at Mr. Bradford's request, to study the expressions on the faces of the cows as they came through. After we moved up to the Eyrie, this gate always seemed to me to separate the two different lives led at Brook Farm: on one side, the rest and recreation of the Eyrie; on the other, the busy, active, happy life of the Hive, where sweeping, dusting, lessons with Mrs. Ripley, and pleasant chitchat filled the morning hours. On a bright morning in May, 1842, soon after Mr. Ripley's announcement, as I was coming down from the Eyrie to the Hive, I saw Charles A. Dana with two strange young men approaching my "magic gate" from the direction of the Hive. Arriving at the gate before me, Mr. Dana threw it open with the flourish peculiar to his manner, and stood holding it back. His companions stood beside him, and all three waited for me to pass through. I saw at a glance that these must be the "two young Greek gods." They stood disclosed, not, like Virgil's Venus, by their step, but by their beauty and bearing. Burrill Curtis was at that time the more beautiful. He had a Greek face, of great purity of expression, and curling hair. George too was very handsome,-- not so remarkably as in later life, but already with a man's virile expression.

Burrill, whom I soon came to know very well, was quite unconscious of himself, and interested in all about him. He talked of the Greek philosophers as if he sat at their feet. He carried this high philosophy into his daily life, helping the young people in their studies, and ready at any time to take his share of the meanest and commonest work. He had that thoroughgoing truthfulness that made him feel that every mood *must* be lived through. One result of this was that he gave himself so completely to the person in whom he was for the moment interested as to create false impressions, and sometimes cause disappointment. But he was so much more attuned to another life than to anything here, so entirely fine in thought, manner, and deed, that one could not resolve to pain him by speaking of this. He was unworldly and wholly indifferent to what others thought of him, as also to their laughter when he changed his opinions, which he often did. Burrill's influence must have been of value to George in keeping him from caring too much for the admiration showered upon him later in life, the pleasures of this world being in many ways more enticing to him than to his brother. George had the greatest love and respect for Burrill, and, I always understood, was led by him to go to Brook Farm. Their intimacy was like that of two sisters. They worked, walked, talked, and sang together. Burrill's power is acknowledged most tenderly in the last chapter of Prue and I. George himself once told me that "our cousin the curate" was in part a portrait of his brother.

About George William Curtis there was a peculiar personal elegance, and an air of great deference in listening to one whom he admired or looked up to. There was a certain remoteness (at times almost amounting to indifference) about him, but he was always courteous. His friends were all older than himself, and he appeared much older in manners and conversation than he was in years; more like a man of twenty-five than a youth of eighteen. I, being a year younger and quite immature, did not then know him so well as a few years later, from which time the privilege of calling him my friend became one of the greatest pleasures of my life. As time passed he grew more genial, but he was always more sociable with some of the older men and women--George P. Bradford, Caroline Sturgis, and Mrs. Shaw, the last two being our near neighbors--than with any of the younger people at that time, excepting Charles A. Dana, with whom he and his brother used to take long walks. I remember Mr. Bradford's telling me that he and the other older men saw more promise in George than in Burrill, perceiving as they did, I suppose, the steady practical side of his nature; but I must always think that the influence of "our cousin the curate" was an important factor in the development of his character.

I passed a happy year and a half as a scholar at Brook Farm; but for the following three years, until I left New England, I was in the habit of making frequent visits there, and was always received as one of their own,--"a child of the farm," as it were. In the course of these visits I made the acquaintance, and in some cases the friendship, of later comers. Among them I must not omit to mention Abby Morton (Mrs. Diaz) who became very dear to me and whose peculiar combination of liveliness and dignity, together with her beautiful singing, made her a favorite with all the members, old and new.

Another whom I first met at the farm, and whose friendship I prized, was Isaac Hecker. It was on one of my earliest visits after leaving the school that I went out to the kitchen to see some of my friends, and there beheld, on one side of the chimney, a strange young man with the regulation baker's cap on his head. His face attracted me. It was pockmarked and not handsome, but it was earnest, high-minded, and truthful. Circumstances--among other things the friendship then existing between him and Georgiana Bruce--led to a somewhat intimate acquaintance and frequent correspondence between him and myself, the latter continuing after Mr. Hecker went to the Catholic college at Worcester. Young as we both were, our correspondence was yet on high, spiritual themes, and his persuasive powers almost made me too a Roman Catholic. Undoubtably, Isaac Hecker's influence had much to do with Mrs. Ripley's conversion to the church in which his restless mind finally found "surcease of doubt." My dear young friend Sarah Stearns became not only a Catholic, but a nun.

Among the unwarranted calumnies formerly circulated about Brook Farm was the assertion that a good deal of flirting was carried on there. I have been much with young people all my life,--a teacher for some years, a mother with several children, and now a grandmother with hosts of grandchildren,--and I have never seen more truly gentlemanly and gentlewomanly relations between youths and maidens than at Brook Farm. I am sure not only that no harm was done, either to young men or maidens, by the healthful and simple intercourse that was invariable between them, but that very much good came, especially to the young men. There seemed a desire in each person to make Brook Farm a happy home. There were few of us who had not enough work each day, either manual or intellectual, generally both, to give a keen zest to the pleasure of the evening. It seems to me, as I look back upon the happy hours of recreation, that we were more amiable and content with ourselves and one another than any circle of people I have ever known since.

Among our daytime amusements were some charming picnics in the pine-tree grove, one of which is almost exactly described in The Blithedale Romance. Hawthorne's one variation from the facts was in making me, both there and in the American Note-Books, the gypsy fortune teller, whereas that part was really taken by Mrs. Ripley, and I was merely the messenger to bring persons to her; but it would seem that I must have done some talking on my own account.

In the happy Brook Farm evenings there were games for the young people at the Hive, while once or twice a week, at the same place, the older classes listened to Mr. Bradford's readings of Racine's and Molière's plays,--delightful readings they were,--or to discussions in Mr. Ripley's moral philosophy class. At the Eyrie we had charming singing by the two Curtis brothers, occasional concerts given by people from "the world," talks by Margaret Fuller, William H. Channing, and others, sometimes dancing in moderation, and once in a while a fancy-dress party.

Everybody on the farm knew that he or she was cordially invited to all these various amusements, and would be kindly received. The result was that all sorts and conditions of men mingled freely and without sense of constraint. There were often side by side three of the most beautiful women I have ever seen from the Shaw and Russell families, a girl who had been nursemaid in my uncle's family, and others of even lowlier station in the world. When the chairs gave out, as they not infrequently did in our more crowded assemblies, our aristocratic guests did not disdain to sit upon the Eyrie floor,--a fact that was made a subject of no little ridicule in Boston at the time, it not being known, perhaps, that it was impossible to get extra chairs.

At one fancy-dress party George William Curtis took the part of Hamlet. Our delightful neighbors, the Shaws and Russells, who were much interested in us, and who had plenty of money and many pretty things to wear themselves, not only came to these simple little balls, but generously lent many of their fine things to Brook Farmers. Jonathan Russell, a not remote ancestor, had been our Minister to Russia, and I remember that some of his court clothes appeared at our fancy parties, particularly a sky-blue silk frock coat, which J. S. Dwight wore. I recollect being dressed as a Persian girl in satin trimmings and tartan, lent by these neighbors, who made our assembly shine by their beauty and charming garments, warming our hearts by their constant kindness.

That many of the Brook Farmers went to church I know; for I remember well the hot walk with them two miles and back on summer Sundays. Most of them fulfilled their duty as citizens by voting, although a few refrained on the ground taken by Garrison and Samuel J. May, that the United States Constitution was a pro-slavery document.

Not long after the burning of the Phalanstery, Brook Farm closed its six years of existence. I cannot regard it as a failure. The influence of the fine, magnanimous living there must have carried blessing to all parts of our land, as its members scattered and planted in distant communities the seeds of the harvest they had themselves gathered at Brook Farm.

Yes, it was indeed a very happy and wholesome life. I wish I had the power to tell in earnest, glowing words how wide its influence seems to me to have been, and still to be. I have not this power, and so quote from an article by my dear friend George P. Bradford, who lived at Brook Farm throughout the six or seven years during which it was maintained:--

"And some there are who still revere all the dreams of their youth, not only those that led them there, but those also that hovered around them while there, and gave a color of romance to their life, and some of whom perhaps still cherish the hope that in some form or mode of association or of co-operative industry may be found a more equal distribution of the advantages, privileges, and culture of society; some mitigation of its great and painful inequalities; a remedy, or at least an abatement, of its evils and sufferings. But it may be thought that I have dwelt too much on the pleasantness of the life at Brook Farm, and the advantages in the way of education, etc., to the young people, which is all very well, but not quite peculiar to this institution, and some may ask what it really accomplished of permanent value in the direction of the ideas with which it was started. This I do not feel that I can estimate or speak of adequately, neither is it within the scope of this paper. But I would indicate in a few words some of the influences and results that I conceive to belong to it. The opportunity of very varied culture, intellectual, moral, and practical; the broad and humane feelings professed and cherished toward all classes of men; the mutual respect for the character, mind, and feelings of persons brought up in the most dissimilar conditions of living and culture, which grew up from free commingling of the very various elements of our company; the understanding and appreciation of the toils, self-denial, privations, which are the lot to which so many are doomed, and a sympathy with them, left on many a deep and abiding effect. This intercourse or commingling of which I have spoken was very simple and easy. When the artificial and conventional barriers were thrown down, it was felt how petty and poor they were. They were easily forgotten, and the natural attractions asserted themselves. So I cannot but think that this brief and imperfect experiment, with the thought and discussion that grew out of it, had no small influence in teaching more impressively the relation of universal brotherhood and the ties that bind all to all, a deeper feeling of the rights and claims of others, and so in diffusing, enlarging, deepening, and giving emphasis to the growing spirit of true democracy."

*Ora Gannett Sedgwick, "A Girl of Sixteen at Brook Farm," Atlantic Monthly, 85 (March 1900): 394-404.

BROOK FARM*

Frederic Dan Huntington

UNITED STATES HOTEL,
July 19, 1842.

TO EDWARD PHELPS HUNTINGTON.

<u>Dearly</u> <u>beloved</u> <u>Brother</u>: Last Sunday I preached for the first time as a real preacher, at Jamaica Plain. Such a world of artistic and natural beauty I am sure I never was in before. They invited me from one country seat to another, and from one garden of fruits and flowers to another, till I was almost bewildered, as if in fairyland. The famous Community, too, near there, was looked at. Dwight hoes corn Sundays. Some sail, some walk, some hear Parker preach. The general feeling with which I came away was one of sadness and commiseration.

Nearly forty years later Bishop Huntington wrote of the Brook Farm experiment: "This was a sanguine attempt of Mr. Ripley, and a few of his friends, to embody in a modified form, on a large tract of land, some of the better suggestions of the French Communists, to give everybody something to do in some bucolic fashion, to afford a convenient rallying-place for the <u>symposia</u> of the coming reformers of religion, literature, society, and so to offer a model of respectable, cultured French Fourierism, with Fourier and much of his nonsense left out. Fine times they had there beyond question, with much that was pure and sincere and lofty in aspiration and conversation, and much that was sentimental, crude and ridiculous. Theodore Parker used to come across the pastures to talk with such good company, the farm lying within the precincts of his parish. Of an evening the group would include very much the same persons, not a few of them already or afterwards eminent, that had been accustomed to gather in the parlors of Mrs. Farrar in Cambridge, Mrs. Parkman in Boston, or at Mr. Emerson's own house in Concord, or that contributed prose or verse, or 'Orphic sayings' which were neither, to the pages of 'the Dial.' Central in the circle, and always oracular in speech, each on a separate tripod, were Bronson Alcott, Margaret Fuller, and Mr. Emerson.

"Hawthorne occasionally looked in, in his silent observant way, but did not commit himself. Of the young listeners and enthusiastic seekers were Wheeler and Bartlett, Jones Very, J. S. Dwight the musician and the lady he married, George W. Curtis and a few foreigners. So the experiment went on, hastening to dissolution and moribund from the start. If there were affinities, so were there antipathies and repulsions. Queer people, impracticable people, disagreeable people, in short bores and dunces, always attach themselves to novel combinations of that sporadic sort. Mr. Ripley was no quartermaster, organizer or financier. The turnips and potatoes languished while the builders of the Future 'cultivated literature on a little oatmeal.' The weeds grew rank while the unanxious husbandmen discussed the Vedas, recited Schiller, laid down the principles of one of the fine arts, or pondered the problems of the universe. Before very long that pleasant place of cattle and corn and poultry knew them no more. The leader of the enterprise went to the Tribune office, Mr. Curtis in due time to his editorial chair, the rest hither and thither to seek their bread. Another was added to the long list of communistic failures, God having clearly ordained that his sons and daughters shall dwell in families, and that the laws of life and duty, labor and thrift, responsiblity and increase, shall not be abrogated by the dreamers of dreams, however amiable or honest or gifted they may be."

It has been seen that neither literary nor social inclination led Mr. Huntington among the followers of Transcendentalism.

---

*Aria S. Huntington, Memoir and Letters of Frederic Dan Huntington (Boston: Houghton, Mifflin, 1906), pp. 68-70.

BROOK FARM REMINISCENCES*

M. Gertrude Cutter

There is now living near Boston one of those who lived at Brook Farm, Mrs. Rebecca Codman Butterfield, whom it is my pleasure to know and my privilege to love.
Mrs. Butterfield is one of the few people, old in years (she is eighty-five), but who retains all the youthful fire and enthusiasm. At no time is this so noticeable as when she is talking of the old life and days at Brook Farm. And whenever I go to see her, I am always impressed anew with the feeling that, though "Brook Farmers" were not rich in worldly goods, they were given an undying heritage of love and hope and joy in life.
On my last visit to her I said, "I am going to write you up, Mrs. Butterfield, and all the years you were at Brook Farm. So prepare for the coming interview!"
She prepared by giving me a comfortable chair and a box of her own home-made peppermints. Then we settled down to what would technically be called an "interview," abut what was really an enthusiastic, spontaneous talk by Mrs. Butterfield, with a very few questions tucked in here and there by myself.
"To begin with the origin of the Brook Farm community," said Mrs. Butterfield, "you of course know that early in the nineteenth century there was a great change in the attitude of many people toward the old theology, with the harsh preaching of brimstone and hell fire. The fatherhood of God and the brotherhood of man became the subjects of sermons, instead of God's everlasting wrath and vengeance.
"This departure in religious belief interested many of the most highly cultured of the day, and they formed a club in 1836 to discuss religious and social subjects. One of the most prominent members was Rev. George Ripley, then pastor of a Unitarian church in Boston. The club took the name of the 'Transcendental Club.' To use Mr. Ripley's own words from a sermon given to his people about

1840--'They are called Transcendentalists because they believe in an order of truth that transcends the sphere of the external senses.'

"Mr. Ripley was a religious scholar, and a man who faithfully fulfilled the duties of his pastorate over his Purchase Street Church in Boston. He was also interested in social reforms, and believed that there should be a new social system. He finally evolved a plan which he set forth to the Club with great enthusiasm, his idea being to live on a farm where agriculture and education should be the foundation of the new social life.

"A number of the Transcendentalists believed that the highest life could only be attained by cooperation in actual daily life, where labor should be honored and where all should take part in it.

"The winter of 1840 was the time when the project was being merely discussed, and when all the plans were being made. Early in the spring of 1841 it was announced that a location was chosen at Brook Farm, West Roxbury, about nine miles from the center of Boston. Very strangely, not one of the original members of the Transcendental Club joined Mr. Ripley's movement, but he had many followers in his endeavor to form the new community."

"What did Mrs. Ripley think of her husband's plan?" was my very natural query, to which Mrs. Butterfield replied:

"Mrs. Ripley greatly encouraged her husband by her deep sympathy with his project, and they both felt that the life at Brook Farm would be the actual fulfilling of the Christian life he had so long preached. Mrs. Ripley's relatives had high social position, and of course her going to Brook Farm caused much excitement in the social world of Boston. She had great natural mental ability and fine training, and was of untold help to her husband throughout the experiment at Brook Farm.

"Soon after the location was chosen, operations were begun at the Farm. When the 'Transcendentalists' (as they were often called) entered on their experiment, the place was a 'milk farm' and some one of the company would start for Boston with the milk at an early hour in the morning.

"The school was opened immediately, and the distinguished men of ability known to be at the Farm brought to it many pupils not only from Boston and its environs, but from distant parts of our own country and from other countries as well.

"Mr. and Mrs. Ripley were at the head of the school. (Mrs. Ripley washed vigorously in the laundry every Monday morning before taking charge of her classes.) Charles A. Dana had classes in German and Greek, and John S. Dwight taught Latin and music, besides whom there were many more instructors.

"It was during this period that Nathaniel Hawthorne, Margaret Fuller, George William Curtis, Mrs. [sic] Elizabeth Peabody and others of the Transcendental school were either visitors or residents.

"This was during the first two years of the existence of the community, when there were no mechanical industries (these not being introduced until about the end of the second year). Until this time, the means of support for the fifty or seventy-five people of the community was furnished by the school and by the products of the farm."

"When was it you went there?" I interposed.

"It was in the spring of 1843 that we left Boston," Mrs. Butterfield replied, a reminiscent smile on her dear old-young face. "Let me see! I was born in 1825, so I was then a girl of eighteen when my whole family left our South End home in Boston to join the community, where we staid until its end.

"We went in a small omnibus that started from Brattle Street, in Boston, for West Roxbury Village and Brook Farm. (West Roxbury was then a village entirely by itself, while now it has been annexed to Boston, though retaining more of the delightful characteristics of a small town than most Boston suburbs.)

"I shall never forget the impression made on my youthful mind when our omnibus first arrived in the yard of Brook Farm, where I saw one of the men members of the community busily engaged in hanging out the morning's washing. This impression was deepened when I afterward learned that he was a very learned and poetical gentleman from Concord.

"Yet was not his work more suitable for a man than for a woman to do in rough weather? All the work at Brook Farm was done by voluntary groups. Every one selected the kind of labor which he liked best, and in this way work was always a delight."

"Can you not tell me more about the work, Mrs. Butterfield, and the way it was done?" I asked.

"Let me give you a description of a typical day at Brook Farm," she said.

"At five o'clock in the summer, the rising horn sounded for those belonging to stable groups or engaged in teaming, also for those whose duty it was to prepare breakfast. I often used to get up early, and go from house to house, giving a peculiar whistle, the signal for certain members of the singing group to make ready to sing under various windows from six until seven. It was soul-inspiring, indeed, to sing Mozart's and Haydn's Masses in the early freshness of the morning air. I shall never forget it!

"At half-past six a second summons came, which meant that breakfast would be ready in half an hour. It was a time of good cheer, the half hour or more spent at table.

"After breakfast men and women all started for the morning's work in classroom, in field, in shop, or about the house.

"It must not be forgotten that there were some men whose duty it was to help the women in the parts of their work requiring special strength (our doctrine of mutual helpfulness rendering it possible to work at anything without injury to our dignity).

"I do not believe that the common tasks of life have ever been done under such charming conditions as existed here. I remember that I once made one of the washing group, of which Mrs. Cheswell was chief. As I have already said, Mrs. Ripley joined regularly in this work, usually termed drudgery, though no work ever seemed so at Brook Farm. Peter Baldwin, our baker, worked the pounding barrel, and there were two or three young men to work the wringers or presses, and do other hard portions of the labor.

"Quotations from Byron and Shakespeare, and from 'Festus,' a recent book (in 1844), made the work which I was doing no task whatever--rather, wholly enjoyable. I honestly think I should have chosen washing as my life work if I could have been certain that I might always do it to the accompaniment of the rhymes of the poets.

"At noon the horn blew half an hour before dinner, to allow plenty of time for those working at a distance to get to the house.

"At breakfast and supper, there were young women waiters, but at dinner young men waited on the table. At one time, Charles Dana was the head of the waiting group, in other words, the head waiter.

"After dinner we worked once more until six o'clock. I forgot to say, however, that there were classes all day in various subjects, which were attended by grown people as well as the young. The shoemaker often left his work to attend a class in Shakespeare, and one of the tillers of the soil would leave his task to enjoy a reading in Greek. But I never [saw] any one to shirk his labor or fall short in the amount expected of him during the week.

"When supper was over, any enjoyment might be indulged in, and there was no rule regarding the hour for retiring, though the house was usually quiet by ten o'clock.

"Now I want you to see this old painting of Brook Farm," said Mrs. Butterfield. "It is so discolored by age that you do not get a very clear idea of the buildings. But I love it because it was actually painted there about 1846, by Josiah Wolcott, one of our members."

She also showed me a water color made from the original painting.[1] This gives the location of the Farm buildings with great accuracy. The approach was about a mile and a half from West Roxbury Village. Near the entrance to the driveway to the Farm was a little brook from which Brook Farm took its name.

Then Mrs. Butterfield went on to tell where her family lived while at Brook Farm.

"On entering the grounds, one came immediately to the 'Hive,' where I lived with my parents and my two brothers. The Hive was a large two and a half story wooden building with a long 'ell' attached. The lower floor contained a reception room, the dining-room, kitchen, washroom and shed. There were sleeping-rooms on the second floor, and others in the attic. Our family sleeping-rooms were at first all on the second floor of the 'ell' of the Hive. But later the place became so crowded that my brothers were obliged to sleep in the attic.

The luxury of the attic may be imagined when I tell you that my brothers would often waken in winter to find that a large mound of snow had drifted in on top of them. During all our stay at Brook Farm, my parents and I occupied the same two chambers in the 'ell,' the windows of which can be seen in the paintings.

"Back of the Hive was the workshop, in which were the shoemaking, woodworking and other workrooms. (About the end of the second year of the Brook Farm community, there were various mechanical industries introduced.) In the illustration, the Workshop shows just a little above the Hive.

"About an eighth of a mile further on, stood the Eyrie, a two-story flat-roofed building, built on rocks on the highest land on the place.

"If you will look at the water color of Brook Farm, just below the Eyrie, you will see the ruins of the Phalanstery, which was burned before it was occupied.

"Near the Eyrie and at the left of it, was a small house called the Cottage, the only one of the buildings now remaining, and not far from this was another wooden house, Pilgrim House. The longest distance between the houses was about a quarter of a mile."

Mrs. Butterfield then called my attention to the fact that for about two years the Farm was supported solely by the school and by the farm products. Then in 1843, mechanical industries were introduced in an attempt to follow the theories of Charles Fourier, the French philosopher. His idea was that all labor can and must be rendered attractive, and that the association of capital, skill and labor for mutual advantage would prepare the way for ideal social conditions. The economies in expenditure and consumption would be prodigious and the pleasure of combined and varied exertion would take from toil its monotony and its repulsive aspects.

It was Albert Brisbane who interested the leaders of Brook Farm in Fourier's theories, when he (Brisbane) returned from France, where he had studied and become a convert to the writings of this French reformer. After becoming converts to Fourierism, the leaders at the Farm tried to rearrange the community in accordance with their new doctrines. As the mechanical industries increased, the number of pupils diminished, until finally there was very little income derived from the school.

"Many men now came to the Farm who were not cultured, but who were strong in their beliefs, and of fine and noble character, and scholars and shoemakers, poets and printers exchanged ideas in the dining-room, where there was the greatest opportunity for sociability."

Mrs. Butterfield spoke of her parents having a special table in the dining-room, with a few others who did not believe in the eating of meat, and when asked if the absence of meat seemed to injure the health of any at the Farm, she replied, "The health of all those at the Brook Farm was uniformly most excellent and with the exception of smallpox, and one or two slight indispositions caused by eating green apples, there were no attacks of illness during my five years' residence there.

"Before the breaking out of smallpox, we had had more visitors than we knew how to take care of, but the disease settled this problem most speedily. There was one other dread disease, with which one of our members was always afflicted, and that was leprosy."

Mrs. Butterfield smiled at my look of horror, and went on as if there were nothing in the least unusual--

"The leper was Lucas Coralles, the son of the Governor of Manila. How we all loved Lucas!"

But then my questions came tumbling out--"Was it generally known? Were you not frightened? And, How soon did they send him away?"

She interrupted my queries with a slight gesture, and recommenced her remarkable story.

"Lucas and Jose Coralles, sons of the Governor of Manila, came to Brook Farm to attend its school when they were in their early twenties. Soon after arriving, Lucas became ill, and was cared for by Mrs. Ripley. I have often heard the wife of our leader called cold and reserved, but I can never think of her thus. The young man's mother could not have been a more devoted nor tender nurse than she. I shall never forget it! It was not long ere we knew that Lucas was suffering from leprosy. No, dear, there was no fright, and no one thought of removing him, for we all loved him so. Of course, he had the disease in its early stages, but even so, his face was swollen, and his already dark complexion was unnaturally darkened by the disease. I cannot tell you the condition of his hands, save that they, too were swollen, for he wore white gloves during all the years he was with us."

"Y-E-A-R-S!" was my exclamation.

There was an amused twinkle in the dark eyes as she went on to say--

"We had no fear. We were not like people today, hunting for opportunities to capture germs. We were at Brook Farm for a greater purpose--to help each other, and to love and serve God and each other, and we had not time to give thought to much else. Our young girls danced with Lucas (I have often done it myself), and he was with us in all ways, and none had thought of harm. The only precaution was that he always wore gloves, as already said. I have but to close my eyes, and I can seem to see him now, as he looked when seated at the dining-table with us. I am apt to think of him there as making cocoa, for he always mixed it, using a small pot, and this stick, which I have always kept in memory of him."

Mrs. Butterfield then brought forth for my inspection a round stick about one foot in length, made of hard dark wood and having a ball-like top, and a handle ornamented with a little clever knife work.

"Lucas left the Farm only because he was obliged to return to Manila. After starting on the voyage, he took a severe cold and died on the way from the effects of the cold rather than the leprosy."

She was silent, thinking of the past so far away, and yet so near. I, too, was silent, marvelling at the tale which I had heard, and wondering if today a large body of the believers in Christian Science or mental science could be kept for so long a period in close proximity to leprosy, and yet be able to maintain a calm, fearless mental state.

But my next question was a far cry from my abstruse musings on the effects of mind on matter, for I suddenly realized that nothing had been said about the question of dress at Brook Farm, and asked about their costumes.

"As to dress," Mrs. Butterfield replied, "there was little occasion for display. No superiority would have been conferred by fine feathers, and the spirit of economy and simplicity prevailed. The favorite dress of the men was a tunic (similar to a Norfolk jacket). It took the place of vest and coat, and was worn with a leather belt. The women generally adopted a short dress, closely resembling the so-called 'bloomers.' The skirt consisted of straight breadths gathered and falling just below the knee. The slightly full trousers buttoned at the ankle. The waist was plain, with collar and belt of the same. In bad weather we wore boots up to our knees, and could go out in the fiercest storms. I continued to wear my Brook Farm costume over a year after leaving the Farm, but of course the dress attracted attention, and my husband could not bear to have me sometimes subjected to ill-natured remarks and so I gave up my costume."

She loving touched the large cameo brooch she always wears, as she spoke of her husband, and I again admired his pure profile, so beautifully portrayed in the cameo. As always, she spoke of her "beloved," who has long since left her, not alone, but accompanied by the memory of their beautiful life together, and wrapped in the knowledge that his love yet enfolds her. Theirs was a Brook Farm romance, of which she told as follows:

"At the Farm the young men and girls saw each other in a healthful, natural way, without the artificialities of modern society. They had an opportunity first to become friends without thought of love, by joining together in the work and amusements.

"I suppose our amusements will seem very simple, as indeed they were, but the entire life admitted of so much sociability that we did not feel the need for complicated amusements. You know that in many of our members there was ability both to entertain and instruct. Our musician, John Dwight, afforded us many hours of pleasure, improvising upon the piano. I well remember one young man, unaccustomed to good music, who would sit night after night by the piano, completely spellbound. He used to say that his entire life was influenced by his entrance into a hitherto unknown world. Frequently there were talks or lectures by the members or by some visitor. Often we had dances in the large dining room, and the dancing would begin when the supper dishes had been washed and the room put in readiness, for no special changes in dress were made. Both young and old joined in the dance, and there was plenty of time afterward for good sound sleep, so there were no dull, listless people with aching heads the next morning. Dancing, as carried on there, was innocent, inexpensive, and beneficial to all, and even the ministers joined heartily with us in the amusements, and I remember one occasion when there were four ministers upon the floor. . . . Our festivals held in the pine grove were always occasions for special enjoyment with musical, intellectual, and dramatic talent given to them. Of course we had many talented members, who afterward became very well known and even famous.

"Nathaniel Hawthorne became most prominent in the outside world, but he was by no means a leader among us. He had left before I came, but I heard much about him. The idealistic phase of the Farm life attracted him, and he fancied that his manual work might aid in the scheme of community life, and thought he could compose magazine articles in his leisure hours. After a very brief stay, he expressed himself as highly delighted with everything--but he soon tired of his unwonted tasks. He was unwilling to teach, therefore manual labor fell to his lot, and though in theory it was very attractive, in practice he failed to find it even endurable. I remember hearing them tell of a remark of his regarding some stable work he had been asked to perform: 'I can not endure being chambermaid to a cow.' Later, he wrote, 'Even my custom-house experience was not such a weariness and thralldom as this.' And again, 'Labor is the curse of the universe, and no one can meddle with it without being proportionately brutified.'

"He could not find the seclusion which he craved, and which was necessary for his writing, and he left the Farm, realizing that he was out of place.

"It is scarcely fair, however, to quote only on this unhappy strain, for he also wrote thus, 'Often in these years that are darkening around me, I remember our beautiful scheme of a noble and unselfish life, and how fair in that first summer appeared the prospect that it might endure for generations. . . . Were my former associates now there, I should direct my world-weary footsteps thitherward, and entreat them to receive me for friendship's sake.'

"And Hawthorne doubtless meant what he said in all these conflicting statements, for his was a nature in which the ideal and the real were ever at sword's points.

"But I must speak of others. Margaret Fuller was only a visitor. She came quite often, however, and talked quite long. I think she would talk all night as well as all day. I have somewhere read that she did not feel that she was treated with sufficient respect during her lectures, and this same writer referred to our attitudes during that time. It was quite true that some of us were seated upon the floor, but we meant no disrespect. It was our custom to sit thus when the talk was given in a small room, for there were not enough chairs. But possibly Margaret Fuller divined our mental attitudes, for we young girls dreaded her coming, she talked so much!

"Among the people afterward well known, was Charles A. Dana, whose name became almost inseparably associated with the New York Sun. In Mr. Ripley's judgment, he was one of the ablest editors in the world. He came to us from Harvard, a young man of about twenty-four. Cultured, refined, of marked ability, and strong in purpose, he soon took a place at the front. Much of his time when with us was spent in work on the farm and in the tree-nursery, of which he was very fond. He was of a very sociable nature, a man whom all liked, and one who was not afraid of work in any form. Method and wonderful activity won for him money and fame, but he never forgot the old days with us. After Mr. Ripley's death, he wrote, 'It is not too much to say that every person who was at Brook Farm for any length of time has ever since looked back to it with a feeling of satisfaction. The healthy mixture of manual and intellectual labor--the amusements, the friendships, the ideals and poetic atmosphere--all these continue to create a picture toward which the mind turns back with pleasure, as to something distant and beautiful not elsewhere met with amid the routine of this world.'

"John S. Dwight was also a graduate of Harvard and had been ordained to the ministry, but he left his pastorate at Northampton, Massachusetts, because he thought that the life at Brook Farm afforded higher opportunities for usefulness. He was extremely musical and was editor of <u>Dwight's Journal of Music</u>, and was one of Boston's foremost musical critics. We called him 'the poet' because he sometimes wrote verses. And we enjoyed very much studying with him Latin and music, which he taught in our school.

"But I must surely mention George William Curtis, a pupil who in after years became very prominent. He had gone before the time of my arrival at the Farm, but I used to see him often, for he was a frequent visitor. His wonderful voice charmed us as he sang all the old, old songs. Mr. Curtis never forgot what he owed to his stay at Brook Farm; in fact, no one <u>could</u> forget. Even now, when I think that it had to end--!"

Mrs. Butterfield paused a moment, subdued by the memory of those dear last days, then continued:

"At the expiration of seven years, the end came, the reasons being wholly financial. The situation selected for the Farm was beautiful, but poorly suited to an experiment greatly dependent upon agriculture. Then there was no sufficiently large stream near by for water power, and so it was necessary to use steam for mechanical industries. All this demanded capital, and in spite of retrenchments the financial problems were difficult of solution. I think, however, that the majority of us would have continued somehow to remain together had it not been for the accidental burning of the Phalanstery which had been built to accommodate the entire community. The building was one hundred and seventy-five feet long and three stories high, and it was planned with special arrangements for families. A part of the second story had been reserved for a chapel, in which it was expected that religious services would be conducted by William H. Channing. The actual expense had been about seven thousand dollars, and three thousand more were to have been added for its completion. Already in straitened circumstances, you can readily see how a blow like the destruction of this building might well have overwhelmed us. Mr. Ripley's method of meeting the disaster serves to show the bravery of our leader.

"After all was over, the firemen were invited to lunch at the Hive. Mr. Ripley thanked them for coming, assured them that, though unexpected, we were glad to offer them hospitality, and said, 'But had we known you were coming, or even suspected your speedy arrival, we should have been better prepared to receive you, and should have given you a worthier, if not a warmer reception.'
"'Good enough!' shouted the firemen.
"The fire took place in the spring of 1846, and during the next year the members began to leave Brook Farm, and it soon ceased to exist as an associative experiment. To think that it all had to come to an end!"

And she sighed deeply. I kept very still while I thought deeply of Mrs. Butterfield, one of the dearest old ladies whom I have ever known. Since we are dear friends, I naturally know much more of her life of eighty-five years than can be given here. And because of that knowledge, I say that not one person in a hundred having had her trials and her losses, would have met them as she has done, or could have kept an enthusiasm which in a person of age would be most remarkable!

"Would she have been thus without the life at Brook Farm, or did she gain there something which she has carried all through her life, and which has kept her younger at eighty-five than many a woman of thirty?"

Let Mrs. Butterfield reply. She says she agrees with Maria Dana, who answered thus when asked if she were not proud to have been a member of the Brook Farm community, "Proud, no, not proud! but deeply and profoundly grateful. All there is of usefulness and beauty in my life I feel I owe to Brook Farm."

---

*M. Gertrude Cutter, "Brook Farm Reminiscences," Good Health, 45 (September 1910): 751-760.
  1. Wolcott's painting has been reproduced a number of times, including Zoltàn Haraszti, The Idyll of Brook Farm (Boston: Boston Public Library, 1937; 2nd ed., enlarged, 1940), and in color as the dust jacket to Edith Roelker Curtis, A Season in Utopia: The Story of Brook Farm (New York: Thomas Nelson, 1961).

A GIRL'S RECOLLECTIONS OF BROOK FARM SCHOOL*

Kate Sloan Gaskill

I shall never forget the first impression that Brook Farm and its people made upon me. It was on a Saturday afternoon, early in June, 1843, that my mother, my young brother and I found ourselves at the door of the "Hive," the principal building of the Farm. We had come in the little one-horse bus that ran from Boston to West Roxbury, a distance of nine miles. On the way I had been dreading the entrance into a new life among a people far removed in aims and habits from our kindly neighbors in the little New England village of Weymouth, where much of my life up to this time had been passed.

My mother was full of enthusiasm. She had met and known some of the members of the association and had been touched and impressed by the new doctrine of the so-called "Transcendentalists" that was working like a leaven through all New England life in the late thirties and early forties. My father had recently died and to her, in her loneliness this new home where she was to find brothers and sisters ready to aid her, inspiration for ideals and higher thinking for herself and more than all, broader opportunities for her children, was most welcome. In her scrap-book I find an article written by her in January, 1845, on the "Purposes and Accomplishments of the Brook Farm Association," printed in The Harbinger, the weekly newspaper printed at the Farm. Near the close of the article she refers most touchingly to the sympathy and kindness shown by the members of the community to those in sorrow, which have convinced her that "humanity has not left the earth."

Upon our arrival we were assigned to Pilgrim House, which for three years was to be our home, and here our community life began. The surroundings were very beautiful. The farm was in the center of what has been called "the wild flower garden of New England." It was surrounded by low hills and its meadows and sunny slopes were diversified by the orchard, the quiet groves and the denser pine wood. The latter was called the cathedral and was a favorite place for picnics, pageants and for religious services. Through the green meadow and by the "Hive," near the roadside, ran the brook that gave its name to the farm. No Brook Farmer ever forgot the meadow or the pine grove or the little stream that flowed so musically on its way to join the Charles river.

Much has been written of the famous experiment in social science which, more than seventy years ago drew most of the intellectual people of America, for a longer or a shorter stay, to the little settlement at West Roxbury. In his bibliography Lindsay Swift gives the name of eighty-six books, magazines and newspaper accounts that he consulted in the preparation of his scholarly and, in the main, satisfactory record of "Brook Farm, Its Members, Scholars and Visitors." Few of the writers quoted by Mr. Swift were residents at the farm. From the men and women most closely associated with the inner life of the community and living at the time when he wrote he secured but "an occasional lecture, an agreeable paper of a personal nature or some remembered conversation." Nearly all the older residents and visitors had found themselves too much occupied in the stirring scenes or in the consideration of great national problems in the years that followed, to record the story of the quiet, busy days that had been the formative period for most of them; a fitting preparation for the days preceding and during our great Civil War. The story was written in their hearts, but such stories are rarely given to the public.

George Ripley was often urged to write the history of Brook Farm and always answered, "When I reach my years of indiscretion I may do so," but he did not live long enough for that. "The Historic and Personal Memoirs of Brook Farm," by Dr. John Thomas Codman, "My Friends at Brook Farm," by John Van Der Zee Sears, and "Years of Experience," by Georgiana Bruce Kirby, all contain reliable and valuable pictures of life in the community during the period of residence of the writers. A few months ago Major Willard S. Saxton contributed an article to the Boston Evening Transcript under the title, "Last Remaining Brook Farmer (but one), Recalls Its Beauty." It is the story of a boy's recollections of the closing years of the great experiment. Many of the incidents and circumstances connected with our life in this delightful home have been recalled to my mind by Major Saxton's article and I have been urged to give a girl's recollections of Brook Farm School and my impressions of the men and women who composed the Brook Farm Community.

Probably to the present generation a brief review of the purposes and circumstances of the founding of the settlement will not prove uninteresting. The Brook Farm Community or Association, as its members insisted upon calling it, was the natural outgrowth of a spirit of democracy that characterized this period, not only in New England, but in the old world as well, which taught that "Life is finer and more beautiful, kinder and happier where men are devoted to each others' good and where the constant struggle for the means of subsistance is made less urgent and exacting." Probably as early as 1838 the famous "Transcendental Club" of New England had suggested plans for an ideal society where thoughtful and cultivated people should be brought together, where each person should do his share of the manual labor necessary for the physical wants of the community, where all should have time and opportunity for mental culture and where life should be simple and wholesome. George Ripley, Ralph Waldo Emerson, the two famous Channings, uncle and nephew, Nathaniel Hawthorne, Margaret Fuller, James Freeman Clark, Elizabeth Peabody and a score of others met during the winter of 1840 and discussed plans for a practical application of these new views of life.

A few months before the project took definite form George Ripley had written a letter to Emerson in which he stated the objects that he wished to accomplish. "We purpose," he wrote, "to take a small tract of land, which, under skillful husbandry, uniting the garden and the farm, will be adequate to the support of the families, and to connect with this a school or college in which the most complete instruction shall be given from the first rudiments to the highest culture." The religious creed should center about the one doctrine of the Fatherhood of God and the brotherhood of man. Labor was to be honored and true democracy was to be practiced and "a fine enthusiasm for humanity" was to take the place of a selfish competition and the sordid struggle for existence. Individual property was to be a fundamental tenet of the association. Every man and women who became a member was to have an equal voice and vote in the management of associational affairs and a strict account was to be kept of all business dealings with members as well as of transactions with outsiders.

Early in 1841 George Ripley, his wife, and sister, Marianna; Charles A. Dana, Nathaniel Hawthorne and six others, bought a farm of 208 acres at West Roxbury, drew up their articles of association of the subscribers to the Brook Farm Institute of Agriculture and Education, elected their officers and moved out to the one large farmhouse which was already on the place. The farm was to provide subsistence for the members of the association and give an opportunity for that healthy mixture of muscular and mental labor which, it was believed, would be conducive to the highest intellectual achievement. The meanest toil was shorn of its disagreeable features as all work was honorable and all workers were on the same level and received the same pay.

The simple, natural life, the hearty goodfellowship, the warm personal friendships, and above all, the elevated sentiment prevailing, tended to create an ideal atmosphere for the student and thinker. Much work of real value was done at Brook Farm by the men and women who found the surroundings conducive to literary thought and who were inspired by association with kindred minds, but the pride of Brook Farm was in its school. There has never been another such school in America or such teaching as was received by the young people at the Farm. Men and women who were soon to become leaders in the thought and life of the nation gave of their best to the little group of students that came to this wonderful school from all sections of New England, from New York, from Cuba and even from far-off Manila.

As the members increased additional accommodations were provided by the erection of new buildings and to these buildings swarmed the former occupants of the old farmhouse now known as the "Hive." During the second year of the association a house was built on the highest point of ground on the farm and was called the Eyrie. It commanded a fine view of the surrounding country and was the home of Mr. and Mrs. Ripley. Margaret Fuller's cottage was the next addition to the association buildings. It was used by the music teachers, and contained two or three pianos. Not far from the cottage and opposite the Eyrie, was the Pilgrim House, so called because it was built by two brothers from Plymouth. Rooms in all these buildings were occupied by members and students, but all assembled for meals three times a day at the "Hive," and in this building most of the social activities were carried on.

Upon the afternoon of our arrival the "Hive" was the scene of activity. A dance was to be given that night and all the girls, several of whom were near my own age, (I was just fifteen), were to wear wreaths of wild daisies. The forenoon had been spent in decorating the dining room and making the wreaths. As we entered the hall of the old-fashioned house we were welcomed by the friendly, smiling faces and greeted in the most familiar terms by the girls, led by Fannie McDaniel, whose sister, Eunice, later became the wife of Charles A. Dana. The girls made a wreath for me and were so cordial and kindly that all feeling of strangeness left me and from that hour I was entirely at home. At supper a welcome beamed upon us from every side. Such faces as were gathered about the rough, plain tables in that low-ceiled dining room! There were men and women from the most select literary and social circles of Boston and New York, scholars from many European countries and happy boys and girls that in a few years were to be leaders in the communities from which they had come and to which they were later to return. Conversation was lively, but the meal occupied less time than usual because of the dance. I assisted in washing the dishes and remember thinking that it was strange that I felt so much at home already.

Mother curled my hair with curling tongs and I wore a simple white dress, as did the other girls. Some attention was paid to dress at Brook Farm, as I remember a few months later notice was given that at one of the weekly parties a wreath bought at a florists would be given to the best dressed girl. I received the wreath and was the happiest person at the Farm. My dress on this occasion was made by my mother. It was very simple and was trimmed with flowers.

The dance was over at 10 o'clock and after the tables were put in place and arranged for Sunday morning breakfast we returned to our quarters at Pilgrim House. Dancing was the favorite amusement in the community and Miss Amelia Russell, who had charge of the social life at Brook Farm, saw to it that there was opportunity for each member, young and old, to learn this accomplishment.

Early on Monday morning, after a quiet, restful Sunday, while the older members were engaged in the necessary duties of the farm and household, school work began for the younger people. George Ripley taught Intellectual and moral philosophy and mathematics. His wife, Sophia Willard Ripley, for years before her marriage one of the most famous teachers in Boston, was instructor in modern languages and history. Charles A. Dana had classes in Greek and German and John S. Dwight imparted a knowledge of music and Latin. There was an instructor in drawing, a lecturer on the theory and practice of agriculture and several teachers for the younger children. Ralph Waldo Emerson, Margaret Fuller, Theodore Parker, Horace Greeley, Bronson Alcott, and indeed, most of the famous men and women of that day came to lecture to us or better still, to talk at their ease in the free, inspiring atmosphere.

The boys and girls of the school were many of them too young to appreciate fully the fact that we were the pupils and companions of men and women who were even then occupying a large place in the literary and civic life of New England. Through all its history the school needed no other advertising than that which was furnished by the names of those associated with it and many were attracted to Brook Farm School who had little sympathy with the fundamental principles of the settlement. Most of the older boys were preparing for Harvard, Williams or Columbia and their success in passing the entrance examinations showed that the teaching was thorough although it was carried on with more freedom in the intercourse of pupils and teachers than is usual in college preparatory schools. Personal influence counted for much and both teachers and students were animated by an enthusiasm that made study a joy and class-room work a delight.

When the school opened George Ripley had written, "We are a company of teachers. The branch of industry which we pursue as our primary object and chief means of support is teaching." He had been a minister for fifteen years in the Purchase Street Unitarian Church in Boston and was already a popular and voluminous author, but it was in his class-room with a group of interested students before him that he felt himself in his element. He was one of the sunniest persons I ever knew and a most attractive teacher. He never entered his class-room without something new or original to bring before us. One day he read to us with great delight one of Mrs. Caudles' curtain lectures just published by Douglas Jerrold, then at the height of his fame. His classes were never dull and his own brilliant thoughts appealed to us fully as much as the authors we read. We never thought of discipline in his classes, but enjoyed the utmost freedom so long as our discussions and digressions were under his control and if we wandered too far from the subject he brought us back by some witty jest or skillful turn of thought.

Charles A. Dana, on the other hand, was a stern disciplinarian. You could hear a pin drop at any time during his recitation and when he spoke we knew that he must be obeyed. We stood much in awe of him and were greatly impressed by the fact that he was said to be able to speak ten languages. He was a musician, having been a famous flutist during his college days at Harvard. At meal times he had charge of the waiters and here, in his checked tunic, he was as stately and dignified as in his class-room.

In Mrs. Ripley's classes every moment was devoted to work. Her French had been acquired abroad and she was most thorough in her drill upon the fundamentals of the language. A half century after leaving Brook Farm I found myself able to converse with a visitor from France although I had had few opportunities to test my knowledge of the language in the intervening years.

The opportunity to study music under John S. Dwight and his talented sisters was one of the attractions of the school. Dwight was, later, one of the most famous musical critics in America. He, like nearly all the instructors, was a graduate of Harvard, and had been a Unitarian minister before joining the association. He was in sympathy with the purposes and practices of the community, but wished to choose his own time and consult his personal feelings in performing his share of unattractive duties. Mr. Ripley once said to Theodore Parker: "There is your accomplished musical friend who would hoe corn all Sunday, if I would let him, but all Massachusetts could not make him do it on Monday." It is added that Parker replied: "It is good to know that he wants to hoe corn any day in the week." Margaret Fuller cottage was given up to the music classes during the day, but we were requested not to use the pianos during the evening without permission. We often persuaded Fannie Dwight to let us have little impromptu concerts or dances in the cottage between the supper and study hours.

Like the college boys and girls of today we were in the habit of giving nicknames to our teachers and favorite fellow students. Mr. Ripley was The Archon, Mr. Dana, The Professor and Mr. Dwight, the Poet. Miss Marianna Ripley had charge of the dining room. She was very tall and straight and the mischievous boys and girls spoke of her as "Her Perpendicular Majesty." Plump little Miss Russell, our dancing teacher, was "The Mistress of the Revels." We never nicknamed the dignified and dearly-loved wife of our principal, although I have heard her referred to as "Her Serene Highness."

Every pupil in the school, as well as every member of the association, was expected to devote from one to four hours a day to such manual labor as inclination or natural aptitude suggested, as farming, gardening, care of animals or some form of domestic labor, always under the direction of an instructor. For this work we were paid ten cents an hour and the amount credited to us was deducted from our regular bills. Brook Farm School was, I believe, the first institution in America to place industrial and intellectual training on the same plane. It was a vocational school of an ideal type and did much to impress upon residents and visitors a sense of the real dignity of the humblest necessary task and an appreciation of skill in the performance of the most commonplace duties. The workers were arranged in groups, changing occasionally from one group to another. I was at various times during the three years of my stay at the school in the dormitory group, the mending group, the typesetting group and in the dining room group. I liked the latter group the least, especially on pleasant summer evenings when I wished to go out for a walk in the groves or by the brook.

But our daily life was not given up entirely to study and work. There was an amusement group made up from the instructors and older members, whose business it was to provide entertainment. Dancing parties, picnics, musicals, pageants, plays, rural fetes and tableaux filled up our leisure hours. The pageants were the most pretentious affairs attempted at the Farm. History was searched for our settings and Scott's novels supplied us with many of our scenes. Costumes were either made by the members, hired in the city or borrowed from Boston friends.

Tableaux were favored above all other impromptu entertainments. Dickens furnished us much material for this form of amusement. On one occasion characters and incidents from Oliver Twist, then but recently published in America, were presented. My little brother represented the hero at that impressive moment when he dares the workhouse authorities and asks for "more." The self possession with which he withstood the attempts of his mischievous mates to divert his attention and make him smile won for him much praise.

We often acted characters and proverbs and impromptu dialogues were encouraged by our teachers. The latter frequently gave Shakespearean readings or related the classic myths of Greek and Rome as we sat about the fireplace during a winter's storm. The "Twice Told Tales" were strangely familiar to all Brook Farmers when Nathaniel Hawthorne gave them to a wider audience long after he had left the Farm.

I wish that I could write at more length of the visitors whom I met; but I was young and we were having so good a time ourselves that we rarely thought much of the distinguished people that came and went. I think that I remember Horace Greeley best of all. He was a strange looking man, quite unlike the other visitors. I sat at the same table with him on one occasion and I remember that he talked well and with a modesty and deference to the opinions of others that surprised me. The New York

Tribune was at that time on its way to becoming, what it was a few years later, the most widely circulated paper in America. It contained many articles on Brook Farm and many of our members were regular contributors to its columns.

We had our own newspaper, too, at the Farm, the Harbinger. I had a file of this paper but after coming to California I loaned it to a friend and it was never returned to me. There are, probably, few copies now in existence but I believe that at the time of its publication it was considered to have a high literary standard. The editors and principal contributors were Ripley, Dana, Dwight and Albert Brisbane, James Russell Lowell, John G. Whittier, Thomas W. Higginson, William W. Story, George W. Curtis, and in fact nearly all the literary lights of that age in America, were occasional contributors. My mother, like many New England women of that day, was a writer of verse and prose and several of her poems and sketches were printed in the Harbinger. She was very modest, and usually left her articles on her desk, which was in a room adjoining the printing office, and the next week they would appear, signed by her initials, in the proper column.

Our life was exceedingly simple. In May, 1841, Hawthorne wrote to his sister, "We arise at half past six, dine at half past twelve, and go to bed at nine." This custom prevailed at Brook Farm throughout all its history and was varied only on evening when dances were given. Then the hour for retiring was ten. The food was plain but wholesome. The favorite breakfast dish was "Brewis" white or brown bread boiled in milk. Meat was served once a day and vegetables were abundant. As many of the residents were vegetarians there was a "graham table" and we young people insisted that better food was served here than at the other tables. During the last year when financial conditions made it necessary to economize we willingly denied ourselves the more expensive foods. We had "meatless days" and butter was rarely served although students who could afford it bought small squares and took them to the table.

During the first year of our residence the women wore a convenient dress when about their work which years later became very popular and was known as "bloomers." For some reason this comfortable working costume was soon given up and we returned to the style prevailing among our neighbors. The men from the beginning discarded the conventional dress coat and wore, on all occasions, a loose tunic about the length of the ordinary coat and confined at the waist with a wide leather belt. Men and women wore wide brimmed hats, the girls frequently decorating their's with wreaths of wild flowers.

As I recall the relations of the various residents at the Farm, we seem to have been one harmonious family. There may have been jealousies and misunderstandings, but they were never allowed to appear on the surface and must have soon vanished in the cheerful, sunny atmosphere that prevailed. One of our visitors wrote after leaving us, "It would be difficult to conceive beforehand how much can be added to the enjoyment of a household by mere sunniness of temper and liveliness of disposition."

The free and natural intercourse among members and pupils never degenerated into undue familiarity. Under the watchful care of our teachers a reserve and personal dignity was developed that was never lost even in our gayest and liveliest moods. A kindly feeling ran through the entire family but, as is everywhere the case, little groups of friends were drawn together by taste and sympathy. Two of my dearest friends were girls of my own age. One of them, Rebecca Codman (Butterfield), died only a few years ago in Boston after a busy and useful life. Her brother, Dr. Codman, has preserved, in his Brook Farm Memoirs, the story of the relations of his family with the closing years of the association.

Louise Kleinstrup was, however, my closest and most intimate friend during the three years of my happy school life at Brook Farm. Her father, Peter Kleinstrup, was a native of Denmark, a man of considerable education and refinement and a botanist of some note. He came to Brook Farm with his wife and beautiful daughter and was placed in charge of the gardens, which soon became a delight alike to residents and visitors. Louise was wonderfully talented in music and Mr. Dwight and his sister predicted a brilliant career for her. When Jennie Lind was in Boston she heard of the little Danish singer and sent her one hundred dollars. She was an artist as well and I still have a dainty little fan which she painted for me. Soon after leaving Brook Farm she began to fail in health and within two years this "charming, tuneful girl" had passed from earth.

In the summer of 1844 it was decided that another building must be erected to accommodate the families that were joining the association in numbers. Plans were made for building the "Phalanstery" which was to be between a modern apartment house and a family hotel. There were to be suites for families and a common kitchen and dining room with two larger rooms for social and literary gatherings. A portion of the money necessary was secured; in August the work began and was carried on during the following year. In the fall of 1847 when seven thousand dollars had been expended, the half-completed structure was closed up to wait for the spring and additional funds.

Meantime the first great misfortune came to Brook Farm in the shape of a small-pox epidemic. John Allen, one of our most active members, frequently went to Boston on business trips, occasionally taking with him his only child, a beautiful boy of four years. A few days after one of these visits the child became ill and it was soon found that he was suffering from small-pox. The Margaret Fuller cottage was turned into a hospital and the child was placed there under the care of a nurse. Within a short time other cases developed until thirty patients had been cared for in the improvised hospital. There were no deaths and all except three cases were very mild. Our simple and sanitary way of living had saved us from serious results.

I was one of the earlier victims. When the doctor decided that a slight cold and fever from which I was suffering were the symptoms of the dreaded disease Mr. Ripley came to Pilgrim House with the carriage, placed me in it and took me to the cottage, walking by the side of the vehicle and talking in the most cheerful manner all the way. I remained there three weeks. Each day my mother made cocoa for me and left it under a tree in front of the cottage. After she had gone I would go out and get it. The first case was discovered early in September and before the first of November the quarantine was raised and we were all at our work again although several students who left in the early days of the excitement did not return.

The winter following passed in the usual way and although the attendance at the school was not quite so large as on previous years our instructors did not allow us to share the anxiety that must have weighed upon them at times. Spring came early that year and new hope was around. In some way money had been secured and the Phalanstery was to be completed. On the 3rd of March the carpenters opened the doors that had been boarded up all winter and placed a huge stove in the basement to dry out the damp rooms. All were cheerful and hopeful and, as usual on occasions of special rejoicing it was decided to have a dance at the "Hive." My mother was at Weymouth visiting friends, but I went over with the other "Pilgrims," leaving my brother asleep in our rooms.

It was the gayest crowd that had gathered in months. Everybody was there. The older members were congratulating each other on the near accomplishment of a cherished scheme and the young people were delighted, as they always were, at the prospect of an evening of pleasure. Louise was at the piano and the floor was filled for the first dance when someone called, "the Phalanstery is on fire!" The dancing stopped and all rushed from the room. The sky was ablaze and the snow-covered ground was red from the reflection. I hurried past the burning building for I feared that the fire might reach our home where my little brother was sleeping. From the front of the Pilgrim House I watched the fire. There was no wind and it did not spread so the other buildings were safe, but our Phalanstery was entirely destroyed.

Fire engines came from the surrounding villages and even from Boston, but they were too late to be of any service. The baker had just taken the bread for the next day's breakfast from the oven, and this, with hot coffee, made and served by the boys and men, were given to the tired firemen. Mr. Ripley, determinedly cheerful as usual, made them a little speech. He assured them that they were welcome to the poor hospitality we offered. He asked that they excuse its meagerness on account of the unexpectedness of their visit and assured them that if their hosts had known that they were coming they would have received a worthier, if not a warmer, reception.

When my mother returned the day after the fire she knew the end was near. We stayed a few more weeks, but even the boys and girls felt that it would be impossible to keep things going through another winter. There was little money coming in, the credit of the association was exhausted and a heavy debt had been incurred which there was now no immediate prospect of paying. Within a few months after the fire the school closed, Brook Farm was deserted and we turned our faces from the happiest home we had ever known.

* "The Last Remaining Brook Farmer (But One)" [Kate Sloan Gaskill], "A Girl's Recollections of Brook Farm School," Overland Monthly, 72 (September 1918): 233-240. The reference to the other surviving Brook Farmer is to S. Willard Saxton, whose article on the community had appeared in the 20 July 1916 Boston Evening Transcript (an expanded version of this article is printed below).

A FEW REMINISCENCES OF BROOK FARM*

S. Willard Saxton

I enter upon the writing of this paper with great hesitation and fear, because the subject is so great and so unique that it needs the pen of a more fluent writer than I am to tell the story as it should be told. It needs the scholarly attainments of a George William Curtis to make this story the beautiful picture that is in my mind, but which I cannot paint in language that will make you see it as I do.

"The period between 1840 and 1850 was one of intense social, intellectual and moral agitation; the greatest probably in our national history. It began with the anti-slavery movement, an attack upon an institution fortified by the Constitution of the United States and connected with the great commercial interests of the country. It was carried on with great fierceness and intensity of feelings on both sides."[1] There was a party of non-resistants who believed it was wrong to use force, and they became a large and influential party. There were many differences and dissensions in the churches, and many who graduated from our colleges to enter the ministry soon broke loose from the churches because there was not sufficient liberality among the people to permit full freedom of thought and speech. Among this class were Ralph Waldo Emerson, George Ripley, John S. Dwight, and others.

During those troublous days there was great unrest in social matters, and many experiments were started in different parts of the country to reform the whole social fabric. There was one called the North American Phalanx in New Jersey, not far from New York. Another was started in Skaneateles, N. Y., and several in other States of the West.

In my judgment, one of the best was the one that was established in West Roxbury, Mass., of which Mr. George Ripley was the leading spirit. He and Mrs. Ripley had spent a summer on the farm he selected, about nine miles from Boston. They were pleased with its location; it was purchased, and early in 1841, they moved out and took possession, followed by the several congenial spirits who had been studying with them the social problems of the day; among them, Marianne Ripley, Mr. Ripley's sister, Nathaniel Hawthorne, the distinguished writer, Mr. John S. Dwight, a Unitarian minister from Northampton, Mass., Charles A. Dana, who, on account of the failure of his eyes, was obliged to leave Harvard College, and Minot Pratt, for some time foreman in the office of the <u>Christian Register</u>. They organized a society called "The Brook Farm Institute of Agriculture and Education," and began work. Most of them belonged to what was known as the Transcendental School. Theodore Parker, Mr. Ripley's intimate friend, lived only a mile away, and preached then in West Roxbury. Francis George Shaw, father of Robert G. Shaw, who was killed at Fort Wagner, lived in the same village.

It was started as a milk farm at first, one of the number taking the milk into Boston every morning. There was much hard work for both women and men, but it was a new life and all entered upon their duties with cheerfulness and energy.

A school was set in operation at once, and it drew together many promising pupils, the corps of teachers being of unusual quality. Every pupil was expected to spend from one to two hours daily in manual labor, being credited with the amount earned.

Hawthorne's stay with the school was quite short, for as James T. Fields once said of him, "He was a man who had, so to speak, a physical affinity with solitude," and he wished to be back with his books. So he returned to Boston, which soon brought out the fact that other interests called him there, and the next year he married Sophia Peabody of Salem.

A passage from "Blithedale Romance," wherein he speaks of his "old and affectionately remembered home at Brook Farm," is of interest: "Often in these years that are darkening around me, I remember our beautiful scheme of a noble and unselfish life, and how fair in that first summer appeared the prospect that it might endure for generations and be perfected as the ages rolled by into a system of a people and a world. Were my former associates now there--were there only three or four true-hearted men still laboring in the sun--I sometimes fancy that I should divert my world-weary footsteps thither and entreat them to receive me for old friendship's sake. More and more I feel we struck upon what ought to be a truth. Posterity may dig it up and prosper by it."

Pupils came from New York and New England, and some from foreign countries, and the school flourished until the small accommodations were filled and a neighbor's cottage was hired. It was not large, but select. Among the pupils were two brothers, George William and Burrill Curtis, one of whom has achieveed a splendid fame and a choice place in the literature of our country. George William Curtis was, in my judgment, an ideal American. It was always hoped by his friends that he, as the most competent to write the story, would write the history of Brook Farm. But, as the editor of Harper's Weekly, and with his many other interests in public and private life, he never reached the time when he could; and quite likely, he did not care to undertake the burdensome task. Mr. Curtis later in life married the daughter of Mr. Francis George Shaw, brother of Colonel Shaw, the hero of Fort Wagner; and another sister married General Francis Channing Barlow, a gallant hero of the Civil War, and also a student at Brook Farm in his younger days.

The organization was continued for two or three years with varying success, when it was decided to make some changes, and add some of the mechanical industries, in order to increase the finances. More money was needed to bring about such great reforms as this ambitious association aimed to accomplish. So in 1844, the Association was re-organized, and some of the principles and methods adopted which were taken from the works of Charles Fourier, a French philosopher and writer of great prominence in the last century. He wrote a great deal on social reforms and laid out the most elaborate schemes for the organization of labor, methods of improving the condition of the laborer, and his home. His works were largely translated into English by Albert Brisbane of New York, who was an enthusiastic believer in Fourier's schemes for the betterment of all the races of the world. A sympathetic chord was touched in the hearts of all Brook Farmers when Fourier argued that "there was a sublime destiny for mankind on this earth, that the Creator was infinitely good, that all the instincts of our nature, when not subverted by bad conditions, pointed toward that destiny, and that humanity was on its way upward; that the past progress argued what the future might be."

The Association was reorganized under the name of Brook Farm Phalanx, with Mr. George Ripley as President, and Mr. Charles A. Dana as Secretary. Mr. Dana was a young man of marked ability, who was matricultated as freshman in 1839, at Harvard College, and at the end of the first year stood seventh in a class of seventy-four. At the end of his second term, he was obliged to give up his studies on account of his eyes, which he ruined, as he himself confessed, by reading Oliver Twist until three o'clock in the morning. He was recommended to go to Brook Farm and work on the farm. He was received very kindly by Mr. Ripley, they became close friends, and he was the principal manager until the close of the affairs in 1847. He was a fine writer, both of poetry and miscellaneous articles on all current topics, had a special aptitude for all foreign languages, several of which he spoke fluently; was quick in his judgments and most agreeable in manner. After being connected with the Boston Chronotype, the New York Tribune, and being one of the editors of the Appleton Encyclopedia, he became the owner of the New York Sun, of which he was the editor until his death. He married while at Brook Farm Miss Fanny McDaniel, sister of Osborne McDaniel.

It was in 1844 that correspondence began in reference to my going to Brook Farm. My Father, Jonathan A. Saxton, of Deerfield, Mass., was a friend of Mr. George Ripley, of Greenfield, Mass., and he was deeply interested in every sort of reform that was started in those times of intellectual and moral tumult. He belonged to the original Garrisonian Abolition party, and fought valiantly with tongue and pen, until he had the happiness of seeing every slave in our land free. He was especially interested in all the social experiments which were started, and was, therefore, a firm believer in the one of which his friend Ripley was the head.

As they were about to start a paper at Brook Farm, and I, a boy of fifteen, had begun to learn my trade as a printer in Greenfield, my father wrote to Mr. Ripley and asked about the chances of my being admitted to work on the new organ, The Harbinger. In due time, a reply came that the matter had been laid before the Board, and that I had been admitted on probation. If at the end of two months I proved satisfactory, I would be admitted to juvenile membership.

As part of the story of my first going to Brook Farm, I copy a portion of a letter of my father, who was at that time in Boston, to his father, Rufus Saxton, who was in the old home, Deerfield, Mass.

Boston, April 3, 1845.
My dear Father:--
I received the promised letter from Mr. Ripley yesterday afternoon. The Brook Farm Association have agreed to accept Willard as an associate. He is to come at first on a probation of two months, and if at the expiration of the time, either party is not satisfied, the connection will cease. After that he will be admitted as a juvenile member. . . . and in view of the moral and intellectual advantages he will enjoy, I could have no hesitation in accepting them for him, even if he should not finally become a member of the association, but should prefer to engage in the rivalries and competitions of the world.

My views of the scheme of society attempted to be carried out at Brook Farm have undergone no change, but rather are confirmed by more reflection--by every new experience (of which in my present position I have abundance) of the evils produced by the false, disjointed and unnatural modes of life which everywhere prevail. . .

The Association wish that Willard should come down as soon as convenient. His fitting out need not be at all expensive, for all the styles of the association, of living and dress, are plain and simple. A man or boy is not regarded for his coat, but for himself.

I wish you would make the necessary arrangements and inform me when he will come. I will meet him at the depot or elsewhere. He will want to spend two or three days in looking around this new world of Boston and then I will go out with him to Roxbury. I long much to see him and to introduce him into the way to a truer life.

Aff'y your son,

JONA. A. SAXTON.

This was an exciting period to a boy of fifteen, who had scarcely ever travelled out of his native county. I was soon made ready for the wonderful journey to Boston, where my father was already. I was placed in charge of his friend, Major Dickinson, and we left Deerfield on a pleasant morning in April, 1845, were driven to Cheapside, where we transferred to the old-fashioned stage coach that ran to Fitchburg about one or two o'clock, if I remember rightly, and there we had dinner. We then took a train for Boston, which was my first ride on the steam cars, and was full of excitement. And it was still more startling when we arrived on the edge of the evening in the huge Fitchburg station, which was then located across the bay in Charlestown. Seventy-one years have brought the endless railroad traffic into the North and South stations, which accommodate millions, where there were then but thousands.

My father met me at the station and I shall never forget that we stopped with some cousins at No. 11, Minot St. A few days were devoted to showing the young man the sights, and I am sure the good father was very glad when my curiosity was satisfied.

It was on the 18th of April, 1845, I think, that my father and I took the one-horse 'bus that made daily trips from the Brattle Street Hotel, out through Roxbury, Jamaica Plain and West Roxbury to Brook Farm. We were received cordially, for that was a Brook Farm habit, with Mr. George Ripley especially. I was made to feel so much at home that I have no remembrance of having been homesick on my first experience of leaving home. And it was a delightful change from being a "Printer's devil" in the Greenfield <u>Democrat</u> office to the pleasant surroundings, physical and social. I went into the office of the Brook Farm <u>Harbinger</u>.

One of the first families with whom I became acquainted was that of Mr. and Mrs. John Codman, their only daughter Rebecca, and their two sons, John and Charles. They were all true and genuine friends from the time I went to Brook Farm through all the years that elapsed until each had finished life's task and wrapped "the drapery of his couch about him," and laid "down to pleasant dreams." Charlie, as we all called him, was a high type of both boyhood and manhood, refined, intellectual and pure-minded. He became my companion in the printing group, and my roommate in all the Brook Farm life, and in after years as well, when we took up the outside life again and worked together at the case. He was the dearest friend I ever had, not excepting my widely scattered brothers, and our confidential intimacy lasted until his untimely end came through a sad accident in Boston.

His sister Rebecca became the wife of one of nature's noblemen, Jonathan Butterfield, who was a true Brook Farmer, and later foreman of the State Printing Office, Boston, where I read proof for some years. Dr. John Codman became a prominent dentist in Boston, and wrote a volume of reminiscences of Brook Farm.

When I arrived, they had completed quite a large building near the Hive for the purpose of carrying on the various mechanical trades that had been introduced. It was a two story and attic building, with a steam engine in the basement for driving the machinery. On the first floor was the carpenters' shop, devoted to the making of shoe boxes, sashes, and blinds, which were taken by the thousands to the wholesale houses of Boston. On the second floor there was a shoemakers' shop, and a Britannia wareshop. On this floor was also located the large and airy printing office, with an old-fashioned Franklin hand press, on which the <u>Harbinger</u> was printed, and mailed to its one thousand eager readers. The top story was used as a dormitory where a number of the men and boys slept and had their daily ablutions. There were none of the modern conveniences for water, and the pump had to do its share of the work, with a water carrier who went from house to house filling pitchers and pails.

All the labor of the Farm, including the domestic part, was organized on the plan of Charles Fourier, into groups and series. The domestic series had the care of the house and all domestic work, and was divided into Consistory, Dormitory, and Kitchen groups, also washing, ironing, and mending groups, many of the people belonging to several groups. The mechanical series covered the shoe and box shops, and the printing office. I, of course, belonged to the Printing group, and was also often detailed to assist in the washing group, the haying group, and not least of all, the waiters' group, where though I say it who should not, I consider we all did ourselves proud. Our waiters' group was made up of some of the best talent at Brook Farm, such as Charles A. Dana, the good-nature Fred. Cabot, of Boston, "unique of face and beard," John and Charles Codman, and myself. A new chief of the waiters' group was elected each week, as rotation in office was the rule. They had their dinner after the others were through, and the scintillations of wit that came from those bright men, the stories that were told, and the bad puns that were made, brought forth shouts of laughter that almost lifted the roof, and brought the ex-diners back to the windows and doors to learn the cause of all the hilarity. Pity it is that Dana could not have made and preserved a short history of that unique group at Brook Farm.

I recall here an incident that occurred in the domestic department one evening when the chief, Miss Ripley, requested all who felt inclined to meet in the room next the kitchen to assist in shelling the peas for the next day's dinner, the peas having been picked from our own vines. There was a liberal response from male and female, old and young, until twenty or thirty had gathered. Rev. Wm. H. Channing was among the number, serene and beautiful of face, and always genial in manner. The dishes and peas were handed around; and the work began in the most social, cheerful manner, some of the girls shelling into the same dish with the boys, to add more joy to the work, and agreeable talk went on naturally. When it was about completed, and some dishes had been handed in, some of us younger ones wanted a little more fun and began by pelting a near neighbor with two or three pods. This was quickly answered by the return of a dozen pods square in the face, and then whole handfuls; and quicker than it can be told, whole dishes of pods were flying through the air in every direction, making a scene of wild confusion and laughter that is hard to picture in words. And the sedate and lovely Mr. Channing was one of the liveliest of the party.

About the time of my arrival, "The Harbinger, devoted to Social and Political Progress," was started in our pleasant office, with the following text at the head: "All things, at the present day, stand provided and prepared, and await the light." It was printed in quarto form, sixteen pages, with clear type and in excellent style. These names appear as its editors in New York:

>Albert Brisbane,
>Wm. Henry Channing,
>Christopher P. Cranch,
>George W. Curtis,
>George G. Foster,
>Parke Godwin,
>Horace Greeley,
>Osborne McDaniel.

The New England editors were:

>Otis Clapp, Boston,
>William W. Story, Boston,
>Thomas W. Higginson, Boston,
>James Russell Lowell, Cambridge, Mass.,
>Jonathan A. Saxton, Deerfield, Mass.,
>Francis G. Shaw, West Roxbury, Mass.,
>John G. Whittier, Amesbury, Mass.

The Brook Farm writers were:

>George Ripley,
>Charles A. Dana,
>John S. Dwight,
>Lewis K. Ryckman.

The printing group was composed of Jonathan Butterfield, foreman, Chas. H. Codman, Edgar Palisse, whose father and mother were members, and part of the time, Thomas Treadwell, from Exeter, N.H., and myself.

It was a congenial and harmonious group that Chas. Fourier himself would have approved. Mr. Butterfield and I did most of the press work each week, and we had the help of some of the young ladies to fold and address the completed papers ready for the mail. Of course, the editors were in daily communication with us all in relation to their articles and all matters pertaining to the papers, and never was a printing office more agreeable to printers and editors. The editors were all high-toned, agreeable gentlemen, and working for the same great cause in which we had enlisted, and we all stood on common ground. Mr. Ripley and Mr. Dana wrote most of the editorial associative articles; Mr. Dana was principal reviewer of new books; Mr. Dwight was deeply interested in the principles of the associative life, and wrote some articles on that subject; but his great forte was music and poetry. In later years he started a paper in Boston called Dwight's <u>Journal</u> <u>of</u> <u>Music</u>, which was greatly enjoyed for many years by all who were fond of the higher class of music.

In the first number of the <u>Harbinger</u>, there was commenced a story called "Consuelo," by Madam Dudevant, whose nom de plume was George Sand. It was a fine translation from the French by Mr. Francis G. Shaw, of New York, who was then living in West Roxbury. So he was a frequent visitor to Brook Farm and the printing office. We boys were always glad to see Mr. Shaw's manuscript, it was so perfect, written in a fine business hand, and with no erasures or interlineations to mar its beauty.

Though there was much hard work at all times, there were willing hands and cheerful hearts accompanying it, so it was never burdensome. We had many amusements during our leisure hours, and it was easy to have a dance after the labors of the day were finished. Some one might suggest it while at supper, and there would be enough to acquiesce to make it go. It was a simple matter to get dishes washed and piled up, and the tables moved out the way. The fiddler was usually brought over from Dedham, when it was "on with the dance, let joy be unconfined." We had the country dance, the waltz, the waltz quadrille, the plain cotillion, etc. All joined very heartily in them; there were no wall flowers, and "all went merry as a marriage bell." Between nine and ten o'clock we finished; the tables were put in place again, everything made ready for the morning meal, and all retired early, at peace with the world.

There were many impromptu dances, when the younger girls and boys would meet at the Cottage for a social sing, when one of the girls would start a favorite waltz on the piano. This would be a signal and an inspiration for all the others to join in a waltz. None of the foreign dances, such as the Fox-Trot, and Tango, had come into our simple life, at that time.

But we did have a great deal of music at Brook Farm and of the best kind. Mr. John S. Dwight was the most musical soul there, and played the piano and the flute. He would often sit down to his piano and improvise in the most delightful manner, and he would seem to be lost in the musical world where his thoughts had led him. His sister, Fanny, was also an accomplished pianist, and there were a number of others who were fine performers. A Miss Harriet Graupner, of Boston, spent a good deal of time with us, and she was a "star" performer. At our meetings on Sunday, we always had a competent quartette, who would give us the grand masses of Mozart and Haydn in the most splendid manner.

When Mr. Curtis would make his occasional visits to the Farm, there was sure to be a gathering at the Eyry to hear him sing. He had a marvelous voice, in singing, and in his public addresses he was most fascinating in both voice and in his choice use of the English language. Mr. C. P. Cranch also came occasionally. He was a poet, an artist, and a musician. He played the flute, and the wonderful imitations he made with the flute and his voice, appealed to the imagination so strongly that we could almost see the barnyard filling with every bird, fowl or animal on the farm, each joining in its own language in the grand rural oratorio. It was an interesting and unique performance, and brought the house down.

In religious matters, there was the greatest freedom of thought and action. Some went to church and some never went. Some nearly always went to hear Theodore Parker, a mile and a half away in West Roxbury. Some preferred their own room for quiet reading or writing. Or small parties would go to the beautiful pine woods nearby and sit around on the ground or rocks, and take turns in reading aloud. Mr. Ripley often had classes in history on Sunday, each one taking turns in reading aloud.

Mr. William Henry Channing would often spend a good deal of time there; and when he did, we would have regular service in the Eyry or Pilgrim House, when we would have sung some of the grand masses of Mozart or Haydn, and then hear one of Mr. Channing's inspired sermons. We had a fine choir which interpreted the masses in beautiful style, the soprano being a charming lady from Boston, Miss Mary Bullard, who afterwards became the wife of Mr. John S. Dwight.

Music was a prominent feature in the Brook Farm life, and we had a great deal of it at all times. And being young, we imbibed it so freely (although I was no musician) that my whole system seemed to absorb it to such an extent, that next to my dear wife and children, I have loved it the most of anything in life. It was no unusual thing for a small party of us to go into Boston toward night, to hear some of the grand operas that were frequently given there by talent that cannot be surpassed even now. They were then given in the old Howard Atheneum. When the opera was over, we would all gather in Higgin's Oyster Saloon on Court St., indulge in a liberal supply of oyster stew and crackers as the preparatory part. We were then ready--the boys and girls--for our walk back to Brook Farm, a distance of about nine miles, reaching there about one o'clock. And all would be on hand for breakfast and the duties of the next day.

It is hard to stop talking of that beautiful life, now so far away in the past. And I have no one left now with whom to talk about it, as I am the last but one surviving working member of that unique body of men and women. There is one lady in San Diego, Cal., who was in the Brook Farm School when I was there, Mrs. Kate Sloan Gaskill. We had not met for over fifty years. Kate and I were good friends, at the time, being nearly the same age. During my visit to San Diego last Summer, I went to see her, and we spent one day at the Fair together, reviving many a pleasant reminiscence of those ancient days.

They were building a Phalanstery when I arrived at Brook Farm, on the plan of Charles Fourier, which was designed to accommodate a large portion of the association, and in a way to be a model for those that might come after. It would have permitted quite a large addition to the membership, which at that time was about 130. Funds had come in for finishing part of the Phalanstery in March, 1846, and all were happy that the work was to be resumed. Carpenters had put a stove in for the purpose of drying out the building. It was thought best to celebrate the renewal of the work by a social dance at the Hive, and it was not long before everything was in readiness for the maidens and their swains to trip the "light fantastic." The dance had begun and there was a joyous crowd present. But suddenly there was a chilling damper thrown over it by a cry through the window, "The Phalanstery is on fire!" There was a rush from the Hive to see it, and I never saw a more magnificent spectacle, when the whole building was enveloped in flames, and not a stick could be saved. The house stood on the side of a hill in front of the Eyry, which stood on the highest ground. So efforts had to be directed to the Eyry, to keep that building from taking fire, and they were successful.

The light from the fire brought people from all directions, even as far as Boston, and engines came from several adjoining towns. But it was of no avail, and the stately pile, on which so many hopes were based for the benefit of humanity, was now a black mass of ruins. The firemen were invited in for refreshments, for it was a cold night with snow on the ground. Dear old Peter Baldwin, our baker, round-shouldered and ungainly, had just taken out of the oven a big batch of bread, which was for our breakfast. They ate it all, and the faithful Peter worked all night to make good the deficit. Miss Ripley had abundant coffee made for them, which disappeared as rapidly as hot cakes.

In the midst of the lunch Mr. Ripley mounted a bench and with his usual beaming face, thanked them for their efforts. Their visit, he said, "was very unexpected to us," but he was very glad to give them the poor hospitality we had. "But had we known," he said, in that bright, pleasant way he always had, "or even suspected you were coming, we would have been better prepared to receive you, and given you worthier, if not a <u>warmer</u> reception." "Good enough, good enough," shouted the firemen.

It was a tragic disaster, but it did not affect any belief that the Brook Farmers had in the social projects that had been formed.

It was a crushing blow to the Association, for nearly all the money the stockholders possessed was involved, and it had at last gone up in smoke. There were talks of revival, and the different works at Brook Farm went on for something more than another year. Then it finally developed that the beautiful experiment of a new social scheme of society, under new and improved conditions must be given up, and the different members began to depart. The funeral dirge seemed to be sounding there for months, as one by one they "folded their tents and silently stole away," to become part of the "outside world" again, at the end of an idyllic life. Mr. Ripley's library became a part of Theodore Parker's library, and the two most valuable libraries in the United States are now a part of the Boston Public Library.

The <u>Harbinger</u> was moved to New York and was followed by Mr. and Mrs. Ripley. He became identified with the <u>New York Tribune</u>, and later joined the staff of the <u>American Encyclopedia</u>.

My dearest friend, Charles Codman, and I went to Boston to work at our trade of printing, going first into the office of the <u>Voice of Industry</u>, an organ of the workingman. There are a thousand more reminiscences that come to my mind but time does not permit my giving them to you at present.

As Hawthorne and Dwight were so closely identified with Brook Farm, permit me to close this desultory paper with a short extract from James Russell Lowell's "A Fable for Critics," which I recommend all to read who have not, even though it is ancient literature. After paying his compliments to Whittier and Richard H. Dana, he goes on to say:

> "There is Hawthorne with genius so shrinking and rare
> That you hardly at first see the strength that is there;
> A frame so robust, with a nature so sweet,
> So earnest, so graceful, so lithe and so fleet,
> Is worth a descent from Olympus to meet;
> 'Tis as if a rough oak that for ages had stood
> With his gnarled bony branches like ribs of the wood,
> Should bloom, after cycles of struggle and scatche,
> With a single anemone trembly and rathe;
> His strength is so tender, his wildness so meek,
> That a suitable parallel sets one to seek,--
> He's a John Bunyan Fouque, a Puritan Tieck;

When Nature was shaping him, clay was not granted,
For making so full-sized a man as she wanted;
So, to fill out her model, a little she spared
From some finer grained stuff for a woman prepared.
And she could not have hit a more excellent plan
For making him fully and perfectly man.
The success of her scheme gave her so much delight
That she tried it again, shortly after, in Dwight;
Only, while she was kneading and shaping the clay,
She sang to her work in her sweet childish way,
And found, when she'd put the last touch in his soul,
That the music had somehow got mixed with the whole."

George W. Curtis, in the Easy Chair of *Harper's Magazine*, January, 1869, said this of Brook Farm:

"But beneath all the glancing colors, the lights and shadows of the surface, it was a simple, honest, practical effort for wiser forms of life than those in which we find ourselves. The Friendships that were formed there were enduring. The devotion to noble endeavor, the sympathy with all that is most useful to man, the kind patience and constant charity that were fostered there, have no more been lost than grains dropped on the field. It is to the transcendentalism, that seemed to so many good souls both wicked and absurd, that some of the best influences of American life today are due. The spirit that concentrated at Brook Farm is diffused, but not lost."

It has always seemed to me that purity and virtue were two of the most striking characteristics of the Brook Farm life; without any preaching, that was the natural atmosphere we imbibed. The prevailing influence was elevating to the intellect and heart. There were sermons for us in the fields, there were love and confidence for us in the wash tubs; there was poetry for us in the pine woods, and in the dormitory; there was mental and spiritual culture in the dining room and in our Sunday meetings; there were wit and humor in our waiting group; there was industry in the shop and kitchen, and there was music everywhere. I might say there were hard times; but we young people did not know very much about it then.

One word I wish to say in closing is, that one of the best stories of Brook Farm was written by one who was never there, my friend Lindsay Swift, of the Boston Public LIbrary. It was published by the MacMillan Co., New York in 1900, and is a fascinating story to all concerned in Brook Farm lore.

*S. Willard Saxton, "A Few Reminiscences of Brook Farm," Pocumtuck Valley Memorial Association Proceedings, 6 (1921): 371-386; reprinted, with additions, from "The Last Remaining Brook Farmer (But One) Recalls Its Beauty," Boston Evening Transcript, 29 July 1916, part 2, p. 4.
  1. From Life of Charles A. Dana, by Gen. James H. Wilson-Harper and Bros., 1907. [Editor's note]

TWO UNPUBLISHED REMINISCENCES OF BROOK FARM*

Joel Myerson

On May 27, 1840, Ezra Stiles Gannett wrote the following in his journal, concerning a fellow Unitarian minister, George Ripley: "He is uncomfortable in his present situation, is dissatisfied with the present religious and social institutions, and contemplates a change in his own mode of action."[1] Ripley had earlier shown his dissatisfaction with the present situation by challenging the literary tastes of the time in his Specimens of Foreign Standard Literature, and by rebuking Andrews Norton and the conservative Unitarians with his "The Latest Form of Infidelity" Examined and similar writings; now, after a few months intensive reading about Albert Brisbane and associationism, Ripley was ready to take another step to demonstrate his dissent. By September his friends were commenting upon how he was "fermenting and effervescing" with new ideas.[2] In October Ripley announced to his parish that he wished to resign and in January 1841 he preached his farewell sermon. He and his followers settled at West Roxbury, Massachusetts, in April and called their experiment Brook Farm.

Ripley's social experiment lasted only six years and ultimately must be considered to have fallen short of Ripley's own ideals for a community in which labor and art co-existed in perfect harmony. Yet in at least one respect Brook Farm was a total success: its school. The latitude and program of the Brook Farm school enabled its students (or "scholars" as they called themselves) perfect freedom to grow and to learn as they pleased. The goal of the school was to draw out the child's inherently good qualities and not to drill or to beat an education into him. All of the subsequent articles and books by former Brook Farmers on their childhood at West Roxbury graphically show the fond memories of their education. The previously unpublished papers which follow are concerned with this school. One, by Frederick Pratt, details the school during the first four years of Brook Farm's existence, while the other, by Mrs. Nora Schelter Blair, recalls Brook Farm during its last days.[3]

ACCOUNTS OF BROOK FARM

By Frederick Pratt

Some 60 years ago, in Boston especially, there began a movement among the progressive, thinking men and women of the time, looking for a more natural method of Living; giving more time for the advancement of the mind, and less for the grosser duties of the body. Ripley, Emerson, Channing, and many others of that class, were among the thinkers, and from these came the Transcendentalists or Social-Reformers: one of the foremost was Mr. George Ripley, who, in 1841 started a scheme which culminated in the spring of that year in the Brook Farm Association, and of that I wish to speak tonight.

Early in 1841, my father's family joined the Community, as it was then called, and were among the first to reach the new home in West Roxbury. There was then but one House, afterwards called the "Hive," and in that house we lived all the time we were there, some five years. There were only 10 or 15 persons in the community when we came, but they rapidly increased, and in a year or two the family increased to 80 or 90 persons: more than half members of the association, the rest scholars and boarders. Three new houses were built, the Eyrie, the Pilgrim House, and the Cottage, which were only used as living rooms, the eating and washing and other household duties being always carried on at the old house, called the Hive.

I have often seen Mr. Ripley and Mr. Bradford helping in the washing room, with the Pounding Barrels, (for it was before the time of Laundries and wringers,) and helping to hang out the clothes in the Drying yards. Miss Marianne Ripley was the head of the Household Group, and had charge of the eating arrangements. My mother came next, and saw to the sleeping rooms, and Mrs. Sophia Ripley attended to the washing and ironing. In those days there were no servants--no hired help, --all work was honorable, and--even at the height of prosperity, there were few drones--Work was done in Groups. One was Chief of the Group, and the rest followed his (or her) direction. Some of the Groups were large, as in the Washing, Kitchen, and some of the Farming ones, while others were small, and, in some cases, one answered for chief and all hands. I was proud in those days to think I was Chief of the Knife-Cleaning Group, and that was a big job too, for in those days there were no plated knives and forks--and twice a day there were from 75 to 125 pairs to scour with cork and Bristol Brick, and well they were done too, if I do say it. But that was not all I had to do. I was one of the Group of Table-Waiters, of which there were five or six. John Orvis was Chief of that Group, and its duties were to wait upon the table: and have our meals after the rest were done. There were 4 or 5 long tables, with one of the older members at the head of each table, who carved the meat, (when we had meat,) and the waiters passed the plates the whole length of the table, and saw that the Bread and vegetables were properly replenished as wanted. As time went on, money was not as plenty as it should have been, and the members had to economize, and for a time, (as I remember, for a year or two,) the most of us became vegetarians, and lived mostly on vegetables and fruits, with Indian Mush and Brown Bread Brewis for our hearty food.[4] We had plenty of Milk, but if butter or meat was wanted, one must pay for it, 3 cents for a piece of Butter, 5 cents for meat. In those times there were a large number of Scholars and Boarders, who, of course were not confined to the Vegetable diet, and so we had two sets of tables, the vegetarian, and the Meat. Mr. Ripley headed the Boarders' table, but he ate his dinner without meat, as did most of the members.

The Waiters' Group were a jolly set of young men and boys. I was the youngest: 11 or 12 years old. John Orvis, and [Frederick] Cabot[5] were always overflowing with fun, and as our dinner came after the others were through, we were not in a hurry. I well remember one day, when we had watermelons for dessert, and we were all full. Orvis took up a rind, stood in his place, and commenced an oration "On this Melon Collar occasion"--and dropped the semi-circle around my neck. He was the only sober one in the company.

We had one of the best of Schools there, with some of the finest Teachers I was ever with. Miss Hannah Ripley had charge of the smaller children, and Mr. George Bradford the older ones. I know I learned easier and faster with him than with any other teacher I was ever under. John S. Dwight was the Music teacher, and Mr. and Mrs. Ripley the general oversight over all. I must have been a busy boy there for I remember I was one of the Onion Group, with John Hosmer as Chief. I see him now with his shuttle hoe running along the rows, while several of the boys [were] weeding out. There was one thing about work at Brook Farm I always noticed:--it was done pleasantly and willingly, even the most disagreeable. I have seen Mr. Ripley and Mr. Hawthorne shovelling over manure, without a murmur, though I believe Mr. Hawthorne did not relish the job.[6]

All the young people that ever lived there as far as I ever heard, all unite in saying it was the happiest part of their lives, and I doubt if there ever was, in so small a home, so many that have since made a mark in the world. Ripley, Dana, Hawthorne, Curtis, Dwight, Margaret Fuller all had lived there, and Emerson, Alcott, Thoreau, Parker, Brisbane, and many others were frequent visitors. I remember in one of the early years of my life there, when visitors were many, the coming of Annie, Louisa, and Elisabeth Alcott one day and the jolly time we children had together, and the use made of our boys' wheelbarrows or wagons in carrying the girls about,--15 or 18 years afterwards my Brother John married Annie Alcott. Louisa became a writer, and John Brooks and the Little Men became famous.

I remember that several happy marriages were the result of the coming together of so many young people, though I do not think any of them were married while at Brook Farm. But there were many engagements entered into there, that were carried out afterwards. I know of six young men that found their affinities there. There was but one death in the Community in the five years I was there, and that was a young woman, sickly when she came, without friends or relatives, who died of Consumption, and, by loving friends the remains were placed in the ground on a lovely knoll near by.[7]

We sometimes had accidents. We boys were playing Tag about the Hive, and, turning the corner of the house, Sam Leatheridge fell and broke his arm, It was the first severe accident I ever saw, and made a lasting impression upon me. Leatheridge, when he left Brook Farm, went to railroading, and has always been employed about the Fitchburg R. R. first as errand boy, then Baggage Master, and for many years as Conductor between Boston & Fitchburg.

Soon afterwards, Mr. [William] Allen, our teamster was going to, or coming from Boston with an ox team loaded, fell off the load, and both wheels went over him. It was many months before he was about again, and I think he never was strong again.

We had some odd sticks in the family. John Cheever was the oldest perhaps. He was an Irishman of good education: for many years the body servant of an English Lord, and lived with him till the Nobleman died, I think in America. Somehow he drifted to Brook Farm, and staid there until it Dissolved. He could do anything. Wash, Iron, Shovel, Hoe, never tired: a good word for everyone, and dearly loved a joke. He got up, a canard on All Fools' Day, that a wild animal, I think an Elephant, had been captured near by, was confined in an adjoining barn, and could be seen through the cracks. He caught a good many of the boys, some of them of older growth, trying to see the Elephant, and seeing they were fooled, kept still, and so trapped others. He came to Concord when he left Brook Farm, and staid about here for a year or two, became low spirited, wandered off to New York, and was never seen afterwards, except by a letter here to someone to tell where his trunk would be found.

There was one there who had a passion for picking up everything laying about:--broken nails, old tins, iron scraps, broken Bricks, old furniture, and packing them away for future use. This he kept up as long as he lived, increasing on him all the time, so as to be a burden to his family at the last. That family were the last to leave when Brook Farm disbanded.

Concord became the home of many of the Brook Farmers after they left West Roxbury, though I believe George Bradford, John Hosmer, and his sister Dolly were the only ones who belonged to

Concord in the first place. But Marianne Ripley, George Curtis and brother Burrill, Hawthorne, Mrs. Barlow and two sons, Mr. & Mrs. Pratt and four children, the youngest, Theodore, being the first child born at Brook Farm, Almira Daniels, John Cheever, and Carrie Stodder, and perhaps some others, made their home here for a longer or shorter period.

I cannot recall all the men and women that made a mark in the world in one way or another, starting from Brook Farm, but it is a long list. Geo. Ripley, Charles A. Dana, John S. Dwight, Nathaniel Hawthorne, John Orvis, Frank Barlow, Georgianna Bruce, George W. Curtis, Geo. Bradford, Father Hecker, are but a few of them.

At the Centennial Celebration at Concord in 1875 George W. Curtis gave the oration, and Frank Barlow was Chief Marshal, both Brook Farmers, and there were 20 or 30 more of them present during the day. Most of them have now passed on, Frank Barlow the last to go only a few days ago,[8] and there are probably not more than 20 members still living. I cannot count but ten that I know of.

The <u>Phalanstery</u>, a large building (175 ft. long) commenced about the time we left, to carry out the newer notions of the Community, was, on account of want of funds, left unfinished for a time, but, about a year after we left, they started to finish the Building. March 3rd [1846], about 1/2 past 9 at night, they were started by the alarm of "Fire" and in an hour and a half afterwards, nothing was left but ashes. This was the finishing touch:--the last hair that broke the Camel's back. In six months the last of the Brook Farmers were gone.

SOME SCHOOL MEMORIES OF BROOK FARM
BY A FORMER PUPIL
MRS. NORA SCHELTER BLAIR
ST. ELMO, TENNESSEE
DECEMBER 22, 1892

In a recent magazine I have read "Reminiscences of Brook Farm," which thrilled me with the fondest recollections of my experience as a pupil, under Mrs. Ripley.[9] To those who, erstwhile, were my comrades, who have not yet passed to the Upper Courts, I believe these crudely written lines will not be devoid of interest, as being rejuvenating.

I must first premise that my father was of sturdy, educated German stock, affiliated, by marriage, to the South. The death of my lovely Southern mother caused me to be transplanted north of Mason and Dixon's line, where I was strictly brought up amongst Germans, who took the liveliest interest in the Community at Brook Farm, resulting in my being retransplanted to that veritable nook.

Never shall I forget the day on which I and my five boy cousins first alighted at the "Hive." The dinner bell had just sounded, and, apparently, the whole community filed by giving us [a] smiling welcome. And, surely, never had we beheld such eccentricities in dress, and such absence of tonsorial effects. The men wearing curious belted blouses, something like the pictures of old English carters, and the women in motley array, some in bloomers. Presently a woman of majestic height and bearing, clad in a dress of checked domestic, was introduced to me as Mrs. Ripley. At home I had seen only colored servants wear such fabrics yet at that moment it struck me as looking essentially royal. It is needless to say that my young heart instantly went out to her in an access of worshipping infatuation, which never swerved, under the closest companionship.

The community was then almost moribund, yet, during that last year, there still remained a choice gathering of every shade of human intellect, wit and wisdom. At least so it impressed a girl of thirteen, and I still cling to my early opinions.

The school itself must have been a curious medley as compared with the educational routines of the day, yet I do believe that what was then so pleasantly learned has never been effaced. One peculiarity was the entire freedom of speech between pupil and teacher. Thus some of the youngest scholars habitually addressed Mrs. Ripley as Sophia,--yet I can recall no instance of willful disrespect to her. She was the Supreme Spirit of the school, and she seemed to permeate her pupils with a joyous confidence in their individual ability to tread the path so clearly and pleasantly indicated by her. Amongst us were gathered divers nationalities, that, under her, were harmoniously blended. French, Spaniards and Germans speedily mastered the difficulties of the English tongue, their marvelous success due to Mrs. Ripley's matchless genius, practice and ingenuity. In like manner were her English pupils inducted into the various modern languages. The veriest dullard, must, perforce, acquire mental illumination under such teaching. Our moral influences were of the highest and purest, albeit there was no special religious training. Certainly, in point of truthfulness, I believe the morale of the school was above the average. Also, outside of school, our advantages were most liberalizing, inasmuch as we held freest intercourse with men who have since won enviable distinction in the literary world.

Mr. Ripley, Chas. A. Dana and John S. Dwight were, to me, the three fixed stellar magnates of that bright galaxy of choice spirits. Brilliant ones from the outside world often mingled in our ideal life, and the recollection of these gatherings is almost a despair to me as something hopelessly gone forever. The Eyrie was the home nucleus for the boarding pupils, the school rooms being in a separate Cottage building. Its construction was adapted rather to summer tenting than to New England ideas of sober staunchness,-- yet how we all loved it, and clutched the Golden Hours as they sped, all too swiftly!

In our sports and walks we were ever under immediate charge of a gracious teacher, who, at such times, seemed as brimming with youthful zest as ourselves. At our occasional dance meetings Mrs. Ripley was invariably partner for the extremely youthful lads, whose six or seven years made them utterly indifferent to any charms but hers.

John S. Dwight was doubtless pioneer to open the path for classic music in New England. Yet such was his gentle diffidence that comparatively few then recognized his high merit as a scholar. His gifted teachers were likewise teachers, whose beautiful lives can never be effaced from my memory. Messrs. Ripley and Dana had charge of the masculine portion of the school, but we, of the weaker persuasion had ample opportunity to stand afar off and listen to the Elders.

One hour, before school, each morning, we took part in such light work as was necessary to keep our chambers tidy, always under supervision of a lady who charmed us into willing housemaidens. "Laborare est orare," was the motto ever inculcated during those pleasant hours, while we were taught to appreciate the real dignity of labor, and to have respect for the wage earner, and, consequently, we treated Bridget, the Irish hireling, with uniform politeness.

Two of us were detailed, in turn, to wait on the table during meals, which duty was vastly enjoyed, as giving frequent opportunity to minister to some distinguished guest or noted foreigner,-- all which proves what trifles may be a rapture to the young. The refectory being at the Hive, we had ample daily walks to get our meals, which were always seasoned by much pleasant conversation and cheerful hilarity. In winter we often had skates and sleds and I well remember the terrors of my first skating bout under convoy of Mr. Ripley. The grove of pines was another favorite resort, sometimes for recitation, or perhaps to listen to such speakers as Mr. [William Henry] Channing or Theodore Parker.

Then the lovely Charles River was source of exquisite enjoyment, paddling for the white water lily, which we found in profusion, and twined into graceful garlands, often singing in gay chorus echoes across the water.

Of the practical workings of the Community I really knew nothing, the school being distinctly apart. I am pleased to know that many others likewise fondly cherish the older memories connected with the place, since embalmed in Song and Story. Take it all in all, my experiences at Brook Farm now seem more richly fraught with kindly memories than any period of my whole life. Though silver threads have thickly interlaced my once dusky tresses, I can never think of the time spent there without emotion, especially when I reflect that, if the school roll were to be called, how very few there would be to answer "Adsum."

* Joel Myerson, "Two Unpublished Reminiscences of Brook Farm," New England Quarterly, 48 (June 1975): 253-260.

1. William C. Gannett, *Ezra Stiles Gannett* (Boston: Roberts Brothers, 1875), pp. 219-220.

2. James Freeman Clarke to his wife, 25 September 1840, *Autobiography, Diary and Correspondence*, ed. Edward Everett Hale (Boston: Houghton, Mifflin, 1891), p. 133.

3. Pratt's paper is published by permission of Mrs. F. Wolsey Pratt and of Mr. William Henry Harrison and the Fruitlands Museums, and Mrs. Blair's by permission of the Boston Athenaeum. I have silently corrected obvious errors of spelling, grammar, and punctuation.

4. Amelia Russell recalled that "Brook Farm brewis [bread soaked in beef broth] has always been a pleasant remembrance to me, and I even yet indulge occasionally in a good breakfast of it" ("Home Life of the Brook Farm Association," *Atlantic Monthly*, 42 [October 1878]: 460).

5. Pratt had originally written "Johnathan Butterfield," then crossed it out.

6. After he had first "commenced a gallant attack upon a heap of manure," Hawthorne jokingly assured his fiancée Sophia Peabody not to come "within half a mile of me." A month later, though, Hawthorne disgustedly looked forward to getting rid of the "treasures" of that "Abominable gold mine!" (13-14 April and 1 June 1841, Henry W. Sams, *Autobiography of Brook Farm* [Englewood Cliffs, N.J.: Prentice-Hall, 1958], pp. 14, 21).

7. Actually, John Orvis was married at Brook Farm to Marianne Dwight by William Henry Channing. Lindsay Swift reports that "Fourteen marriages have been traced to friendships begun at Brook Farm, and the record of unhappy unions is small" (*Brook Farm* [New York: Macmillan, 1900], p. 117).

8. Francis Channing Barlow died 11 January 1896.

9. George P. Bradford, "Reminiscences of Brook Farm," *Century Magazine*, 45 (November 1892): 141-148.

INDEX

INDEX

Adams, George, 179
Adams, John Quincy, 179, 180
Adams, Samuel, 180, 181
"Adonis," 120, 121, 126-128, 136, 156, 158
"Agricola," 146
Alcott, Amos Bronson, 41, 42, 138, 191, 223, 225, 234, 258, 261, 285, 304, 332; "Orphic Sayings," 284
Alcott, Anna, 270, 332
Alcott, Elizabeth, 332
Alcott, Louisa May, 270, 332
Allen, Fred, 310
Allen, John, 63, 74, 224, 229, 236, 310
Allen, Mrs. Sylvia, 271
Allen, Tom, 198
Allen, William B., 242, 260, 270, 333
Alvord, Mrs. A. G., 274
American Union of Associationists, 43
Anaxagoras, 33
Anthon, Charles, 229
Antonines, 33
Aristides, 33
Arnold, Matthew, 176
Associationism, 87, 132

Bailey, Philip James, 289
Baldwin, Peter, 234, 236, 289, 325
Ballou, Adin, 25, 130, 131, 224, 225, 241
Bancroft, George, 223, 258
Bancroft, George, Jr., 269, 273
Bancroft, John, 269, 273

Barlow, Almira, 334
Barlow, Edward, 334
Barlow, Ellen Shaw, 315
Barlow, Francis Channing, 167, 209, 315, 334, 338
Barrett, Elizabeth: See Elizabeth Barrett Browning
Barrows, Belle C., 185-190
Bartlett, Robert, 285
Beecher, Lyman, 95
Beethoven, Ludwig van, 30, 165, 188, 250
Betham-Edwards, M., 253-255
Blackwell, Anna, 253-255
Blackwell, Elizabeth, 253
Blackwell, Emily, 253
Blair, Nora Schelter, 330, 334-337; "Some School Memories of Brook Farm," 334-337
Booth, Popelston, 220
Boston Athenaeum, 338
Boston Public Library, 326
Boston Quarterly Review, 26
Bradford, George Partridge, 55, 196-213, 249, 270, 271, 274, 275, 278, 279, 281, 282, 330, 332, 333, 338; "Reminiscences of Brook Farm," 196-213
Bridget, 337
Brisbane, Albert, 27, 69, 74, 186, 196, 215, 231, 251, 261, 291,

308, 315, 321, 329, 332
Brook Farm Association of Agriculture and Industry, 260
Brook Farm Institute of Agriculture and Education, 1, 242, 302
Brook Farm Phalanx, 69, 74, 316
Brown, John S., 55
Browning, Elizabeth Barrett, 135, 172
Browning, Robert, 98
Brownson, Orestes A., 130, 172-175, 180, 191, 206, 258; "Brook Farm," 26-38; "The Laboring Classes," 6; The Mediatorial Life of Jesus, 38
Bruce, Georgiana: See Georgiana Bruce Kirby
Brutus, 33
Bullard, Mary: See Mary Bullard Dwight
Burleigh, Charles, 192
Burns, Robert, 236, 270
Burton, Warren, 131, 196, 225, 270
Butterfield, Jonathan, 262, 294, 319, 321, 338
Butterfield, Rebecca Codman, 286-298, 309, 318, 319
Byron, George Gordon, Lord, 127, 289

Cabot, Frederick, 74, 320, 331
"Camilla," 140, 156, 171-173
"Carlos, Don": See Charles A. Dana
Carlyle, Thomas, 109, 149, 162, 191, 223, 240
Carter, Robert, 222, 225, 226
Channing, Ellery, 109, 126
Channing, Walter, 258
Channing, William Ellery, 33, 93, 95, 176, 240, 257, 258, 301, 330
Channing, William Henry, 76, 91, 105, 188, 216, 222-225, 229, 236, 251, 258, 261, 263, 268, 281, 297, 301, 320, 321, 323, 337, 338
Cheever, John, 105, 198, 221, 236, 333, 334
Cheswell, Mrs. William, 289
Child, Lydia Maria, 223
Christian Register, 259
Clapp, Otis, 321
Clarke, James Freeman, 91, 301, 338
Clough, Arthur Hugh, 193
Codman, Charles H., 290, 318, 320, 321, 326
Codman, John, 290, 292, 318
Codman, Mrs. John, 290, 292, 318
Codman, John Thomas, 256-267, 274, 290, 300, 309, 318-320; "The Brook Farm Association," 256-267; Brook Farm: Historic and Personal Memoirs, 267
Codman, Rebecca: See Rebecca Codman Butterfield
Coleridge, Samuel Taylor, 96, 158, 172, 176
Collins, John A., 68-71
"Commodore," 110, 113
Communitist, 69-70

Cooper, James Fenimore, 229
Cooper, Samuel, 181
Coralles, Jose, 292
Coralles, Lucas, 221, 292
Cornwall, Barry: See Bryan Waller Proctor
Cousin, Victor, 122
Cranch, Christopher Pearse, 139, 180, 258, 263, 321, 323
Curtis, Anna Shaw, 315
Curtis, Burrill, 187, 189, 194, 225, 227, 250, 274, 277-279, 281, 315, 334
Curtis, Edith Roelker, 298
Curtis, George William, 187, 189, 194, 209, 217, 225, 227, 250, 260, 263, 274, 277, 279, 281, 285, 288, 297, 308, 313, 315, 321, 323, 327, 332, 334; "Brook Farm and Transcendentalism," 176-181; "Hawthorne, Brook Farm, and Transcendentalism," 92-100; Prue and I, 279
Cushing, Caleb, 218
Cutter, M. Gertrude, 286-298
"Cynthia," 107, 109, 122

Dana, Anne M., 55
Dana, Charles Anderson, 52, 55, 74, 80, 123, 132, 147, 161, 165, 166, 182, 183, 186, 187, 189, 194, 197, 216, 218, 225, 229, 230, 235, 242, 249-251, 254, 262, 264, 265, 270, 272, 274, 278, 279, 288, 290, 296, 302-306, 308, 314, 316, 320-322, 328, 332, 334, 336; "Letter from Charles A. Dana," 63-67
Dana, Eunice Macdaniel, 182, 303
Dana, Maria, 298
Dana, Richard Henry, 268, 326
Daniels, Almira, 334
Dante Alighieri, 210
Deane, Sophie, 112
Dial, 27, 192, 223, 244, 285
"Diana," 146, 148
Diaz, Abby Morton, 219, 250, 280
Diaz, Manuel, 55
Dickens, Charles, 240, 307, 316
"Dolores," 156
"Dominie," 110, 113, 116, 118, 121, 128, 134, 146, 147, 152, 166, 168
Doucet, J. Homer, 222-239; "Reminiscences of the Brook Farm Association," 222-239
Dwight, Frances Ellen, 305, 306, 323
Dwight, John, 259
Dwight, John Sullivan, 30, 55, 74, 80, 130, 164, 165, 182, 183, 185-188, 209, 217, 223-225, 229, 236, 249, 255, 258, 259, 261, 262, 265, 268, 270, 282, 284, 285, 288, 294, 297, 304, 305, 308, 309, 313, 314, 321-324, 326, 332, 334, 336; "How

BROOK 344 FARM

Stands the Cause?",
82-84
Dwight, Marianne, 305,
309, 338
Dwight, Mary Bullard,
236, 285, 324

Edwards, Jonathan, 277
Eliot, John, 242
Ellis Farm, 268
Ellsler, Fanny, 125
Emerson, Lidian, 223
Emerson, Ralph Waldo,
91, 92, 95, 96, 100,
104, 136, 138, 150,
152, 159, 162, 170,
178-180, 182, 191,
193, 194, 213, 223,
224, 243, 244, 258,
263, 270, 273, 284,
301, 304, 313, 330,
332
Emerson, William, 179
Epictetus, 168
"Erasmus": See Charles
King Newcomb
Everett, Edward, 179

F., Julian, 109
"Fabian," 156
Farley, Frank, 94
Farrar, Eliza Rotch, 284
Fawkes, Guy, 174
Fields, James T., 314
Finch, John, 51, 53-55
Follen, Charles, 123
Follen, Mrs. Charles, 134
Folsom, Abby, 97
Foster, George G., 321
"Foster, Silas" (The Blithedale Romance), 218
Fourier, Charles: See Fourierism
Fourierism, 24, 27, 65, 72-74, 165, 166, 184, 186, 187, 191, 214, 231, 251, 253, 254,
261, 263, 274, 284, 291, 315, 319
Fox, George, 149
Frothingham, Octavius Brooks, 176, 177, 179, 185, 240, 241; Transcendentalism in New England, 181
Fruitlands Community, 41, 42, 225
Fruitlands Museums, 338
Fuller, Sarah Margaret, 86-91, 100, 105, 107, 139, 150, 159, 165, 179, 186, 206, 219, 223, 224, 235, 244, 246-248, 250, 258, 263, 268, 273, 281, 285, 288, 296, 301, 303, 304, 306, 332; "Brook Farm," 86-91; Günderode, 158; Memoirs of Margaret Fuller Ossoli, 91

Gannett, Ezra Stiles, 329
Gannett, Mary, 274
Gannett, Ora: See Ora Gannett Sedgwick
Garrison, William Lloyd, 102, 179, 282, 316
Gaskill, Kate Sloan, 299-312, 324; "A Girl's Recollections of Brook Farm School," 299-312
Godwin, Parke, 184, 231, 251, 261, 321
Goethe, Johann Wolfgang von, 123, 222
Graham, Sylvester, 191
Grant, Ulysses S., 184
Graupner, Harriet, 323
Greeley, Horace, 184, 191, 229, 251, 261, 304, 307, 321
Greenfield Democrat, 318
"Gregorio," 156

Guyon, Madame, 112, 149

Hancock, John, 181
Hannah, 220
Haraszti, Zoltàn, 298
Harbinger, 43, 229, 234, 262, 265, 299, 308, 317-320, 322, 326
"Harlan", 109, 138, 151, 152
Harmony Community, 51
Harrison, William Henry, 338
Hart, A. Bloomer, 56-62
Hatch, George, 234
Hawthorne, Nathaniel, 92-100, 178, 186, 196, 201, 202, 219, 225, 227, 242, 246, 247, 254, 258, 259, 263, 268, 269, 271-273, 276, 285, 288, 295, 301, 302, 308, 314, 326, 332, 334, 338; American Notebooks, 92, 93, 177, 270, 271, 275, 281; The Blithedale Romance, 92-100, 177, 186, 201, 218, 247, 253, 267, 270, 271, 281, 314; The Marble Faun, 92; Twice-Told Tales, 307
Hawthorne, Sophia Peabody, 223, 258, 259, 314, 338
Haydn, Franz Joseph, 165, 188, 289, 323
Hecker, Isaac, 209, 280, 334
Hedge, Frederic Henry, 100
Hegel, Georg Wilhelm Friedrich, 222
Heine, Heinrich, 128
"Heloise," 153
Herbert, George, 178
"Hercules," 120

"Hero," 101, 103, 105, 108-110, 112, 118, 121-125, 128, 133, 134, 140, 144, 146, 153, 159, 163
Higginson, Thomas Wentworth, 308, 321; "The Brook Farm Period in New England," 191-195
Hillard, George S., 271
"Hiram," 151
Holmes, Oliver Wendell, 258
Homer, 105
Hooper, Ellen Sturgis, 194
Hopedale Community, 25, 41, 131
Hosmer, Dolly, 333
Hosmer, Edmund, 244
Hosmer, John, 332, 333
Huntington, Frederic Dan, 284, 285; "Brook Farm," 284, 285
Hutchinson, Abby, 130
Hutchinson family, 191, 194, 206

Isaiah, 32

"Janet," 121
"Jerome," 148, 149
Jerrold, Douglas, 305
"John," 144

Kant, Immanuel, 176, 208, 222
Kingsley, Charles, 165, 240
Kirby, Georgiana Bruce, 177, 248, 270, 277, 280, 300, 334; "My First Visit to Brook Farm," 101-118; "Reminiscences of Brook Farm," 119-175

Kleinstrup, Louise, 309, 311
Kleinstrup, Peter, 309
Lacuna, Ramon, 220
"Lady Superior": See Sophia Willard Dana Ripley
Lamb, Charles, 93
Lamson, Father, 97
Landor, Walter Savage, 162
Lane, Charles, 136, 138; "American Correspondence," 41, 42; "Brook Farm," 44
Law, William, 112, 149
"Leander," 101, 105, 108, 115, 121, 145, 163
Leatheridge, Sam, 333
Lessing, Gotthold Ephraim, 222
Lind, Jennie, 309
Longfellow, Henry Wadsworth, 258
Lowell, James Russell, 192, 223, 258, 308, 321, 326
Loyola, Ignatius, 125

Macdaniel, Eunice: See Eunice Macdaniel Dana
Macdaniel, Fanny, 303, 316
Macdaniel, Osborne, 74, 316, 321
Mack, David, 268
"Madonna," 151
Mann, Mary Peabody, 223
"Marcus," 103
"Margaret," 108, 120, 133, 148, 161, 163, 169, 170
Martineau, James, 240
May, Samuel Joseph, 282
Milnes, Richard Monckton, 126
Molière, 281

"Molly," 151
Morton, Mr., 219
Morton, Abby: See Abby Morton Diaz
Morton, Edwin, 229, 274, 303
Morton, Ichabod, 229, 274, 303
Mozart, Wolfgang Amadeus, 165, 188, 250, 289, 323
Myerson, Joel, 329-338

Newcomb, Charles King, 124-126, 133, 136, 138, 149, 154, 164, 167, 168, 275
New York Sun, 184
New-York Tribune, 69, 184, 307
North, Christopher, 126
North American Phalanx, 104, 313
Northampton Industrial Association, 41, 51, 53, 55, 131
Norton, Andrews, 185, 329
Novalis, F. von Hardenberg, 169

"Oland," 132
"Olden, Professor," 109
Oneida Community, 237
"Oraculum Basilius": See Orestes A. Brownson
Orange, Thomas J., 75, 99
Orvis, John, 74, 229, 331, 334, 338
Ostinelli, Frances, 206
Owen, Robert, 27, 206, 237

"Pacha," 102
Page, William, 192
Palisse, Edgar, 321
Palisse, Jean M., 321

Palisse, Mrs. Jean M., 321
Palmer, Edward, 191
Palmer, George, 75
Palmer, Thomas, 75
Parker, Lydia Cabot, 223
Parker, Theodore, 95, 98, 100, 105, 110, 130, 179, 191, 206, 208, 216, 223, 224, 241, 242, 246, 258, 263, 268, 270, 273, 284, 304, 306, 314, 323, 326, 332, 337; Discourse on Religion, 133
Parkman, Mrs. Francis, 284
Peabody, Elizabeth Palmer, 219, 258, 288, 301; "A Glimpse of Christ's Idea of Society," 11; "Plan of the West Roxbury Community," 11-23, 38
Peabody, Sophia: See Sophia Peabody Hawthorne
"Pedro," 144
"Pericles," 110, 111, 120, 121, 124, 126, 127, 136, 143, 156
Pestalozzi, Johann Heinrich, 48
Phalanx, 43
Phillips, Wendell, 105, 106, 134, 135, 273, 274
Phillips, Mrs. Wendell, 223
"Plainly, Dora," 121
"Plainly, Harry," 120
"Plainly, Jemima," 120, 143, 144, 151
"Plainly" family, 120
Plato, 33, 135
Poe, Edgar Allan, 229
"Portia," 105-109, 126, 134, 141, 142, 144, 146-148, 150-158, 164, 167, 168, 170
Pratt, Carrie, 334
Pratt, Frederick, 270, 329-334; "Accounts of Brook Farm," 330-334
Pratt, Mrs. F. Wolsey, 338
Pratt, John, 270, 332, 334
Pratt, Maria T., 242
Pratt, Minot, 52, 197, 242, 259, 260, 265, 270, 274, 314, 330, 334
Pratt, Mrs. Minot, 265, 270, 274, 330, 334
Pratt, Theodore Parker, 270, 334
Prescott, William Hickling, 179
"Priscilla" (The Blithedale Romance), 255
Proctor, Bryan Waller, 127
"Professor, The": See George Ripley
Putnam, George, 189
Putnam, Mrs. George, 223

Racine, Jean, 281
Regulus, 33
Richter, Jean Paul, 222
Ripley, George, 4, 9, 25, 27, 39, 43, 51-54, 59, 69, 73, 80, 86, 87, 90, 93, 94, 112, 122, 129-131, 160, 162, 165, 174, 175, 177, 182, 183, 185-187, 189, 196, 198, 203, 206-208, 215, 216, 224-226, 228, 229, 236, 240-244, 246, 249-251,

254, 256-259, 261-270, 273, 274, 277, 278, 281, 284-288, 296-298, 300-308, 310, 313, 316-318, 321-323, 325, 326, 329-332, 334, 336; "The Angels of the Past," 85; "Brook Farm School," 80-81; "Fire at Brook Farm," 75-79; "The Latest Form of Infidelity" Examined, 329; Specimens of Foreign Standard Literature, 329
Ripley, Hannah B., 55, 332
Ripley, Marianne, 55, 196, 197, 235, 242, 258, 259, 265, 269, 302, 306, 314, 320, 325, 330, 334
Ripley, Sophia Willard Dana, 9, 55, 70, 80, 87, 88, 112, 113, 118, 122, 148, 162, 166, 186, 187, 189, 193, 196-198, 202, 206, 211, 223, 228, 234, 235, 241, 242, 249, 250, 254, 258, 259, 265, 266, 268-270, 274, 276, 278, 280, 281, 287-289, 292, 302-305, 313, 326, 330, 332, 334-336
Robbins, Samuel D., 130, 259
Roy, Rammohun, 51
"Rückhalt," 159, 172
Russell, Amelia E., 55, 213, 304, 306, 338
Russell, Jonathan, 282
Russell family, 281
Ryckman, Lewis K., 74, 321

St. Augustine, 20, 126
St. Paul, 32
Salisbury, Annie M., 240-252; Brook Farm, 240-252
Salisbury, Charles, 248
Sand, George, 322
Saxton, Jonathan A., 316-318, 321
Saxton, Rufus, 317
Saxton, S. Willard, 300, 312, 313-328; "A Few Reminiscences of Brook Farm," 313-328
Schiller, Johann Christof Friedrich von, 123, 222, 285
Scott, Walter, 307
Sears, John Van Der Zee, 300
Sedgwick, Ora Gannett, 268-283; "A Girl of Sixteen at Brook Farm," 268-283
Shakers, 49
Shakespeare, William, 105, 236, 281, 289, 290, 307
Shaw, Mrs. Anna, 223, 279
Shaw, Francis George, 74, 189, 314, 321, 322
Shaw, Quincy, 189
Shaw, Robert Gould, 188, 314, 315
Shaw family, 281
Shelley, Percy Bysshe, 127, 135
"Sibyl," 163
"Sibylla," 135, 136, 138, 150-152, 158, 161, 166, 169-171
Sidney, Philip, 120
"Siren," 140-142
Skaneatales Community, 71, 313
Slade, Ellen, 270, 272
Sloan, Mrs. Catherine, 308, 310
Sloan, Jeremiah, 307

Sloan, Kate: See Kate Sloan Gaskill
"Smith, Grant," 109
"Smith, Mrs. Grant," 102, 109, 140, 148, 156, 160, 164
Socrates, 33, 168
Solon, 33
Southey, Robert, 96
Stearns, Sarah F., 242, 270, 277, 280
Sterling, John, 162
Stodder, Carrie, 334
Story, William Wetmore, 258, 308, 321
Sturgis, Caroline, 223, 279
Sturgis, James, 188, 189
Sumner, Arthur, 214-221; "A Boy's Recollections of Brook Farm," 214-221
Sumner, Charles, 219
Sumner, Horace, 219
Swedenborg, Emanuel, 33, 137, 162
Swift, Lindsay, 300, 328, 338
"Sybil," 102, 105, 107-109, 111, 113-118, 120, 126, 128, 140, 141, 143, 144, 148-150, 157

Taylor, Father Edward, 168, 172
Tennyson, Alfred, Lord, 98, 149, 162
"Thane," 109, 143, 144
"Theodore": See "Tom"
Thoreau, Henry David, 223, 225, 332
Ticknor, William D., 179

"Tom," 101-103, 107, 109, 111, 114-118, 120, 163
"Torquemada," 126, 151, 172-174
Transcendental Club, 257, 286, 287, 301
Transcendentalism, 22, 92-100, 97, 108, 176-181, 223, 240, 241, 257, 299, 327
Treadwell, Thomas, 262, 321

Vedas, 285
Very, Jones, 285
Virgil, 278
Voice of Industry, 326
Von Arnim, Bettina, 158

Warren, General, 242
Washington, George, 123
Washington, Martha, 123
Wells, George, 209, 218, 277
Westacott, Robert G., 74
Wheeler, Charles Stearns, 285
Whitmore, Charles O., 242
Whittier, John Greenleaf, 258, 308, 321, 326
"William," 167
Wolcott, Josiah, 290
Wright, Henry G., 136

Xavier, Francis, 125

"Zenobia" (The Blithedale Romance), 218, 255, 270